One And One Equals Eleven

Edited, typeset and cover design by Michael Fischer
Used fonts: Oswald (Book Cover) | Adobe Caslon Pro, Oswald (Book block)

Images
Part I: Photo by Mwangi Gatheca on Unsplash
Part II: Photo by Simon Zhu on Unsplash
Part III: Photo by Luke Stackpoole on Unsplash
Part IV: Photo by Riccardo Annandale on Unsplash

Names: Ákos Balázs, Nitin Aggarwal, Michael Fischer, Gurmeet Naroola.
Title: One And One Equals Eleven : The Power of Silicon Valley and German Collaboration.

One And One Eleven 2021.

Identifiers: ISBN 9781736382509 (coverback) | ISBN 9781736382516 (ebook)

Subjects: Venture capital. | New business enterprises. | Entrepreneurship. | Worldwide collaboration.

Printed by Kindle Direct Publishing

10   9   8   7   6   5   4   3   2   1

To our families, friends, and all the crazy entrepreneurs enabling one and one to equal eleven. We love you all.

Testimonials

The innovation power of the Silicon Valley is unmatched on a global base. With its rich history of technology developments and the raise of very successful enterprises, it has formed and will continue to lead technology ecosystems worldwide. For Siemens, the Silicon Valley represents foundational learnings, and opportunities. That's why we established our venture arm Next47 in Palo Alto. This well-timed book showcases the power of collaboration between FAU-Germany and SJSU-Silicon Valley as well as highlights the importance of cross-fertilization between academia and industry.

— Roland Busch
Deputy CEO, Siemens AG

Reproducing the success of Silicon Valley is not an option, however, learning from, and co-creating, success with partners in Silicon Valley is. This book opens up our learning and sharing capabilities and invites us to become a member of a global innovation community. It is a tool for making innovation happen – between our ecosystems, our networks, between leaders and learners, between the interviewees and interviewers, the contributors and readers.

— Joachim Hornegger
President, Friedrich-Alexander University
Erlangen-Nürnberg (FAU)

This book captures the essence of Silicon Valley – the risk taking, perseverance and passion that make this one of the most innovative places in the world. Some of the Valley's most innovative minds showcase their entrepreneurial skills and knowledge in such areas as artificial intelligence, big data, blockchain, clean energy, e-mobility, fintech and medical technology.

— DAN MOSHAVI
Dean, Lucas College & Graduate School of
Business, San José State University

At Siemens Healthineers, we combine a long tradition of leadership with the urgency of a startup company because we believe the digitization of healthcare holds enormous potential for the lives of patients. As we work closely with our partners in the Medical Valley EMN, learning from cross-industry best-practices and embedding them into healthcare's context, we continue to expand our global footprint. Healthcare is local, but innovation in medical technology requires a global network of pioneers, that's why fostering entrepreneurship while connecting the brightest minds with long-term experience is key. This book reaffirms the power of collaboration and creative thinking – and the untapped potential of digital natives.

— BERND MONTAG
CEO, Siemens Healthineers

"Collaboration is the only pathway to success" – that is what this book showcases on every single page. If we could establish this basic principle as a guideline, we would no longer dwell in mediocrity, but dare to dream big and form companies with global leadership in technology and business. Collaboration on a global scale turns audacious visions into outstanding business ideas.

— HANS-GEORG KRABBE
Managing Director, ABB Germany

The planet is reaching its limits – we need fundamental changes. Digitalization can only lead to a sustainable world if we work together; innovations only bring about the desired change if we utilize them efficiently and effectively; social-ecological improvement worldwide can only happen if we leverage new technologies the right way. And this is what "One And One Equals Eleven" is all about: The scaling effect. One And One DOES Equal Eleven, and perhaps even more, if individuals, organizations and politics are committed to work hand in hand together. A sustainable world? "Collaboration" is the magic formula.

— AYA JAFF

Forbes 30 Under 30 & Co-Founder,
CoDesign Factory

This program – established by leading global universities FAU, Germany, and SJSU, Silicon Valley, California – shares how entrepreneurship and technology are merging together in the digital globalization era and this book is an output of that. I look forward to seeing the companies built as a result of this partnership.

— DAVID WORTMANN

Founder and Managing Director, DWR-eco

This book captures everything you need to know about inspiring entrepreneurship in emerging mega-growth-mega-market opportunities. A very timely book that showcases the secrets of Silicon Valley. It's great to see how this ambitious ecosystem has not only defined the pace of our world for decades but that it has kept identifying the next big thing while establishing world-leading companies. Luckily, mindsets here in Germany are changing; people are fostering entrepreneurship through start-up ecosystems and we are seeing them shoot up like mushrooms all across the country.

— CHRISTOPH OSTERMANN

Co-Founder and CEO, Sonnen

The COVID-19 crisis we are currently living in opens up a window of opportunity to accelerate sustainable solutions to overcome key challenges. The year 2020 has forced everyone to build awareness, reshape their mindset, and drive collective interactions and agendas through a global network. As the epicenter of technology, Silicon Valley has laid the foundation for the igniting field of innovation, entrepreneurship, and science. This book is actively leading stakeholders towards a successful rebrand on digital and technological transformation. "One And One Equals Eleven" – A pioneer of change.

— SUSANNE DEISSENBERGER
Finance & Consulting, Thermo Fisher
Scientific Messtechnik GmbH

The timing of this book is impeccable. We are living in a time where accelerated technological development, digital transformation, and extremely volatile business environments are the new normal. This book features extraordinary entrepreneurs telling their stories of success and one thing was consistent between all of them: the belief that a company is only successful to the extent that its network allows it. I am even more convinced that collaboration and networking are decisive keys to entrepreneurial success – whether as a self-employed person, as a small and medium-sized company, or as a global player.

— CONSTANZE OSCHMANN
Vice President, IHK Nürnberg

I have lived in Silicon Valley for the past thirty-six years, the first sixteen at Stanford University and the next twenty as a venture capitalist. What has struck me is the mindset of cross-fertilization of ideas, innovation, collaboration and risk taking. It is no accident that this book covers a wide range of topics because technology will disrupt all industries. This is a must-read book for budding entrepreneurs anywhere in the world.

— RAMAN KHANNA
Managing Director, Dell Technologies
Capital

From my experience at GE, we are always impressed and happy to combine German technology with our Palo Alto digital business. Any phenomenally successful company has always had strong partnerships. The challenges and speed of innovation that arise from new technologies mean that solo attempts are most likely to fail. Intelligent partnerships, like those described in the book, and the development of start-up ecosystems are fundamental prerequisites for success in a constantly changing world.

— STEPHAN REIMELT
Former President & CEO, GE Germany & Austria

.

ONE AND ONE
EQUALS
ELEVEN

The Power of Silicon Valley and German Collaboration

Ákos Balázs
Nitin Aggarwal
Michael Fischer
Gurmeet Naroola

ORIGINAL EDITION

Let's make "One Plus One Equals Eleven" our guiding principle for the innovations ahead!

Joachim Hornegger

President FAU

Foreword by Joachim Hornegger

Joachim Hornegger
President
Friedrich-Alexander University Erlangen-Nürnberg (FAU), Germany

Silicon Valley has changed the world we live in: we all use apps on our smartphones, easily book private homes and cars, and share our pictures with a global community. Many technologies that we consider indispensable today come from "the Valley". This place, although it is quite inconspicuous, raises both anxieties and fascination due to its high innovativeness and disruptive power. Many articles on Silicon Valley seek to understand its mystery: What makes it so special? What is the core of the renowned Silicon Valley culture? What does it take to become a part of it?

Reproducing the success of Silicon Valley is not an option, however, learning from and co-creating success with partners in Silicon Valley is. Everyone who has lived and worked in "the Valley" experienced its impressive ecosystem, unique mindset, communication strengths, risk-taking culture and open network that facilitates building scalable high-tech startups. Everyone who also lived and worked in the Bavarian ecosystem in Germany, especially the innovation ecosystem around the Friedrich-Alexander University Erlangen-Nürnberg (FAU) knows how different it is. It builds on incredibly stable, long-lasting university-industry relationships, relatively low individual mobility, outstanding loyalty to institutions, a patent-focused mindset and – among others – a tendency to start sustainable businesses with a clear engineering and ownership culture. The strength of this Bavarian ecosystem is also unchallenged and widely known, but the contrast to Silicon Valley could hardly be bigger.

When I first met Gurmeet Naroola for a joint breakfast, the idea was born: together with both our networks, we would run a challenging experiment. Matching and mixing individuals from both ecosystems, building links between our institutions and creating opportunities for joint learning, joint projects and joint startups. This could result in a combination of strengths and vast win-win opportunities. It might also, however, make different mindsets and attitudes visible. Would it lead to immediate successes? How much time would it need to evolve? One aspect was clear: we would jumpstart, run and learn – together.

This book is one of the early joint projects. It makes individual success stories from Gurmeet Naroola's incredible network visible, but it also does not hide the challenges those individuals experienced during their innovation journeys. It brings in many individuals from the FAU ecosystem as contributors, interviewers, co-creators and participants of our joint innovation journey. This book now opens up our learning and sharing project and invites you, the reader, to join our journey and become a member of our global innovation community.

This book is not a product. It is a tool for making innovation happen – between our ecosystems, our networks, between leaders and learners, between the interviewees and interviewers, the contributors and readers. This project is not about copying or reproducing each other's successes, it is about celebrating innovation with diversity and passion. It truly fits our FAU motto "Knowledge in Motion" and turns ideas into value. This would not have been possible without many innovators joining the journey.

I am deeply grateful to my friend Bernhard Beck for starting the matchmaking and to my wonderful colleague and entrepreneur Gurmeet Naroola who quickly turned our joint experiment into a joint venture with full Silicon Valley style, speed and spirit and who always respected our FAU innovation ecosystem style. I thank Dan Moshavi, Dean of the Lucas College and Graduate School of Business at San José State University, who trusted our ideas and provided his full support. Thank you to all participants and partners, contributors and co-creators in this early step of our joint innovation journey. Thank you to two outstanding FAU students: Markus Schober who co-created the design of our first joint program and Michael Fischer who took the German lead in the joint book project.

Let's make "One And One Equals Eleven" our guiding principle for the innovations ahead!

Joachim Hornegger
President
Friedrich-Alexander University Erlangen-Nürnberg (FAU)

"Risk taking, perseverance and passion make the Silicon Valley one of the most innovative places in the world!"

Dan Moshavi

Dean of Lucas College and Graduate School of Business at SJSU

Foreword by Dan Moshavi

Dan Moshavi
Dean of the Lucas College and Graduate School of Business,
San José State University

"In the long history of humankind (and animal kind, too) those who learned to collaborate and improvise most effectively have prevailed."

— Charles Darwin

About 20 months ago, two universities – San José State University (SJSU) and Friedrich-Alexander University Erlangen-Nürnberg (FAU) – embarked on an entrepreneurial collaboration leveraging the immense research capabilities of FAU and SJSU's powerful and robust Silicon Valley ecosystem.

The result – a custom executive education program delivered by SJSU that has morphed in new and exciting ways. What began as a robust exchange of knowledge and ideas has grown into much more – the commercialization of intellectual property, the formation and incubation of new companies and … this book.

This collaboration would not have been possible without the tremendous support of FAU President Joachim Hornegger and Vice President Kathrin Möslein, and the aspirational thinking and program execution of my colleague Gurmeet Naroola, who has led the SJSU efforts.

This book captures the essence of Silicon Valley – the risk taking, perseverance and passion that make this one of the most innovative places in the world. In the following pages, you will gain insights from some of the Valley's most interesting minds as they showcase their entrepreneurial skills and knowledge in such areas as artificial intelligence, big data, blockchain, clean energy, e-mobility, fintech and medical technology.

Dan Moshavi
Dean of Lucas College of Business
San José State University (SJSU)

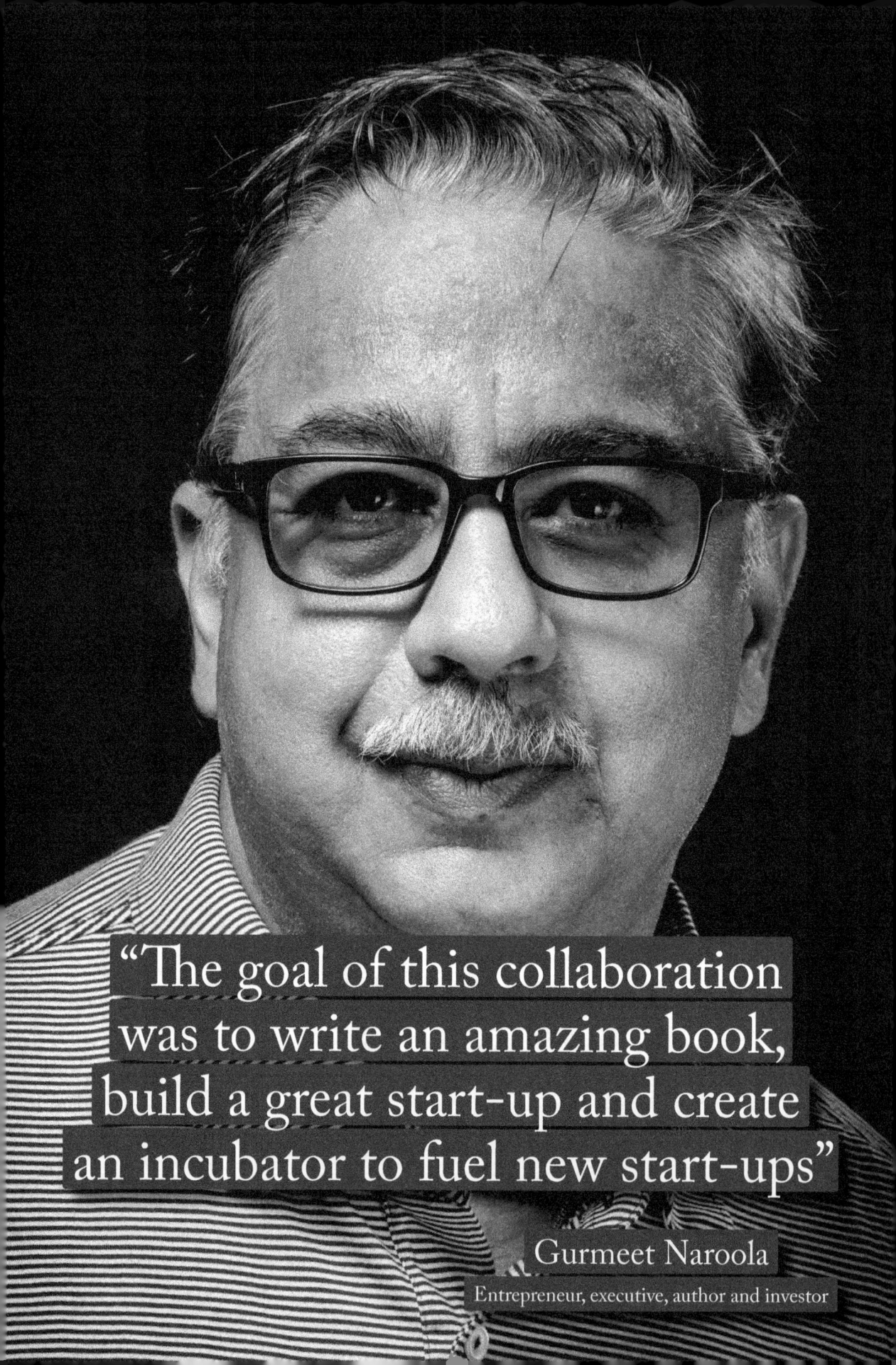

"The goal of this collaboration was to write an amazing book, build a great start-up and create an incubator to fuel new start-ups"

Gurmeet Naroola
Entrepreneur, executive, author and investor

Preface

This book shows the power of how "one and one" becomes "eleven" in the Silicon Valley. We share stories of how entrepreneurship, collaboration, friendship, students, faculty, blue ocean strategies, and break-neck execution, all come together from around the world to create magic.

Here is how the FAU and SJSU collaboration began:

Believe it or not, I ran into Dan Moshavi, Dean of the SJSU business school, in the university's parking lot. He was on his way to his office and I was heading to a classroom to teach. Coincidentally, I had watched him on a TED Talk a few days ago that I really enjoyed. I made sure to share with him a copy of my last book, The Entrepreneurial Connection, that I had put together in 2003.

A few weeks later a dear friend and business colleague of mine from Germany, Bernhard Beck, called me. He mentioned that his close friend Dr. Joachim Hornegger (Achim) – President of Friedrich-Alexander University Erlangen-Nürnberg (FAU), one of the top 15 innovation leaders among universities worldwide and No.1 in Germany – was visiting the Bay Area and that I should meet him. I immediately reached out to him and we met for breakfast the very next day. Achim was keen on meeting a few Silicon Valley executives so I called Dr. Harry Partridge, CTO at NASA, to see if he was available for breakfast and luckily, he was. The three of us had a great discussion over an equally great breakfast right by AMES NASA. After breakfast, I thought it would be a good idea to show Achim around SJSU. After all, it is the university planted right here, in Silicon Valley. On our way there I decided to push my luck and see if Dan was available. Again, luck was on our side and Dan was available. A few minutes later, Dan, Achim and I were having coffee in Dan's office. In between conversations, the idea of an immersive Silicon Valley program came up. We thought about hosting a week-long program for FAU students and faculty to come to Silicon Valley. Some dates were proposed and we eventually shook hands for March 2019, only 3 months away. Achim, a Stanford postdoctoral, moved at typical Silicon-Valley speed. All this happened in 2 days. There was no formal planning, meetings, discussions, or approvals. Speed, a focus on creating 10X value for the participants, collaboration, and risk-taking all came into play. Of course, our respective visions and goals were aligned

– enabling One and One to equal ELEVEN. This is a prime example of how Silicon Valley works.

Dr Kathrin Moeslein and I began to define the program. Our criteria for the program was simple: make it innovative, make it different and let's create outstanding and unexpected value for leaders and learners alike. It would have the best speakers presenting on the latest technologies. We would explore some of the best corporations in the Valley, cover mega-market mega-growth topics that lead to start-ups. This program had to be bold and intensive. At the end of the program, we wanted the participants to feel two things: "thank God the program is over" and "I wish it was longer." There were two desired outputs: 1) publish a book based on the presentations and 2) start-up a few companies based on the program.

We rolled up our sleeves and got to work. One of my ace students, Novee Thondee, joined the team to help with the logistics and management of the program. He introduced me to Professor Nitin Agarwal who I automatically hit it off with. He became my partner in crime for the program and this book. Nitin and I opened up our Rolodex and we networked our way through friends and family to an incredible set of people that shared their knowledge.

We built an amazing team of speakers: Dr. Harry Partridge – CTO of NASA • Dr. Meyyappan – CSO of NASA • Danny Kennedy – Managing Director of California Clean Energy Fund • Tom Davies – President of world-renowned Vineyard V. Sattui • Jeremy King – Head of Engineering, Pinterest and former CTO, Walmart • Shubham Goel – Co-founder of Affinity.co • Professor Banafa – renowned Blockchain & Quantum computing expert at SJSU • Siegfried Balleis – former mayor of Erlangen • Bernhard Beck – Cofounder of one of the largest solar EPC companies in the world: Belectric • Vish Palekar – CEO of Mahindra GenZe and Solar • Marcus Lehmann – CEO of CalWave • Stanley Chang – renowned Bay Area IP Lawyer • Mike Todasco – head of innovation at PayPal • Sukhi Singh – Founder, Sukhi Foods, a leading provider of delicious Indian Food • Kanwal Rekhi – Serial Entrepreneur and leading Venture Capitalist • Ram Sriram – XeroxParc Technologist • Nitin Vaish – Technology Incubator, Vikaram Takru – Serial Entrepreneur and Founder of KloudGin • Gurtej Sandhu – seventh most prolific inventor in the world and holder of over 1300 patents. We included chapters on Silicon Valley from my previous book and Dr. Anil Gupta (Top 50 Global Thinker) to bring a global dimension to the book.

We covered an array of topics: Impact of COVID-19 on Silicon Valley entrepreneurship, emerging technologies like precision medicine, imaging, biosensors, terahertz, nanotechnology, cybersecurity, blockchain, quantum computing, IoT, AI innovation, big data, mobility, machine learning, printed sensors, triboelectricity, e-mobility, smart buildings, viral marketing, hypergrowth, Solar, organic hydrogen storage and li-ion batteries, food technology, Napa Valley wine region, business planning, venture capital, mega-growth mega markets, go-to-market, intellectual property, seed capital, venture funding, startup exits, R&D technology roadmaps, and digital globalization to name a few.

We had amazing visits: At Tesla, we saw the incredible automation and intense manufacturing culture that builds these world class disruptive cars. You can feel Elon Musk's energy as you walk through this Californian factory in the heart of the Bay Area. At Amazon we saw Jeff Bezos' vision come to life: logistics, supply chain technologies, and infrastructure seamlessly delivering millions of packages. SJSU and Stanford visits shared a snapshot of how critical a role these educational institutes play in fueling and supporting entrepreneurship in Silicon Valley. A visit and lunch at Google corporate office exposed us to the open and amazing culture of innovation and caring for employees. And of course, a visit to Sattui Vineyards shed light on why Napa Valley is the Silicon Valley of wine.

At FAU, Michael Fischer took the lead when it came time to put the book together. He worked with every participant/student to turn these thought-provoking presentations and discussions into chapters of learning. Michael became an author entrepreneur on a mission and his drive continuously fueled motivation amongst the FAU and SJSU teams, especially during the times of winter, when everyone claimed this an impossible endeavor.

At SJSU, my ace student and teaching assistant (TA) Ákos Balázs played a vital role. He worked tirelessly to shape up every chapter and work on the introductions and outlines. Ákos even conducted a few interviews with Kanwal Rekhi – renowned investor, Sukhi–CEO of Sukhi foods and Tom Davies– President of V. Sattui Vineyards, one of the best vineyards in the world. Ákos then learned the required software needed to put the book in its final format that you see now. I predict a bright future for Ákos.

Amaranta Quintero, another bright student of mine, jumped in to review a dozen chapters and finetune each chapter before sending it to Tiana Khong and Diana Cooper for formal editing. I met Tiana through Professor Nitin and Diana had edited my previous book – The Entrepreneurial Connection. Everybody in the team has always been astonished about how Amaranta edited multiple chapters at lightning speed with absolute dedication and commitment to the vision. She truly represented the one plus one equals eleven spirit at its core.

Professor Nitin, Michael Fischer, Ákos Balázs, Amaranta Quintero and all the participants and students became co-authors and editors of the book.

Here is the book. One output accomplished. As you can see this book is about knowledge, connecting the dots, getting the job done, thinking out of the box, and not letting your intelligence get in the way.

We all had a tremendous amount of fun, experience, and learning as we put this book together. We hope it does the same for you.

Gurmeet Naroola
Serial Entrepreneur

Overview

Start-up ecosystems have sprung up all over the world, but the original is still number one, in terms of access to talent and capital. Silicon Valley has developed its own culture that emphasizes openness and break-through innovation and inspires start-up scenes around the world. The vibe is not for everyone and of course there are challenges, such as the high cost of housing and office space, but between 14,000 and 19,000 start-ups have now settled here. More than half of the entrepreneurs come from around the world, so it makes no difference where in the world you are right now. A good idea is always welcome here – and has a chance of success, provided you play your cards right. In much the same way, learning the essentials of building a start-up as well as profiting from others experiences, is the reason we've conducted these interviews and assembled them in this book.

The book is divided into four overarching sections. The first section focuses on the ecosystem on which a successful start-up is based. Silicon Valley has been recognized as the flagship ecosystem – not only for co-location of large and high-profile technology companies like Google, Apple, and Facebook, but also for the clustering of entrepreneurs, venture capitalists, research institutes, and support infrastructure. In the second section, you will learn about the business, financial and legal foundation that needs to be established when setting up a start-up. In the third part we discuss mega growth mega market opportunities at hand: cybersecurity, nanotechnology, biosensors, printed sensors, blockchain, wave energy, etc. The fourth and final part you will dive into the success stories of well-known companies, as well as start-ups that have the potential to become the next unicorns.

Book Team

Special thanks to all the featured entrepreneurs and contributors. It was a lot of fun and immense learning experience.

Concept, Design and Implementation Team

Michael Fischer received a B.Eng. in Mechanical Engineering and is currently doing his master's degree in Mechatronics at FAU. After gaining the entrepreneurial spirit in the Silicon Valley, Michael initiated a mobility startup and co-founded Climate Connect, the Facebook for climate activists and projects. He's a speaker and facilitates workshops for people to market their inner brand.

Ákos Balázs completed his bachelor's degree in International Business with a focus in Global Operations Management at San José State University. As a former professional athlete from Hungary, he has cultivated a multi-cultural background with extensive knowledge in the health and wellness industry. Combined with his entrepreneurial spirit, he started his own business in said field which allowed him to grow love and passion for business development and digital marketing strategy.

Nitin Aggarwal is an Associate Professor of Business at the School of Information Systems and Technology at SJSU. He received his Ph.D. in Business Administration from Texas Tech University. He has published in reputed journals like the MIS Quarterly, Decision Sciences, International Journal of Electronic Commerce, and Electronic Markets. He has also presented his research in a number of national and international conferences such as ICIS, HICSS, and AMCIS.

Gurmeet Naroola is a seasoned entrepreneur and executive having held key executive positions at SunPower, Apple, Panasonic, Sanmina and Mahindra GenZe. Gurmeet has both business and technology experience and has conducted business in over 25+ countries. He received a EPGC from GSB Stanford, a M.Sc. in Engineering from SJSU, and a B.Eng. in Mechanical Engineering from MIT India. He is the recipient of the US Department of Commerce award and Apple quality award. Gurmeet has authored three well-known and highly endorsed business books on entrepreneurship, automotive business systems and quality.

Editing Team

Diana Cooper received her bachelor of arts degree in English Literature, with a minor in French language and literature from the University of California at Berkeley. She has worked as a substantive copy editor for over thirty years. She has edited novels, numerous short stories, memoirs and non-fiction articles. Several of the articles were written in English by authors who speak and write English as their second language. She also sings in a professional chorus and a small Renaissance music group. She is semi-retired and lives with her husband in Santa Cruz, California.

Tiana Khong obtained a bachelor's degree in Business Management from San José State University. Her studies focused on project management, operations and manufacturing, and quality assurance. She won 1st place in the 2017 American National Standards Institute essay competition during her final semester at SJSU. She has project management experience working in the health care, commercial signage, and solar industries. Born and raised in the Silicon Valley, Tiana and her family moved to Georgia in 2018 for a change of pace.

Amaranta Quintero is currently working on her bachelor's degree in Business Administration with a concentration in Global Operations Management at San José State University. She loves the drive that comes with the business world, especially in such a fast-paced environment like Silicon Valley. Some of her passions include learning, challenging herself, and traveling.

We've put this book together at Silicon Valley speed. The interviews are edited to keep the style and intent of the speakers genuine. Forgive us as you find any errors and feel free to reach out to Michael (michi.fischer@fau.de).

Interviewers and Content Development

Anatoli Kalysch

Associated Postdoc at FAU with a research focus on mobile security.

André Hochreiter

Ph.D. student at FAU in light-matter interaction on SiC-MEMS.

Benedikt Bischof

M.Sc. in Industrial Engineering and Management at FAU. CEO Sewing Technology at Bischof Nähmaschinen. Co-Founder gesichtsmaske-bayern.de.

Carl Marius Garzorz

M.Sc. in Industrial Engineering and Management at FAU. Founder of BERRY & CONE

Christian Grenz

Head of Project Development and Investment for Europe and CIS States at Siemens Energy and PhD Student in economics focusing on decarbonisation of electricity systems until 2050.

Christoph Heynen

Head of Spin off Services and Entrepreneurship. Management of projects fostering entrepreneurship culture in academia, counselling of academic spin offs at FAU.

Christoph Stoll

Founder of Climate Connect.

Claudia Lehmann

Executive Director of the Center for Leading Innovation and Cooperation (CLIC) at HHL Leipzig Graduate School of Management.

Dominique Schröder

Professor for Computer Science. Cryptography expert. Teaching "Introduction to Modern Cryptography" at FAU.

Fabian Sperling

B.Sc. in Industrial Engineering and Management at FAU.

Holger Hackstein

Professor for Transfusion Medicine and Cell Engineering at FAU.

Jörg Robert

Postdoc at FAU with research focus on IoT physical layer technologies.

Jonas Schlund

Ph.D. student in smart energy systems at FAU, Lead Data Scientist at ampcontrol.io and Executive Board Member at Technology without Borders.

Julian Weishaupt

Entrepreneur in Residence at LivingPackets.

Lucia Grom-Baumgarten

Co-Founder and CMO at arLife, creating a location-based content platform in augmented reality.

Malvina Supper

Ph.D. student participating in iRTG-PST program (CRC1411) on process concepts for nanoparticle chromatography at FAU.

Marcel Ritter

Acting director of the Erlangen Regional Computing Center (RRZE) at FAU.

Markus Schober

Co-Founder & CEO of INVRTUAL, creating a platform for collaboration and training in VR. M.Sc. Student Industrial Engineering at FAU.

Martin Lauer-Schmaltz

M.Sc. in Mechatronics at FAU.

Martin Knöfel

M.Sc. in Advanced Optical
Technologies at FAU.

Matthias Lochmann

Professor at Department of Sport
Science and Sport, Chair of Sport
and Exercise Medicine, FAU.

Matthias Ring

Data Scientist at
HUK-COBURG

Nicolas Butterwegge

Innovation & Incubation
Manager at Siemens
Healthineers.

Paul Schärfe

M.Sc. in Mechatronics and
M.Sc. Industrial Engineering and
Management at FAU.

Reinhard German

Professor for Computer
Networks and Communication
Systems at FAU.

Sophie Nehrig

M.Sc. in Economics at FAU.
Student representative at
Bundesvereinigung Logistik e.V.

Sagithjan Surendra

M.Sc. in Molecular Medicine
at FAU. Founder of Aelius
Förderwerk e.V.

Spyridon G. Koustas

M.Sc. in International
Information Systems at FAU.

Stefan Blos

Software Engineer with a focus on mobile, web and machine learning. Aspiring to build technology that makes the world a better place.

Thilo Bauer

PostDoc in the Department of Chemistry and Pharmacy Computer Chemistry Centre (CCC), FAU.

Tobias Salbaum

Co-Founder and CEO of Atlas Aero GmbH – Reinventing transport for the people. M.Sc. in Sustainable Chemical Engineering.

Veniamin Morgenshtern

Professor of Machine Learning in Signal Processing, FAU.

Xenia Dolguschew

M.Sc. in Cybersecurity & Privacy. Associate at PwC WPG GmbH.

Contents

IV. Success Stories

Afterword

Part I

Entrepreneurial Eco-System

Introduction about Globalization 4.0

by
Anil K. Gupta

Dr. Anil K. Gupta is the Michael D. Dingman Chair in Strategy, Globalization and Entrepreneurship, and Distinguished Scholar-Teacher at the Smith School of Business, The University of Maryland at College Park. Anil also serves as chairman, The China India Institute, a Washington DC-based research and consulting organization. He earlier served as a Chaired Professor in Strategy at INSEAD and a visiting professor at Stanford University and Dartmouth College. He received a doctorate from the Harvard Business School, an M.B.A. from the Indian Institute of Management at Ahmedabad, and a B. Tech. from the Indian Institute of Technology at Kanpur. Anil is widely regarded as one of the world's leading experts on strategy, globalization, and entrepreneurship. Ranked by Thinkers50 as one of the "world's most influential management thinkers," he has also been named by The Economist as one of the world's "superstars" for research on emerging markets in a cover story on "Innovation in Emerging Economies". Anil Gupta shares his insights into the next phase of globalization – the transformation currently underway: A new era of digital globalization: Globalization 4.0.

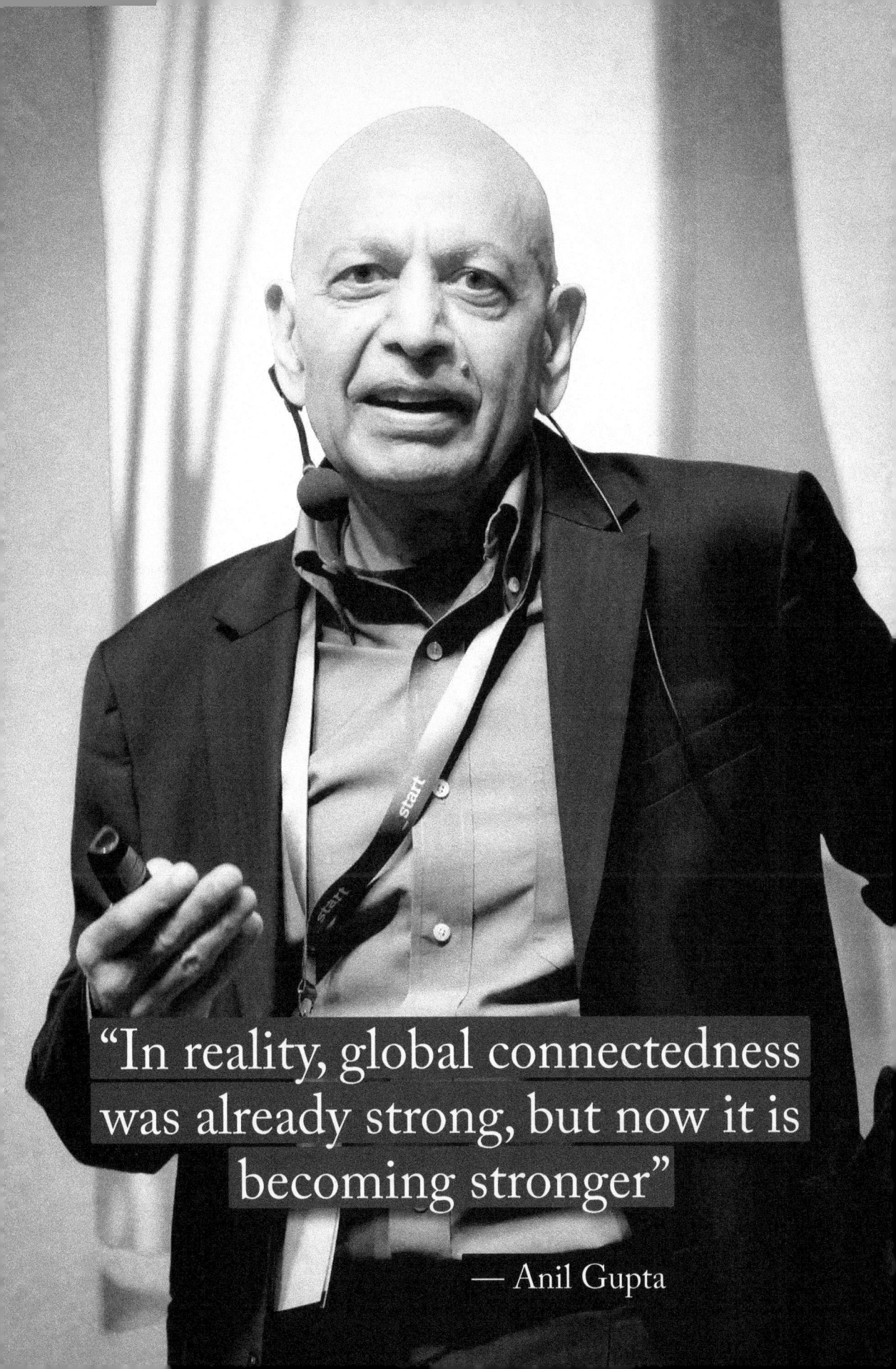

"In reality, global connectedness was already strong, but now it is becoming stronger"

— Anil Gupta

Globalization 4.0:
New era of digital globalization

I have been studying and writing about globalization for over thirty years and I find the transformation currently underway in this phenomenon absolutely fascinating and massively important.

The first era of globalization, let's call it Globalization 1.0, started out as going abroad in search of new markets, whether for the seller's natural resources or manufactured goods. The second era, we can call it Globalization 2.0, started around 1980 with outsourcing of manufacturing to Asia, particularly to China. So, globalization of manufacturing got added on as a second layer on the cake above the globalization of markets. The third layer, Globalization 3.0, was the globalization of R&D. That started around 1990 when companies such as Microsoft, IBM, and GE started building R&D centers around the world. The fourth layer now is Globalization 4.0. This layer on the cake is really the era of digital technologies, and how these digital technologies are actually affecting, permeating, and transforming all of the first three layers.

How is this new era of globalization affecting inter-linkages among countries? Many analysts seriously misinterpret what's happening today. Using terms such as "slowbalization," they assume that we're witnessing the end of globalization as if globalization is dying. That's absolute baloney. It's almost as if these analysts are like an observer in 2000 who looked at the demise of chemical films and started wondering if this meant the end of photography.

In reality, global connectedness was already strong, but now it is becoming stronger. Yes, global connectedness by trade in goods, when adjusted for the size of global GDP, is slowing down. But, there is increasing connectedness via trade in services, stock of foreign direct investment, and cross-border movement of know-how and other types of data – again, after adjusting for the size of global GDP. So, now, we're in an era of connectedness by data and capital rather than connectedness by trade in physical goods.

McKinsey estimates that the contribution to worldwide GDP by cross-border flows of data already exceeds the contribution from trade in physical goods. Thus, the last thing we should do is to bemoan the decline of trade in physical goods and say that globalization is dead. What is slowing is the "old" globalization via trade in physical goods. To paraphrase what people say about transitions in the British monarchy, "The old globalization is dead. Long live the new digital globalization."

Look at Tesla for example. They have just built a Gigafactory in China and are building one in Germany. This has eliminated Tesla's exports from the U.S. to China. Even if China were to eliminate all tariffs on the import of cars, it would not make sense for Tesla to be exporting cars to China. Rather, it would make more sense to build a Gigafactory in China and export data, know-how, technology and then manufacture in China for China. Why would you want to incur a thousand dollars in shipping costs when it's completely unnecessary and makes you uncompetitive?

Another example of the new era of globalization would be Netflix or Amazon video. When somebody in India or China downloads Game of Thrones, that's digital globalization.

Then, of course, if we look at other developments, other examples of globalization – for instance, global platforms such as Facebook, Android, WhatsApp, or Instagram – we see the same phenomenon. In this new era of digital globalization, we're also witnessing the transformation of the traditional trade in goods. Even the traditional merchandise trade has become a whole lot more efficient because customs clearance and coordination now can take place through paperless mechanisms, through blockchain.

Is Globalization 4.0 good for the global economy? I think the answer depends on what countries one is talking about. If we take the rich economies, you're talking about fundamentally slow-growing economies. In the new era of Globalization 4.0, the returns to knowledge, and the returns to people who create that knowledge become very high. You have superstar firms with superstar employees who are paid rather handsomely. But the returns to physical labor go down. So, in the rich economies, Globalization 4.0 exacerbates inequality. This development can be pretty nasty when the overall growth rate is very low.

On the other hand, if you look at emerging markets, in the aggregate, their GDP is growing at 2-3x of that of the developed markets. So, even with growing inequality, people at the bottom of the pyramid see their lives becoming better off. Further, in emerging markets, the vast chunk of the population has historically been disconnected from the financial sector, from education, from health care, and so on. That bottom of the pyramid, or even the middle of the pyramid, now gets connected to online education, to telemedicine, to the banking and insurance sector, in fact, also to the rest of the world. Suddenly, the world opens up for these hundreds of millions of people in emerging markets.

I think, as a whole, Globalization 4.0 is a net plus for the global economy. Emerging markets, which account for 80% of the world's population and 40% of the world's GDP, will clearly benefit. At the same time, Globalization 4.0 will not necessarily be good for all countries, especially those with very low rates of growth and high and rising inequality. Every one of us has to watch out for these concerns and think about how to counter the nasty side effects.

Anil K. Gupta

Entrepreneurial Eco-System

Interview 1

Culture and Competition in Silicon Valley

AnnaLee Saxenian

Author of the book "Regional Advantage: Culture and Competition in Silicon Valley and Route 128", UC Berkeley

This interview is featured from the book "The Entrepreneurial Connection", with permission from Gurmeet Naroola.

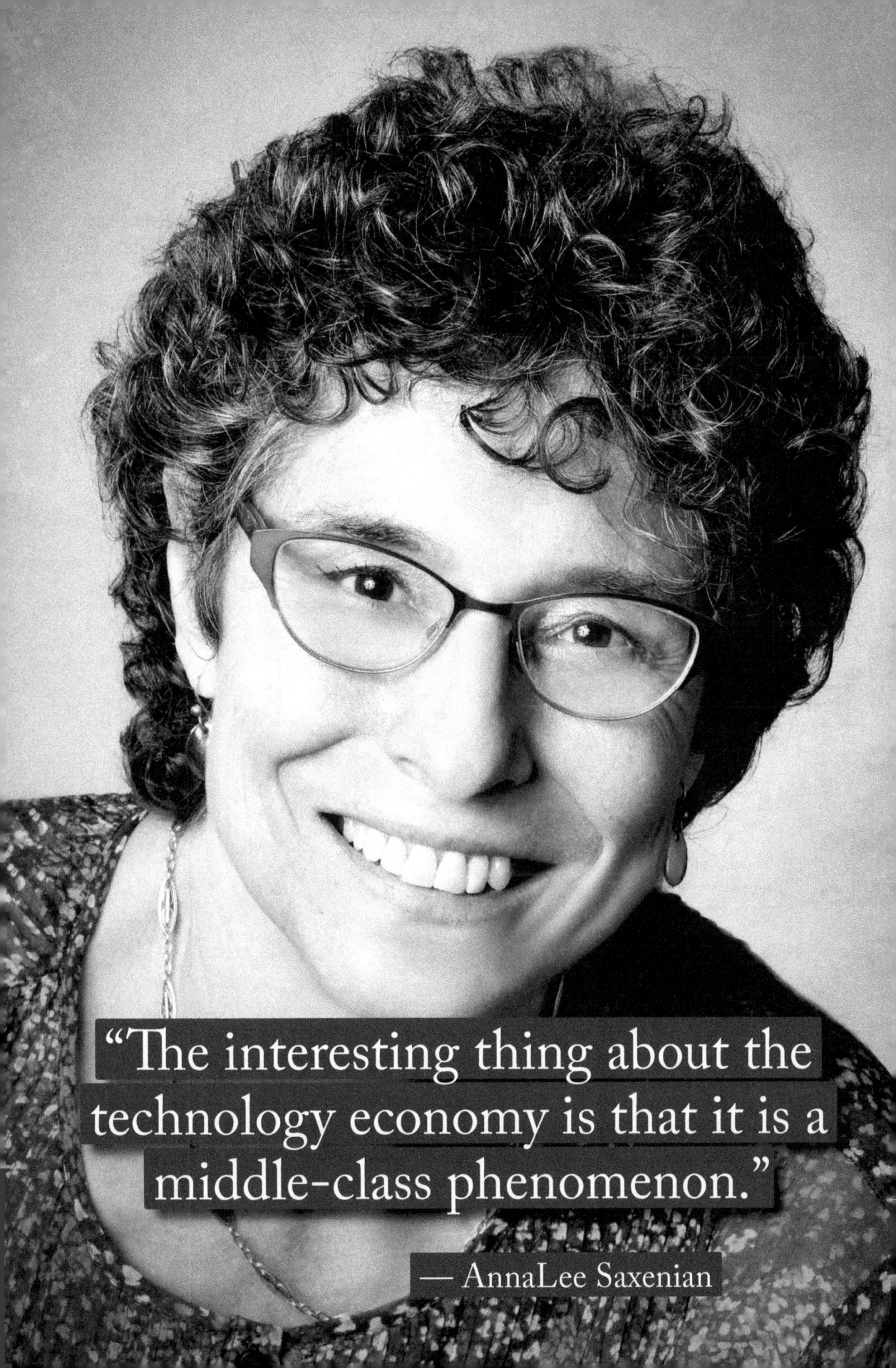

"The interesting thing about the technology economy is that it is a middle-class phenomenon."

— AnnaLee Saxenian

Dr. AnnaLee Saxenian is a professor and the current Dean of the UC Berkeley School of Information, known widely for her work on technology clusters and social networks in Silicon Valley. She received her BA from Williams College and her Ph.D. from Massachusetts Institute of Technology. Her publications include Silicon Valley's New Immigrant Entrepreneurs and Regional Advantage: Culture and Competition in Silicon Valley and Route 128. She has written extensively about innovation and regional development, urbanization, and the organization of labor markets in Silicon Valley.

R aghu Batta and I met with Dr. Saxenian at her residence in Berkeley. We all sat around her dining table that was covered with her son's toys and began looking at the core ingredients that make Silicon Valley the center of entrepreneurship. She shed light on the culture capital, venture capital, support capital, and intellectual capital that fuel the chemical reaction that makes Silicon Valley the most fertile area for entrepreneurs. We then discussed, through examples, what it would take to emulate the Silicon Valley in different parts of the world, and how such an ecosystem fosters the recombination of experience, skill, and technology into new enterprises.

What makes Silicon Valley a center for entrepreneurship?

Silicon Valley is an unusually open environment, allowing skilled professionals to experiment freely with new technologies, new products, new markets, and new applications in a relatively unfettered fashion. This is a radical departure from the way business has been done in the rest of the U.S. and probably in the rest of the world in the postwar period. One of the region's most important innovations is the institutionalization of venture capital as a mechanism for financing high risk, high return ventures. The other critical element in this environment is a set of attitudes and relationships between individuals and companies, a very open attitude towards sharing ideas and information.

Silicon Valley is notable for its dense social networks that grow out of a high rate of mobility. Professionals move between companies at a very high rate. As a result, ideas and know-how are transferred very quickly between individuals and firms within the regional economy. People maintain their social networks when they move between jobs, so when they decide to start another company they draw on a much broader network. Engineers frequently move between industries and sectors – from university to industry, from semiconductors to telecommunications, and from industry to finance and venture capital. This contributes to the cross-fertilization of ideas and know-how and leads to unanticipated technological recombinations.

Cross-cutting social networks and venture capital allows for the seeding of multiple experiments. When combined with the presence of intellectual resources in universities such as Stanford and Berkeley, they create an environment that supports repeated parallel experiments; far more experiments than would be tolerated within a large corporation. Finally, risk-taking is part of the culture in Silicon Valley, and failure is not a stigma. Instead, there is recognition that learning can only happen through failure. So, a very different cultural environment emerged in Silicon Valley in the post-war period than that which existed in most other industrial regions.

Can you elaborate on what you mean by "open attitude"?

Information and know-how circulate faster and more freely in Silicon Valley than anywhere else I've seen. The traditional business attitude has been one of secrecy and pursuit of corporate self-sufficiency. This involved protecting corporate resources and technology by building boundaries around the company. Silicon Valley's pioneers broke away from this model by opening up the boundaries both between firms and other local institutions like universities and venture capitalists.

For example, let's go back a few years and compare Silicon Valley with its counterpart, the Route 128 area in Boston. This is the story I told in my book, Regional Advantage. Although Boston had a strong pool of technical talent, outstanding educational institutions like M.I.T. and Harvard, was a nice place to live, had a fledgling venture capital industry, and a long industrial history, the Boston corridor failed to keep pace with technological change in Silicon Valley in the 1980s. The region's leading minicomputer companies, such as DEC and Data General, pursued vertical integration and built hierarchies as they grew larger. They also became very autarkic; they built corporate boundaries that made it difficult for people to leave or to share information outside of the firm. As a result, the skills and technology in the region were trapped within the boundaries of a small number of very big companies, while in Silicon Valley they were being continually recombined. Moreover, vertical integration made it very difficult for companies like DEC to adapt as markets shifted. This problem intensified as the pace of technological change accelerated in the 1990s and the big integrated East Coast companies could not keep up with the more flexible and entrepreneurial startups in California. Geography is also important. The geography certainly both reinforces and reflects these corporate differences. The Route 128 companies actively pursued geographic isolation in the 1980s while Silicon Valley firms and other institutions are very densely clustered within a small area. This proximity supports the continuous exchange and face-to-face communications that characterize the region.

Do you see the Boston area becoming more like Silicon Valley?

Absolutely. The Boston area fell into crisis in the early 1990s because its leading producers failed to keep up with the pace of technology and market change. But as companies like DEC and Wang declined, they freed up thousands of engineers and managers who went out and started new companies. These entrepreneurs learned from the mistakes of their predecessors; this new generation of firms are more focused and integrated into a more open and horizontal network business model. As a result, the Route 128 corridor today looks more and more like Silicon Valley.

Of course, it takes time for individuals and institutions to change. It is not just the technology companies that have been changing. The region's universities, professional service firms, and the financial community are all adapting to support a faster-paced, more decentralized, and entrepreneurial industrial system. This helps explain why the Boston area remains the second-largest center of entrepreneurship in the US.

What attracts immigrants from all over the world to Silicon Valley?

Silicon Valley has always been unusually open and meritocratic. People of different backgrounds, including first-generation immigrants, feel comfortable here and can progress in the region in a way that is not possible in many other parts of the world. In the 70s and 80s, large numbers of immigrants came to the U.S. to study engineering and sciences. This influx of immigrant engineers coincided with the boom of Silicon Valley and these newly-minted graduates got pulled into the Silicon Valley economy. Immigrants went to graduate schools all over the country, from Iowa to New York to Texas, but they eventually migrated to the Valley in huge numbers because the jobs were here.

These people were primarily Indian and Chinese, the best and the brightest from their countries, graduates of the elite technical institutions like I.I.Ts in India, National Taiwan University in Taiwan, and Beijing University in China. They were also risk-takers by nature, having left their homes to come to the US. When they came to Silicon Valley, one of two things happened; they either succeeded in a big company or faced a glass ceiling. Some of those pioneers faced barriers or were forced out of the leading positions in the companies that they founded. But the thing about the Silicon Valley environment is that if you face a glass ceiling in one environment you have a very easy run-around; you simply leave and start your own company. And that's essentially what happened; the response to such limits has been successive waves of entrepreneurship. The openness of the environment and the opportunities for entrepreneurship go a long way toward explaining the tremendous success of immigrant entrepreneurs in the Valley today.

Why are the majority of entrepreneurs mainly from India and China?

I think it has to do with the desire for knowledge and the desire for economic success. The Indians and Chinese came from developing countries with tremendous ambition, with no pressures or immediate reason to return. Most Indians and Chinese would say, "What would I do? I have a Ph.D. from Illinois Institute of Technology but there is nothing that I could do back in India or China." The best opportunities are in the U.S.

Immigrants from other countries typically feel pressure to go back home after completing their studies. A lot of Koreans and Japanese who came to the US to study could return home to stable, high paying jobs in their countries' biggest, most successful companies. Europeans often felt a similar pressure. If you were a French student, you could go back home to France and get one of the most elite jobs in the country

So the immigrants who have stayed and worked here in large numbers are the ones from the poorest countries; initially Taiwan, then India, and then China. The Mainland Chinese are the most recent arrivals in the U.S., but they also represent the largest group of immigrant engineers. They haven't proven themselves yet, but I am certain they will.

How have Stanford and Berkeley become top-notch educational institutions?

The most interesting fact about Stanford is not simply that it is an excellent institution but that it has overcome the Ivory Tower syndrome. It's deeply integrated into the industrial economy that surrounds it. People move quite freely from Stanford to various corporations. Stanford University is a critical part of the open culture of Silicon Valley.

In fact, Stanford itself played a key role in developing this culture. Fredrick Terman, the former dean of engineering, is often referred to as "the father of Silicon Valley" because he envisioned "a community of technical scholars" in Northern California. He sought to create a technical community where there was, in his words, "continuous ferment of new ideas and stimulating new challenges." And perhaps most importantly, he collaborated closely with local industry and entrepreneurs in achieving this goal. So he not only amassed resources aggressively and hired top-notch people, but he created a new model of a university, one with much more open boundaries to the surrounding industrial community.

Of course, other educational institutions have been central to the Silicon Valley's success, including not just the University of California at Berkeley, but also San Jose State University and DeAnza and Foothill Community Colleges. All of these institutions are part of the state-funded California education system that excelled in the postwar period and contribute to the supply of skill and intellectual capital that are central to Silicon Valley's continued dynamism.

Is education a common platform between India, China, and Taiwan?

Absolutely. If you look at India, Taiwan and China, they have all created first-rate science and engineering universities, even if in small numbers, and have all developed unusually meritocratic processes for entrance in spite of the corruption elsewhere in the society. This allows middle-class families to push their kids to obtain higher education, and in each of these societies, engineering is regarded as one of the most desirable pursuits. The kids that excel at home in India, China, and Taiwan are the ones who go on to study in the U.S. and ultimately become part of the skilled labor force in places like Silicon Valley and the Boston area.

The interesting thing about the new technology economy is that it is a middle-class phenomenon. It's being spearheaded by young engineers from the middle classes of their societies. Silicon Valley is not the home of the established American corporate or political elites, nor is it attracting the older elites from places like India and China. These are the hard-working kids of the middle class.

Would it be correct to say in order to emulate the Silicon Valley environment, universities and corporations need to work hand in hand?

Collaboration between universities and companies is at the core of the Silicon Valley experience. My sense is that in most of the world, educational institutions remain separate from the world of industry and there is little knowledge flow between them. This is the legacy of the Ivory Tower. Take India, for example. I visited the Indian Institute of Science in Bangalore. It's beautiful, but it is like a separate world from the local software industry.

There are people trying to build links, but as elsewhere in the world, the tradition is to maintain distance from the industry. These institutional habits are often slow to change.

Why are there so many more entrepreneurs in Silicon Valley than elsewhere in the U.S.?

When you work in the Silicon Valley environment you become part of it and you learn how it works; you learn how to network, how to find venture capital, how to start a company. You learn what the support infrastructure looks like, how to deal with the venture capitalists, the lawyers, all the things that make it easy to start a company very fast and succeed. It's very hard to learn that outside Silicon Valley. In the Valley you kind of marinate in it, you learn it almost by osmosis. But if you are an equally good engineer who takes a job in Chicago, I'm not sure you're going to understand how to do it.

Take a look at The Indus Entrepreneurial group (TiE). The fact Kanwal Rekhi has started an institution like TiE that helps other Indus entrepreneurs is very much a reflection of the Valley culture of helping one another, of networking, of trying to build a set of horizontal networks that help. You will find that there are dozens of associations like that for different ethnic groups.

Is it the case venture capital in Silicon Valley and the Boston corridor comes primarily from people who've "been there, done that" rather than bankers or traditional financiers?

Venture capital grows right out of the environment. The most successful venture capitalists are individuals who understand the industry first-hand, who know how to start a company, who have networks of relationships they turn to help build teams. Unlike traditional bankers, the U.S. venture capitalists are very much part of the local industrial infrastructure and it's essential they are part of it. In Silicon Valley it is like an evolutionary process; first, you start a company, then if you succeed and make lots of money, you become an angel and invest small amounts in companies run by friends and acquaintances. Later in life, when you're ready to leave management, you might become a venture capitalist. Very few people in Silicon Valley actually retire; rather, they become angels and venture capitalists in their old age, sharing their knowledge, experience, and networking skills with the next generation of entrepreneurs.

Is it possible for India to mimic the Silicon Valley Phenomenon?

Rather than making a checklist of factors such as university, venture capital, science park, and so on, that contribute to the "high tech recipe", I think the first step in a place like India is to begin to create a more open environment. It should be one that encourages horizontal flows of information and joint problem-solving across traditional boundaries. This means bringing together traditionally separate communities: university researchers, corporate managers, aspiring entrepreneurs, financiers, and policymakers to address shared problems. This could include everything from problems of the physical infrastructure and telecommunications system to the availability of venture capital and skilled labor.

The key is to create a context where people come together repeatedly and start to build relationships with one another. They start to recognize they have shared interests and shared problems. In India they might get together first and say, "Damn it, we need to fix the roads because they are driving us all crazy." Later it might involve providing training in management or marketing or supporting research in a particular area. Over time, as these relationships mature and evolve, they can provide the foundation for entrepreneurship as well. It's interesting many of the promising startups you see in a place such as Bangalore come out of WIPRO which is a large technology company that has served as an important training ground for many Indian engineers. These individuals were able to build a set of relationships and gain managerial skills and knowledge within this large company. These skills and relationships become an invaluable resource when they start new businesses. It's no different in a region. You have to create opportunities for people to get to know one another, build up the cross-cutting social networks, and the process of collective learning in the region

There are important aspects of the institutional context that matter, and one thing that is interesting about India is the non-resident Indians like Kanwal Rekhi and KB Chandrasekhar have been working to influence policy. For example, they have worked with the Securities and Exchange Board of India to develop the venture capital industry. I think creating some kind of exit option like the American NASDAQ for venture capitalists is a very important element of this model.

In each of the places trying to imitate Silicon Valley, there are particular items that need to be addressed collectively. None of them are insurmountable. India still needs to improve its telecommunications infrastructure. China needs to develop its capital markets and the rule of law. Both need to deal with intellectual property rights.

Each place has its own particular history, institutions, and resources, so no place will be exactly like Silicon Valley. The key is to create an environment that supports entrepreneurship, experimentation, and learning. For these, the main prerequisites are well-trained people, sources of technology, high-risk financing, and open flows of people and information between the universities, industry, and the financial community.

What are some issues other regions face when trying to mimic the Silicon Valley phenomenon?

There is a general pattern that I have observed, not just in Europe but in parts of Asia as well. The places that were most successful in the old industrial model are having a harder time adapting to this new "bottom-up" entrepreneurial model. I'll term the old model the "National Champion model." Success in this era depended upon an alliance between the state and the large corporations that were designated as national leaders. In this era, every country sought to create its own IBM.

In Europe, the big, established electronics and communications companies typically developed privileged relationships with the state. Those relationships worked when markets were national and technologies were stable, but they also tended to hinder local entrepreneurship. First, the most talented engineers and managers worked for these established corporations, depriving aspiring startups of skill. Moreover, the "national champions" typically dominated the government market for telecommunications and electronics-related products, thus limiting the opportunities for startups. Meanwhile, the lack of competition for these "champions" often resulted in a lagging pace of technological advance.

It is interesting to note the places that are emerging as successful in the new era are those that have traditionally been considered peripheral to Europe. Ireland, Israel, and Finland have all emerged as centers of innovation and entrepreneurship, while France and Germany continue to lag behind.

Or think back to the 1980s, when Japan was the model. When I started writing about Silicon Valley people said to me, "You're crazy. The big Japanese corporations are going to gobble up all the small companies in the Valley." The large and integrated Keiretsu in Japan provided lifetime employment to the most talented professionals. Like their European counterparts, they were successful in an era of mass manufacturing but failed to keep up with the accelerated pace of market and technological change in the 1980s and 1990s.

How can the "top down" mold be broken?

I think that it's going to be a long process. It is likely to take generational change to achieve the institutional changes needed to shift from the old model to a more flexible and bottom-up one. It's proven very hard to break up the alliance between the politicians and bureaucrats in the powerful ministries on one hand and the leading corporations on the other. There is a lot at stake. Many people recognize the problem, but the changes are much harder to make.

Will we see a localization of industry segments?

I think you will see localized specialization continue to emerge and I believe that innovation will increasingly occur outside of Silicon Valley as well. Innovation in different segments and sectors will take place in different places as each location builds up its own distinctive technical capabilities. Taiwan, for example, has shifted from a source of low-cost manufacturing labor into a center of state-of-the-art computer and semiconductor manufacturing. India has the potential to develop as a center of innovation in the software and service sectors. Most front-end product definition and design will remain in Silicon Valley as long as the leading customers are here. But as new markets open up, I can imagine new product definitions emerging in other places as well. The case of Nokia in Finland is a good example.

What are misconceptions other countries attempt to adopt from Silicon Valley?

First, they should recognize it takes more to replicate the Silicon Valley phenomenon than a science park. There are many places in the world that are building science parks and these are, as far as I am concerned, just real estate deals, or perhaps an alliance between real estate developers and politicians. A science park is just a building. It alone has little to do with innovation or entrepreneurship aside from providing infrastructure. Second, they should learn they cannot create venture capital from the top down. There are many government-funded and government-run venture capital efforts emerging around the world. These efforts ignore the fact that venture capital must be part of the local technical infrastructure and networks in order to succeed.

Planners and policy-makers typically adopt some variant of the "high tech recipe," believing that if they combine a research university, a science park, skilled labor, and supplies of venture capital in a nice environment they can "grow the next Silicon Valley." What they fail to recognize is the relationships and social networks are as essential to Silicon Valley's continued dynamism as the presence of educational institutions or supplies of skill and capital.

Do you believe Silicon Valley will be self-destructive or continue to grow?

People have been predicting Silicon Valley's demise for a very long time. The first thing I wrote about the Valley in 1980 was it was going to stop growing. I argued Silicon Valley would stop growing because the housing prices were too high, transportation was too congested, and that all future growth in high tech would occur in Austin or Seattle. But this did not happen. That's what led me to understand that the Silicon Valley environment offers advantages that outweigh its high costs.

Silicon Valley will continue to attract the best and brightest talents in the world. And they will continue to benefit from its open and mobile and meritocratic environment. There have been a lot of great companies built in the Valley in the past. This is the environment that spawned Intel, Oracle, Cisco, Chiron, Yahoo, eBay, and many more of the world's leading IT companies. There is no reason to believe that process will stop now.

Of course, there are still physical and economic limits to large-scale expansion in the Valley, which is why you will always see Silicon Valley companies expanding to other regions of the U.S. and other parts of the world. This is good for Silicon Valley because you can't do everything here. Nor is this a zero-sum game. Silicon Valley companies benefit from the emergence of new centers of technological excellence. Meanwhile, the region will continue to serve as a crucible for leading-edge entrepreneurship and innovation in the near term. I don't expect that in the next decade either the technology will slow down or the environment here will deteriorate significantly enough to undermine its accumulated regional advantage.

Entrepreneurship DNA

Kanwal Rekhi

MD at Inventus Capital Partners
& Founder of Excelan

Written by Ákos Balász, Michael Fischer and Amaranta Quintero

"It is only when you are out of your comfort zone that you grow."

— Kanwal Rekhi

Kanwal Rekhi is an Indian American businessman, investor, and entrepreneur, currently serving as the managing director at Inventus Capital Partners. Rekhi founded Excelan in 1982. When Excelan merged with Novell in 1989 he joined Novell's board of directors and was later named executive vice president and CTO. Rekhi serves on several public and private company boards. In 1986 he was named "Entrepreneur of the Year" by the Arthur-Young Venture magazine. He earned a B.Tech. from IIT-Bombay and a master's degree in electrical engineering from Michigan Tech. Rekhi is a person of clear views who knows where he stands. He is a man with the heart of a lion and will go out of his way to offer help. He is known to be very fair and passionately devoted to cultivating entrepreneurs and helping them to succeed. With this man, what you see is what you get. He speaks his mind and does not mince words.

R ekhi was kind enough to attend a San Jose State University/ Fried-rich-Alexander-Universität Erlangen-Nürnberg (FAU) dinner event as the guest of honor. During the evening, over a few glasses of wine, he captivated the students with his lessons in entrepreneurship. He shared his views on topics ranging from the impact of Covid-19 on Silicon Valley entrepreneurship, venture capital, the importance of "Cash is King", IPOs, strategy and tactics, the importance of a balance between profitability and growth, the inner workings of a VC's mind, and much more. Rekhi has a spectacular history and invaluable insights, which is why he has over 100,000 followers on LinkedIn, where he frequently shares his business acumen. These insights are shared in the section following the questions and answers.

Part 1: Invaluable insights from Kanwal Rekhi

On success

I became an entrepreneur by thinking totally outside the box, not by focusing on design alone. I focused on how to deliver good value, how to price things right, and how to bring in the customers. One thing that was of key importance was my realization that you stagnate when you get stuck in your comfort zone. It's only when you're outside your comfort zone that you can grow. I have seen this over and over again. Every time I step outside my comfort zone I begin to think more effectively and really use my brain.

On mentorship

The one person I really look up to is Mahatma Gandhi. He was an innovator and a true leader; a man who thought outside the box. He was able to bring everybody together for a cause. Sharply focused on a single cause: India's freedom.

On recession

Recessions are necessary for a free market economy to function. They signify the end of one era and the start of a new one. Consumer behavior can get pretty bad. People become overly exuberant, money seems to have no value, they burn billions of dollars, and a recession is the end-result of that nonsense. A recession begins to discipline all the players. Recessions are the best time to start a company. The activity levels go down, the resources free up, and so does the competition for entrepreneurship because only the hardcore entrepreneurs will be willing to stick it out. All the fair-weather entrepreneurs just want to get a steady job and lie low. Salary expectations drop, as there's not as much of a demand. This gives you time to develop your technology or service without feeling you have to rush. The bottom of a recession is always the prime time. VCs, flush with cash, find valuations more attractive and are eager to invest. When you are at the top of the mountain, your next step is always downward. But at the bottom of the valley, your next step is always going to be up. So, when the markets return, and they will, you will climb back up again. This is a once-in-a-lifetime opportunity, a time when the sun, moon, and stars are in alignment. It's time to Carpe Diem!

The current recession driven by the pandemic means that things will not restart as easily and new ways of doing things will have to be discovered. This means there'll be an opportunity for someone to supply the things that these new businesses will need. I'm sure the Plexiglas companies are doing great right now because Plexiglas is being used everywhere. New needs will offer new opportunities for entrepreneurs.

On Silicon Valley' success

My sense is that Silicon Valley has become a fountain of wisdom, a source of inspiration. I think the electronic renaissance will last another half-century. That's the Grandfather Theory. The grandfather comes up with a new idea and works hard to develop it. He is the innovator, the doer. The son, though used to a good life, remains aware of how it came about, and he works hard to sustain it. But the grandson simply assumes this to be his birthright; he has no idea how it happened or what is necessary to sustain it. As a result, he unwittingly destroys it. Now the process must begin all over again. In the Valley, we are going through this cycle and I think we're currently in the "son" phase.

On corporate objectives and guiding principles

» Profit: To make a sufficient profit with which to supply the finances required to meet the other corporate objectives.

- » Customers: To supply our customers with products and services of the greatest possible value in our chosen business.
- » Growth: To grow at a rate which keeps Excelan the premier company in its market of choice, and to provide its employees with an opportunity for personal growth.
- » Employees: To ensure that our people can benefit from the company's success that their achievements are recognized, and that they are managed in such a way that they can enjoy personal satisfaction from their accomplishments. To continue to hire the very best people possible.
- » Management: To manage our company so that an equitable balance is struck between the needs for short-term financial performance and long-term product and customer growth. To allow individual freedom in attaining well-defined objectives.

On entrepreneurship and discipline

The Indian middle-class ethos is pretty clear. There are constant exhortations: Beta Doctor Bano (son become a doctor); Beta engineer Bano (son become an engineer). No parent ever says, "Beta entrepreneur Bano" (son become an entrepreneur). There is further advice to settle down, find a good job, make time to get married and become responsible. The son should never forget the advice to be disciplined, meaning to always do what is expected of you. Finding a job with a multinational corporation and marrying a family-chosen girl are seen as the smart things to do.

The problem is that these are things that steer you away from following your heart and doing your own thing, such as becoming an entrepreneur. Becoming an entrepreneur goes against everything that is expected of you.

Furthermore, it's a hard and lonely journey when you choose to go down that path. You should not expect, and will not receive, any sympathy from anyone. People will laugh at you for being what they consider a foolish person. So why do some people choose to become entrepreneurs anyway? It's because they have to prove something to themselves. You must keep that fire inside you burning brightly. No one from outside will encourage you to put yourself through that hardship. It's your choice alone.

On the odds of becoming an entrepreneurial success.

Only one in fifty people, from the general population, will succeed as an entrepreneur. These are not very good odds. It's no wonder that parents aren't in favor of it. But if you take that first step of leaving your job and following your dream for a year, your odds of succeeding improve ten-fold. That's because you are now a part of a select few, about 10%, who have opted in. Your odds of success have gone from about 2% to 20%! Those odds are not so bad when you consider that just one big win could set you up for life. In any case, most entrepreneurs succeed on the second or a third try. I was lucky enough to make it on my first try.

So are entrepreneurs' gamblers? In a sense they are, but they're taking a calculated risk. Logic alone is not enough; one also has to take that leap of faith. Entrepreneurs blend the primal with the intellectual and concoct a unique recipe. Instead of finding 10 reasons why they can't do it or shouldn't do it, they find one reason to actually do it. The longer you wait, the harder it is to act. You slowly begin to become more sensible, more practical, more responsible, and more set in your ways until you eventually lose the will to take that necessary leap. You have to be a bit foolish to go for the gold, but it's worth it!

On entrepreneurs and broncos

I loved the old westerns that were very popular when I first got to the U.S. in 1967. One thing I remember is that cowboys were always trying to break bucking broncos (tame wild horses). Broncos have minds of their own. They jump around wildly and try to throw the rider off while the rider struggles valiantly to stay in the saddle. This battle of wills occurs many times until both rider and horse begin to understand each other.

I think of entrepreneurs as cowboys and markets as broncos. It takes a while for them to understand each other. What does the market really want? What is it willing to pay? What does it value? Speed? Price? Quality? Of course, a very high-quality product, priced really low and delivered yesterday will be a winner any day of the week! A methodology known as "lean startup" has developed in Silicon Valley over the years. It says that entrepreneurs should come out with a minimum viable product (MVP) as soon as possible and start testing – riding – the market. The product should then evolve and perfect itself in the market under commercial conditions. The entrepreneur should understand what the market wants and how much it's willing to pay. No scaling should happen before that. Using any other method is just playing with fire.

On VC crapshoot

Investing in start-ups, especially in the early stages, is a very risky business. This is evidenced by the fact that most VC funds don't earn the same returns that the very safe ten-year treasuries do. As a matter of fact, most VC funds don't return the capital back to their investors. Only two percent of people succeed as entrepreneurs, and only twenty percent of funded start-ups make a reasonable return. It truly is a crapshoot! So why invest in such risky businesses? Because a 100x return is common enough and even a 1,000x is not unheard of. One big hit can cover a multitude of sins. The latter category includes Microsoft, Google, Facebook, and Amazon, to name a few.

VCs use standard risk management techniques to mitigate risk. For every dollar they invest on an unproven entrepreneur, with unproven technology, they reserve two for investments in the clearly emerging winners. VCs build a diverse portfolio of 15-plus companies, with the hope that one or two will hit it big. They negotiate hard to have as low a valuation as possible to get a reasonable ownership position. In many cases, they will not invest unless they can see a potential return of 20x or more. They reserve a sizable portion of the equity for talent hired to improve the odds of success. They also build in many protective and control mechanisms to make sure that they're able to assert some modicum of control over troubled situations. Even the best teams with good funding often fail for a myriad reasons beyond their control. Markets don't emerge, competition overwhelms them, unit economics and business models don't click. But an inept entrepreneur is the single most common reason that start-ups fail. Losing investments must be weeded out quickly in order to conserve the cash for winners.

A good VC does his due diligence to verify facts and spends an inordinate amount of time picking the right horse to bet on. He then provides enough funding to meet agreed-upon specific and fundable milestones. The goal of the early-stage VCs is to show enough tangible progress to convince the late-stage VCs to invest at stepped-up valuations. The more they progress, the better the valuation. Not being able to attract the next-stage money can prove catastrophic for both the entrepreneur and the early-stage VC. VCs and entrepreneurs sit on the same side of the table and have a shared interest in the success of the venture, except during funding episodes when they sit across from each other with divergent objectives about the valuations. To get a good valuation, an entrepreneur has to attract multiple VCs who are willing to invest. The VC business, like the movie business, is a business of hits. It is not a business for soft-hearted individuals. You have to walk away from emerging losers. You have to double down on winners. There's no room for muddled thinking here.

On VC economics

VC economics is very risky and requires a disciplined approach if it is to provide satisfactory returns. The dirty little secret of the VC business is that most of the returns are made by the top ten percent of the funds; the remaining ninety percent barely return the capital back after 10 years. Let's do some math here:

Assume an early-stage VC fund of $100 million, with the typical 2% annual fee and 20% carry. It has a 10-year life, so it siphons off a 20% fee over 10 years and will invest only $80 million unless it recycles the profits from the early winners. A typical early-stage fund invests in about twenty companies, in this case averaging about $4 million each, and will easily lose all its capital in at least half of its investments. So, for it to return 5x to its investors after the carry (a good but not great return) it must produce 6x overall or 12x on its winners. But since only 80% of the money is invested, it must produce 15x on its 10 winners. That means each must produce a $60 million return to produce $600 million so that $500 million can be returned to investors.

A good fund manager starts to starve its early laggards and nurture its winners. The goal is to deploy most of the capital in the emerging winners to increase their odds of winning and maximize returns. This requires the VCs to watch their investments like hawks for early signs of trouble. It requires the discipline to make hard decisions about not spending the limited resources of time and money on your troubled investments. The VC business is simple but heartless.

On his approach to problem-solving

Early in my career, I earned a reputation of being a firefighter. I would be brought in to help salvage troubled projects. I would come in and look at it from a firefighter's perspective; take a step back and assess the situation; see what could be saved and what couldn't; what must be saved, and what could be let go. I'd look at the resources and the time available to get the job done. I got very good at developing a plan to achieve, in the shortest time possible, the maximum desired results. Since that time, I have become more strategic in my approach to everything in life. Thinking through what needs to be done and what can be done, given the time and resources, has been my strength.

It is sad to see that there is no such overall strategy driving the U.S. response to COVID-19. We're going to have a significant number of deaths by the time this is over.

The general assumption is that all states will once again have to go into lockdown. President Trump is reluctant to tell his followers that they must "get with the program". These incremental lockdowns are very ineffective and expensive. I believe we're likely to lose a lot more people as a result of this dangerous hesitation on President Trump's part.

On profitability vs growth

It is interesting to see the TechCrunch article that says Paytm is raising $1 billion in a new round of funding. The article says that it has raised a total of $3.3 billion to date. I don't have any details, but reading between the lines, I can see that it's prioritized growth over profitability.

The risky part of the business comes from thinking that there is an unlimited amount of money available, so you can burn tens of millions of dollars every month. It's going to be hard to sustain that. I find Uber as a very useful service and started writing about them two years ago. I don't care how much money they have right now, but with the current spend levels, they're bound to get into trouble.

I know for sure that capital flows are not steady and can change overnight. Let me tell you another story of Exodus, a darling of the dotcom era. Exodus was started by K.B. Chandrasekhar and B.V. Jagadeesh and pioneered the Internet Data Center business. It grew rapidly as the internet grew in the late '90s. It was doubling every six months and reached a $100 million-a-month revenue by 1999. It went public in 1998 and reached a public market valuation of $30 billion. One hundred percent growth implied that it needed to double its number of data centers every six months. Money was easily available, as its banker, Goldman Sachs, could raise a billion dollars in convertible debentures overnight. Conventional wisdom says not to sell equity to dilute shareholders, but to raise debt. I was the only one on the only board who advised against doing so. I resigned from the board and decided to sell my shares. The problem was that as the company scaled, its losses also scaled. It never made a profit and it had $3 billion-dollar debt that needed to be serviced. It borrowed more to service the debt and build the data centers. When the music stopped with the dotcom bust in 2000, the money dried up. Its customers started to default, and the new data centers stayed empty. The company went from being worth $30 billion to nothing – I mean zilch, in no time at all.

My shares had grown 1000+fold and I was super rich on paper, but I was not able to sell, as I was locked out as an ex-insider for 90 days. I sold as much as I could as soon as I could, but the value had dropped by ninety percent when I was allowed to sell. By the time I was out, it had dropped another ninety percent. I learned the hard lesson that you can't count on financing when you most need it if you are not profitable. A profitable company can pull in its horns and ride out the market storms. Loss-making companies go under.

I am an avid believer in strong balance sheets, early improvement of your model, and early profitability. That's how it used to be done. But look at Google; how much money did they burn before they became profitable? Less than $2 million. With Microsoft, it was less than one million. Bear in mind, however, that these are very rare examples.

On the importance of giving back

Kanwal founded the Kanwal Rekhi Schools of Information Technology at both IIT-Bombay and Michigan Tech. He is a prime benefactor of a foundation in India that identifies talented students without funds and provides them with both their college tuition and their living expenses. He is currently a board member of Pan IIT USA, Inc., the alumni organization of the Indian Institutes of Technology. Kanwal has been honored with the 2010 Haridas Award and received the Bina Chaudhuri Award for Distinguished Service by the California Institute of Integral Studies. He was also named Entrepreneur of the Year in 1987 by the Arthur-Young/Venture magazine. He won the Distinguished Alumni Award from IIT Bombay in 2000. Later, Kanwal was appointed to the Board of Advisors to the President of Michigan Tech and is a board member on the IIT Bombay Heritage Fund (IITBHF).

Finally, advice to the younger generation

I raised my kids to believe that the most important thing in their life is education. Second is their health, which keeps them fit, strong and clear-minded, and third in importance is their family.

Part 2: Q&A on the current business environment

What impact do you see COVID having on Silicon Valley?

Silicon Valley can function remotely better than any other place. Even before COVID, a lot of presentations were made on Google Hangouts. Out of five meetings with entrepreneurs, maybe one of them might be in person. We were already using technology, but now five out of five meetings are virtual. Driving for an hour to get somewhere and another hour to drive back was really unproductive. These virtual meetings are eliminating that. You can talk to VCs, your mentors, and investors without ever seeing them in person. Some of my employees are functioning really well without the offices being open now, so I don't think COVID is having the same type of impact here as it would in Detroit or even Hollywood. That's not to say it won't have any impact at all. I'm not sure how much, but we'll see. Either way, this will present a lot of opportunities for us. As the world evolves and changes, we adapt. Take Zoom, for example. Complex technology will have to be applied everywhere; imagine the complications and difficulties involved in trying to successfully run a university remotely.

In the absence of social networking, how will entrepreneurs adapt, in coming up with or nurturing the next business idea?

The networking aspect is definitely going to be more difficult. We usually hold an event every year in May called TiECON, but we had to cancel it this year. There were supposed to be 4,000 people there, with a lot of opportunities for networking. They are now trying to do that over Zoom. So, instead of one or two days attending the TiE con event, it will be spread over seven or eight days. Silicon Valley is pretty inventive, so they'll find a way to make it work. I'm actually doing more mentoring now than I've ever done before. The distance aspect has disappeared. During a Zoom meeting I'll ask a person where they are at the moment and they might be in Atlanta, DC, even India.

How does Silicon Valley startup culture compare with other cities of the world?

I love it here. Nice weather, liberal attitudes, an interactive environment. It's hard to imagine that anywhere else will have this rich of a concentration of venture capital and entrepreneurs. Silicon Valley is a like nuclear reactor. Still, London and Berlin have a pretty active startup culture too, and Chicago had the Groupon immersion. But this level of branding and concentration of people doesn't happen overnight. When people from other countries say they want to come to the United States, they aren't thinking of Philadelphia or Boston. There's a massive startup culture that has emerged in India. Silicon Valley companies outsource IT services there, and some have offices in Bangalore. Startup culture outside Silicon Valley is definitely accelerating.

Do you think this pandemic is going to change consumer behavior?

This pandemic will definitely change consumer behavior. I was actually surprised that we didn't have a plan in place for this pandemic. Yeah, we have the CDC and WHO, but we had no guide to follow. This is basically Coronavirus 3.0 if you include MERS and SARS. I think we'll be a lot more prepared in the future. We, as individuals, must be responsible for our own health. At the very least we will become more aware of the unnecessary risks that we take. One thing people have discovered is that they will have to save more money, and business balance sheets will have to improve. You have to be prepared to take a hit for a two-to-three-month period without going under.

Are there any particularly new ideas lately that excite you?

A person like me doesn't have to think about those things anymore. I'm 75 years old, so I'm not going to be starting anything new on my own. I meet a lot of people, and I hear a lot more about automation and a lot more about AI stuff. It's been happening for quite a while now, and this pandemic is speeding it all up. President Trump talks about wanting to bring manufacturing back to the U.S., but it will have to be done by robots because we no longer have that amount of manpower on tap.

The internet's held up well, but there are days when you get very frustrated with it. Sometimes it's extremely slow when another person in your home is streaming; other times it just mysteriously doesn't work, and you have no idea why. I sense a greater need for technology in the near future than we've ever had before.

Entrepreneurial Eco-System
Interview 3

German Medical Valley

Siegfried Balleis

Previous mayor of Erlangen and
Honorary Professor at FAU

Written by Michael Fischer

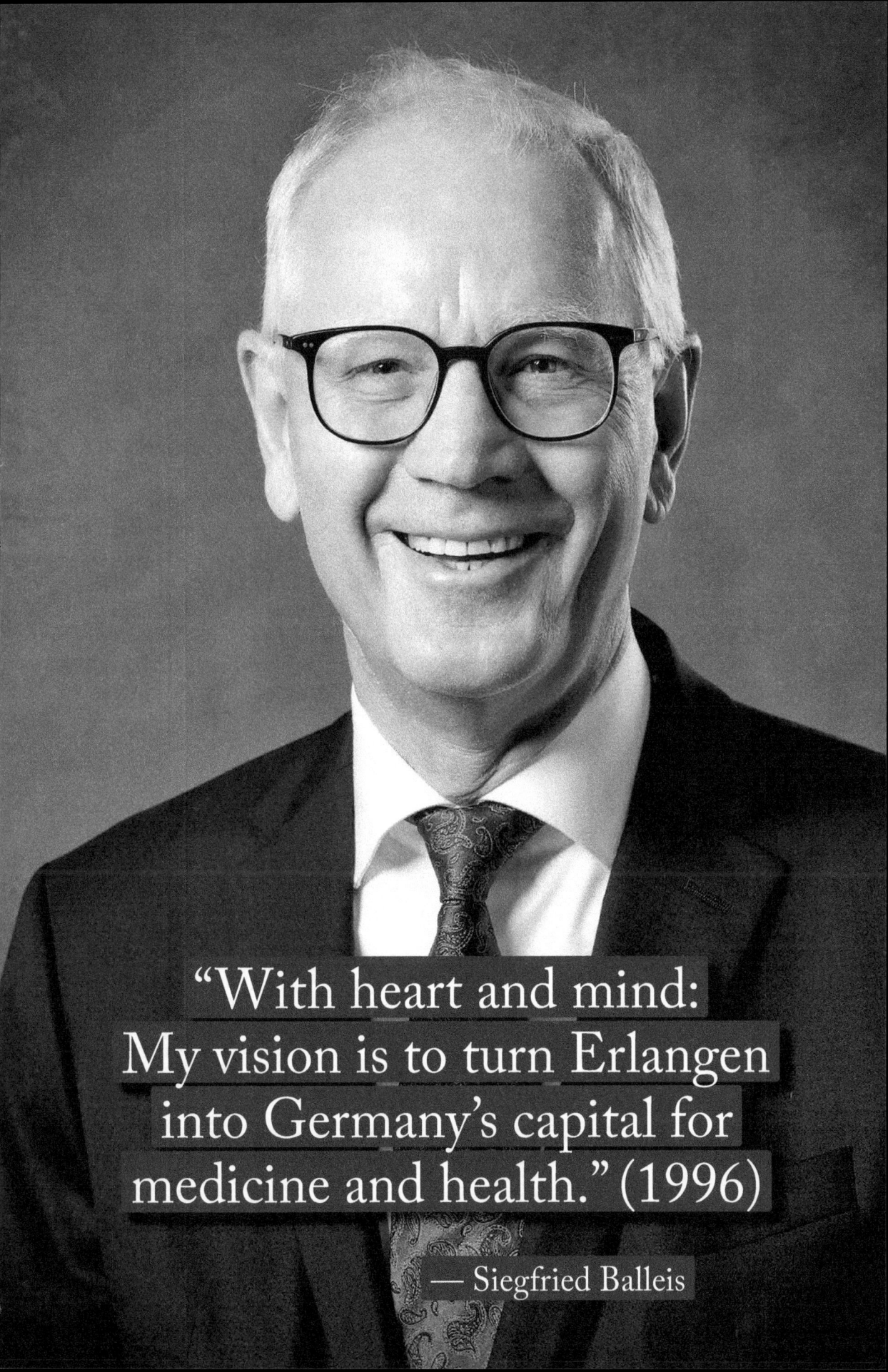

"With heart and mind: My vision is to turn Erlangen into Germany's capital for medicine and health." (1996)

— Siegfried Balleis

Siegfried Balleis was the mayor of Erlangen from 1996 to 2014 and was key in establishing the Medical Valley Center (MVC) in Erlangen. He's a politician, representing the Christian Social Union of Bavaria (CSU).

Balleis holds and has held (partly in his function as mayor of Erlangen) numerous offices in clubs, associations, and supervisory bodies. On a supra-local level, for example, he was a member of the presidium and board of the German and Bavarian Association of Cities and Towns. From 2002 to 2014, he served as Chairman of the Board of Directors of KGSt Kommunale Gemeinschaftsstelle für Verwaltungsmanagement – a think tank of the municipalities in Germany and Austria. From 1997 to 2015, he was a member of the CSU party executive committee, and of the party presidium from 2007 to 2011. On October 28, 2011, he was elected Council President of the European Metropolitan Region of Nuremberg and held that position until 2014. In addition, Siegfried Balleis has long been associated with the Friedrich-Alexander University Erlangen-Nürnberg (FAU), as Chairman of the University Association and Honorary Senator, and, since 2018, as an Honorary Professor at the Institute of Political Science. Siegfried Balleis is an honorary citizen of the city of Erlangen and bearer of the Bavarian Order of Merit.

I n this interview, Siegfried Balleis explains how he, as Mayor of the City of Erlangen, was key in establishing an ecosystem especially for start-ups in the medical sector. MVC is the ideal place for anyone looking to start a business in the medical field. Besides giving people a space, the MVC also provides valuable start-up services, consulting in financing and funding, networks, marketing services, and international services.

Dr. Balleis, tell us a little about yourself?

Let me tell you a short story about myself. I grew up in a suburb of Nuremberg in the 1950s. My father, who was captured in the Soviet Union at the end of the Second World War, was very familiar with the term "Carpe Diem" – the instant of our existence. Every moment in your life is crucial. When I was young, he told me "Boy if you don't take risks, you're not doing anything." As a young boy, this sounded pretty harsh, but it made me a man who's never afraid to make decisions – and a man with an ambitious vision.

How did you identify the need for a medical innovation hub?

Germany has experienced a reasonably stable economy for decades. But it has not always been that way. From 1993 to 1996, Germany experienced a very sharp recession that resulted in a steep loss of jobs. This was especially devastating in the city of Erlangen. Nearly ten percent of the seventy thousand workplaces had disappeared. In this difficult period, the city administration of Erlangen discussed strategies on how to tackle these problems. One strategy developed was to start a consistent innovation policy which turned out to be the right path. We also focused on a second approach with the idea of a SWOT-analysis to identify the strengths, weaknesses, opportunities, and threats of the Erlangen economy.

The results were of these analyses were amazing. They showed that Erlangen's working population had the highest percentage of people employed in the health sector compared to all other eighty-three cities in Germany. It became obvious that Erlangen had a unique selling point compared to all other German cities and it was a logical step to emphasize this individuality.

In my inauguration speech, as recently elected mayor, I outlined my plan for the further development of Erlangen, "it's my vision, and it should be our common vision, to develop Erlangen as a national capital of medical research, production, and services".

What were the initial difficulties and what were the key enablers of this project?

Although there had been many doubts in the city of Erlangen at the beginning about whether this was the right approach, an intense discussion and cooperation process started between the different stakeholders such as local politicians, local businessmen, and the members of the Friedrich-Alexander University Erlangen-Nürnberg. A very important milestone of this development was when the CEO of Siemens, Heinrich von Pierer, announced that at the end of 1997, his company would make its largest investment, €100 million, in the so-called old "Bundesländer" after the German reunification. This decision was highly supported by national and federal policies as, then Germany's minister of finance, Theo Waigel, enabled Siemens to buy a 60,000 m² area from the federal government.

Under the rule of Prime Minister Edmund Stoiber, the development of the Medical Valley is strongly connected with the privatization policy of the Bavarian government. His mission statement was, "the main task of politics is not to possess assets but to shape the future". He developed an innovation strategy for the free state of Bavaria in which all-in-all nearly €5 billion were invested in innovation projects. In Germany, this policy is known as the Bavarian "Hightech-offensive". Nearly $1 billion were invested in the Erlangen region in innovation projects and modernizing the hospital infrastructure.

How did professional networks push the project towards success?

On the regional level the "Competence initiative medicine, pharmaceutics, and health" was founded. The members of this network met face-to-face several times every year, connecting specialists from politics, medical business and services, and official institutions. The key concept was that the participants presented their ideas and business plans within a "five-minute talk" to find the connection between ideas and capital. The result of this network were many new corporations and foundations of new enterprises. Looking back from the year 2020, one can see at least twenty thousand new jobs have been created in this newly found ecosystem.

Parallel to this network on the regional level the "Forum Medtech Pharma" has been founded on the Bavarian level, organizing corporations and contacts and informing on the latest trends in the health sector by offering workshops, sessions, and fairs.

What made this project unique?

With the Bavarian Government's strong commitment, the new Medical Valley Center was designed and built up. It was opened in May 2003 and after six months, it became Germany's most successful incubation center. It's not surprising that this innovation center was expanded to 5.000 square meters within two years. The MVC hosts more than thirty-five startup companies and institutions connected with innovation activities, such as the Medical Valley cluster management and the chamber of industry and commerce.

The unique selling point of this Medical Valley Center is it is not only a business incubation center but also a scientific research unit. The central Institute for Medical Technology and the Institute of Biomedical Technology work closely together with the activities of the start-up companies in the MVC. The young entrepreneurs and scientists meet nearly every day in the common cafeteria or common lecture halls of the MVC.

At the beginning of 2007 the society "Medical Valley European Metropolitan Region Nuremberg" was founded, coordinating all stakeholders in politics, business, and the scientific community in the region. This organization continues to be the motor and coordinator of all activities in the Medical Valley.

The Medical Valley experienced its next big step by winning a national excellence competition of the German Ministry of Education and Research (BMBF) Professor Reinhardt designed the draft together with Professor Juergen Schuettler, the dean of the medical faculty, and received €40 million. They matched it with another €50 million from the private sector. Today, the Medical Valley is a national Leading-Edge Cluster upon its application as a 'Centre of Excellence for Medical Engineering'.

What is the cluster's key to success?

The cluster's strength is its power of innovation. Businesses and research institutes in the Medical Valley EMN benefit from the short distances to develop best-in-class research and development processes. These, in turn, result in competitive advantages and growth

500+	70+	850,000	80+	20+
Companies active in medtech & digital health	Hospitals & strong outpatient sector	Inpatients treated per year	Institutes focused on medtech & digital health	Non-university research institutions in the med-tech field

opportunities in a global market. Healthcare providers benefit from access to state-of-the-art technologies and cost optimization. Cluster management encourages these developments and strengthens the market positioning of the brand Medical Valley EMN. Thus, the region is associated with excellence in healthcare provision and is perceived as more and more attractive both in Germany and internationally. As the global market share and sales revenues are increasing, the economic power of the region is strengthened. This approach enables us to create and secure jobs.

What is Medical Valley's vision?

Medical Valley European Metropolitan Region of Nuremberg (EMN) is one of the strongest, most active medical technology research clusters in the world. Renowned partners from industry, research, healthcare, and politics have come together to form this interdisciplinary network. Their common goal is to innovate successful solutions for the healthcare of tomorrow.

Medical engineering products and services are currently being developed in over forty projects. These products and services are aimed at making prevention, diagnosis, treatment, and rehabilitation, in connection with a variety of illnesses, more efficient and effective. Activities in the cluster and communication among the stakeholders are coordinated by the Medical Valley EMN Association, which also supports its members with numerous services.

FAU is a member of Medical Valley and has close connections to many of its partners thanks to its research projects. Furthermore, research and teaching in this field have become a well-established part of the University through the Central Institute of Healthcare Engineering and the medical technology degree program.

The long-term strategy of the Medical Valley EMN is to optimize the structures of healthcare provision. Medical Valley EMN brings together all parties to establish an international model region of optimized healthcare provision.

What is 'Communities of Practice' and how does it help entrepreneurs?

The Communities of Practice (CoP) in Medical Valley EMN are groups of people that communicate on a regular basis and learn from each other in their particular field. In cooperation with the board of the cluster, the CoP topics are discussed regularly and, if necessary, new communities are established. Thus, the CoPs play an important role to cover the topics that are relevant for the implementation of the cluster strategy and to use them to enable real projects.

The Digital Hub Initiative, developed by the Federal Ministry for Economic Affairs and Energy, seeks to support the establishment of digital hubs in Germany. The underlying idea of establishing hubs is that cooperation between companies and business start-ups within a confined area, like in Silicon Valley, will boost innovation, especially in the digital age.

Cooperation and networking in a common space is the breeding ground for new innovative products and business models. In this way, a regional "hub ecosystem" can be created where new ideas emerge, and digital transformation is taken forward. Therefore, hubs with international appeal/reach are necessary, in which German and international business start-ups, scientists, investors and established companies mutually support and strengthen each other.

Part II
A Start-Up Building Tool-Box

Establishing the Legal Foundation

Stanley Chang

Founder of Perspectives Law Group, Western Digital Corporation, Quantum Corporation, IBM, Hewlett-Packard, and Agilent Technologies

Written by Malvina Supper, Thilo Bauer and Veniamin Morgenshtern

"You must be careful about inadvertently losing your legal rights in the process of building a business as a founder."

— Stanley Chang

Stanley M. Chang is an engineer, patent attorney, and high-tech entrepreneur. He is the founder, and managing attorney, at the Perspective Law Group. His law practice spans many areas like corporate and real estate law, patent prosecution, and portfolio management. Before practicing law, Stanley was a successful engineer and held various senior management positions in companies like Western Digital Corporation, Quantum Corporation, IBM, Hewlett-Packard, and Agilent Technologies. He holds a Bachelor of Science in Electrical Engineering from UCLA, Master of Science in Electrical Engineering from the USC, and Juris Doctorate from Santa Clara University School of Law. He is admitted to practice law in California and also before the United States Patent and Trademark Office.

Intellectual Property (IP) has become a valuable asset for many organizations. Without strong IP protection, a business can quickly lose its competitive advantage. As a domain expert, Stanley was asked to walk us through the different types of IP, their characteristics, IP protection, and legal issues surrounding IP, when starting a new business. Stanley discusses the essential steps that an entrepreneur must take early on in the process of company formation, such as assigning responsibilities amongst the team and the importance of timing when filing for IP protection. He talks about what to consider when dealing with a venture capitalist (VC) and how to avoid accidental loss of IP rights. Stanley shares the secrets for an entrepreneur to create a successful unicorn.

Tell us about your unique background in engineering, business, and law.

I have a unique blend of experience in law, technology development, and business management. I was in engineering for seventeen years before practicing law. As an engineer, my role spanned from design engineering to senior management and management of product lines. I've also created a high-tech start-up. My firm, Perspective Law Group, supports companies ranging from start-ups to Fortune 100 companies. I understand Intellectual Property (IP), the role of IP in different stages of creating a company. I consult in the area of IP, the role of IP in company formation and funding, and how IP relates to start-ups. This combination enables me to connect the dots and support a start-up from different perspectives. Therefore, the name Perspectives Law Group.

What are the different types of IP?

IPs are exclusionary rights. In other words, you can exclude others from using your IP rights. There are four types of IP: patents, trademarks, copyrights, and trade secrets.

Essentially, a patent is to protect functions and features; a trademark is to protect branding and logos; a trade secret is to protect important information in perpetuity, and a copyright is to protect works of authorship. There are different nuances in different countries, but these four types are generally applicable.

1. Trademark

A trademark aids in product differentiation. It helps in identifying the source of a product or service and can be used by a company in its marketing and branding strategy. Anything can be trademarked, whether it's a word, style, color, shape, or design. There are a lot of notable trademarks, for example, Google, Apple, Coca-Cola, and BMW. On a single Coca-Cola product, there are a lot of different trademarks like the name, the stylized word, the white ribbon, and the red color. A trademark is the only IP where you must enforce your IP rights and requires constant monitoring and enforcement. If you do not exercise your trademark rights, it could be deemed that you have abandoned that trademark.

2. Trade secrets

A trade secret is something so important that you want to keep it a secret in perpetuity. It covers information that is not public and has independent economic value giving you a competitive advantage. For example, the Coca-Cola formula is one of the best-kept trade secrets in the world and has been around for more than 100 years. The Google search algorithm and the improvements made to it are not patented; they are trade secrets. Trade secret lawsuits can be expensive. Waymo settled its trade secret lawsuit against Uber for $245 million and a 0.34% equity in Uber. With all other IP rights, like patent, copyright, or trademark, there is a specific time limit on how long you can own that IP right. A trade secret is perpetual if you keep it a secret. However, simply calling it a trade secret does not make it one. Some formalities must be put in place for an entity to have a chance for gaining trade secret protection.

3. Copyrights and copyright licensing

Copyright is very important in the area of creative arts such as literature, music, and movies, so it's quite common to think of copyrights in the area of non-tech entities, but there are also copyrights in the tech and biotech industries. You can copyright your software code, your firmware, or even how you express your genomic data. Take, for example, a semiconductor chip design. The mask used to fabricate a semiconductor device is considered eligible for copyright protection. Copyright is automatic in that once it is captured in a tangible medium you own a copyright in the U.S., assuming it meets all the legal requirements. However, if you ever want to litigate against it, you must register that with the Copyright office.

4. Patents

Patents, universally, give you the right to exclude others from using your invention. There are three types of patents in the United States: the utility patent, the design patent, and the plant patent. Utility patents cover the functionality of an invention. In other words, how does something work? Design patents cover how things look from an ornamental standpoint. Apple and Samsung were parties to a design patent lawsuit about icons and iPhone's rounded corners. Plant patents cover a new variety of plants, for example different cannabis strains are eligible for plant patents.

As an entrepreneur, where do I start in terms of IP?

The first thing to do is to understand that you do not have to just settle with one IP type. You can use any number of IP types. Find out what fits your business the best, and which ones help you in your particular environment, with due consideration to your budget and timing. You should also consider factors like; does it give you a market, performance, or reliability advantage? As an example, let's say you have genomics information, but it takes perhaps three to five years to get a patent. Consider using the copyright option at the same time you work on your patent. Patents cost the most and take the longest to achieve, but they may also get you the biggest damages in case of an infringement. Trademarks are the second most expensive to maintain. Now, trade secret, that's a wild card. What industry are you in? What are you trying to protect as a trade secret? It can be expensive and an extremely long process.

What does "patent pending" mean and are they valid worldwide?

Patent-pending means exactly what it says. The patent has been filed, but it has not yet been issued. Under the US laws, you can sue for damages, including the time when the patent was still pending. There is no such thing as an international patent. Each patent is based on its legal jurisdiction. Even the European Patent Office (EPO) doesn't represent a patent office for all of Europe. To enforce a patent issued by EPO, it must be validated in each EU country. However, there is an international Patent Cooperation Treaty (PCT), which allows international applications and gives about eighteen months for you to file patents in individual countries. Taiwan is not in the PCT, so if you want that right, you must file separately in Taiwan.

How do businesses leverage their patent portfolios?

Businesses monetize their patents by licensing their patent portfolios. For example, Ericsson, with a portfolio of about thirty-seven thousand patents, earns approximately a billion dollars a year in royalties. That's about 4.3% of their total revenue for 2014.

Another method of leveraging your existing portfolio is by selling it. Nortel Networks, as a part of their bankruptcy proceedings, sold their six thousand patents, to a consortium led by Apple and Microsoft for $4.5 billion. That's $750,000 for each patent.

Patents are also used defensively or as a bargaining chip for a business deal. They can be used to sue or counter-sue a party. The bigger and more successful you get, the bigger target you become for lawsuits. People will try to find a way to poach your profits. Broadcom was sued by a much smaller company for patent infringement, nearly putting it out of business. Fortunately for Broadcom, a patent portfolio bought from a bankrupt start-up held some strong patents that were used to counter-sue and both companies settled. This is the reason companies spend money, not only developing their organic patent portfolio but also purchasing them from others.

Universities used to license or sell their patents, but that method wasn't very successful. Now, some universities use their portfolio to strategically support start-ups instead. If you look at the entrepreneurial websites in the University of California system, you'll find that they offer startups their office space, funding, and their patent portfolio.

Can I file my own patent application? Should I do my own patent search?

I'll tell you a little secret about the U.S. patent system that does not exist in any other country. We have what's called a provisional patent that serves as a placeholder, for one year, while you decide what to do with your innovation. As an individual inventor, the filing fees are around two hundred dollars. However, you cannot just say, "This product is great and it's going to change the world." You must define functional benefits as a part of your application in case you want to change your provisional patent to a non-provisional patent in a year.

As far as patent search is concerned, I never recommend that engineers or scientists do their own patent search. From an engineering perspective, I often found inventions that were not considered new. They were just used somewhere else or the functionalities they provided were used differently, there was no difference. But as a lawyer, there is a big difference, one that makes the invention patentable. Engineers see similarities while lawyers see differences. If you find something that looks interesting, I'd advise you show it to your patent counsel rather than taking it on yourself.

When should I consider filing for patents? Are there scenarios where I can inadvertently lose legal rights to my inventions?

You should file for patents as early as you can, or you may lose your IP rights. If you talk to me about your ideas and I do not have a Non-Disclosure Agreement (NDA) with you; you may lose some of your patent rights. As a matter of fact, in some countries, by talking without an NDA, you might lose your rights because of something called an "absolute novelty requirement". Absolute novelty is the public disclosure or disclosure without expectation of confidentiality. Unfortunately, VC's will typically not sign NDAs; therefore, technically speaking, once you talk to a VC, you have already destroyed absolute novelty. Thus, don't be handing out your business plan and your secrets willy-nilly. VCs will pressure you for more information, they'll fill you with doubts about yourself and they'll say things like, "Well, unless you give me more details, I can't go any further with this discussion." However, you need to keep your secret sauce to yourself, so to speak.

What should founders consider from a legal point of view when starting a business?

Everyone gets excited about what they will do as a start-up entrepreneur, but people don't understand the risks they may be taking. Unless you fully understand this, you can get yourself embroiled in a world of hurt. For example, one of the most heavily litigated areas of civil litigation is the litigation between partners, either VC partners or founders of the company. That's important to know because you should never work with other people as founders without having proper legal agreements. You don't want to go into a business saying: "We're friends, so nothing can go wrong." This will almost always backfire. At the very least, put your initial agreement down on paper. You don't want to have any mis-understandings. If you value your friendship, get the agreement on paper. This will help ensure that both you and your partner understand each other. Sometimes I may say some-thing, and you may hear something very different because we each hear it in a different context. This might lead to you losing a good friend.

What are the issues when multiple founders are involved and how do you resolve disputes?

It is important to have a discussion with all co-founders upfront. Have an open discussion about who is responsible for what, who takes on which tasks, who invests what. Otherwise, you will have conflicts with your co-founders. By "invest" I mean both capital contribu-tions and sweat contributions. Are you going to quit the job you have right now? Are you going to work only half time but want to earn a hundred-thousand-dollar salary? You want to work only part-time but want equal shares in the company? Is that acceptable? It may be if you have most of the key knowledge. If you don't, then maybe not. You can pro-vide additional compensation to the person who works more. You can give them a salary and even more shares as a bonus.

Unfortunately, no matter what the mechanism is, disputes are inevitable. You need to have a plan in place for resolving these disputes. Do not be afraid to disagree with each other. You simply need to deal with it constructively to keep things moving forward. Focus on the issues and not on the person. Once it devolves into a personal attack it's no longer business-focused and will end up being non-productive.

What are shares and how do you distribute them?

A corporation has a certain number of authorized shares, let's say ten million, and those ten million shares are issued to you, the founders. Now you want to bring someone in as a CEO and she wants four million shares. That's when the company's board authorizes another ten million shares. Now you have twenty million authorized shares, but the ad-ditional ten million are not issued. When you give the four million to the new CEO, the question is: what is the valuation of the shares? In stocks, there's dilution and there's also an anti-dilution clause. For the sake of clarity: stock dilution is the decrease in existing shareholders' ownership percentage as a result of the company issuing new equity. New equity increases the total shares, which has a dilutive effect on the ownership percentage of existing shareholders. There are many ways of handling this with both common stock and preferred stock.

If you bring on people as strategic partners, those who will help you grow, then don't worry too much about dilution. Once I screwed up when I offered too little to a CEO. I'm going to tell you right now, and I say this from the bottom of my heart, do not make that mistake. Do not be greedy and unwilling to give up a little control of the company. In the end, you may lose out in terms of forward growth.

How can the equity structure be used to maintain your control over the company?

I will explain this using an example from the equity structure of Alphabet, the parent company of Google. Alphabet's equity structure is composed of Class A common stock, Class C common stock, and Class B stock. Class A and Class C stocks are publicly traded in the market. Class A has voting rights, one share equals one vote. Class C has no voting rights, but you still have publicly traded security. Class B is not publicly traded. It is owned by three people in Google, the two founders, and one of the executives. Each one of those shares has voting rights. The way the math works out, those three people can out-vote everyone else. This is how you have control of the company.

Snapchat is another company with an interesting equity structure. They have certain stock classes where the original investors have ten voting rights per share, the lead investors have one voting right per share, and the common shares on the market have zero voting rights.

What is a corporate veil in a corporation and how does it protect the shareholders?

A corporate veil is a legal concept that separates the liabilities of a corporation from its shareholders. Under this doctrine, a company is responsible for its business debt and liabilities. You as an entrepreneur will only be responsible to the extent of your investment in the company, whether it be cash, work, or whatever. You want an entity type that has this corporate veil. One entity type that provides this security is a corporation. There are other entity types, like a sole proprietorship and general partnerships, that do not provide the corporate veil. In a sole proprietorship, you're the only owner, which means you are responsible for everything, including all the debt, all the liabilities, and all the lawsuits.

Another way to cover your liabilities, without a corporate veil, is to obtain insurance such as business liability insurance or a personal umbrella policy. Some people say "I'm going to make my life simple; I won't get into all the legal hassles about forming an entity. I'm just going to run it as a sole proprietorship or as a general partnership, and I will just buy insurance based on that." Great, but you must thoroughly understand the insurance policy. What are the limits? How much coverage do you have? What is the coverage per incident? How good is the insurance company? Is the insurance company still going to be around when you have a problem?

Is the work done before forming a corporation automatically covered under the corporate veil?

Promoters are personally liable for a company before it is formed. Be careful what you do when getting ready to sign on for a new start-up. There are a lot of personal risks that an entrepreneur takes without realizing it. If you inadvertently made agreements through a written contract or even just verbally, that could result in a lot of personal debt and you will be personally liable unless you deal with it in the right way.

For example, a lot of you have already started thinking about a start-up. Someone talks to a manufacturer or a supplier and these are verbal discussions. Then they take actions based on these discussions. Guess what? That discussion can eventually create a binding agreement and make you personally liable because the company is not yet formed.

What legal advice do you give young students when building a start-up?

Students often say, "I have nothing in my pocket. What could they sue me for? I'm still broke anyway." Here's the problem, you're doing a start-up because you think it will be successful. Let's say, a few years down the line, it indeed becomes successful and you have, let's say, millions of dollars in the bank. Now you have a lot to lose. Or worse yet, you close your start-up and you work at Google and you get a nice salary. Guess what? If there's someone who wants to sue you, they can go after your wages. Every time you get paid, they get paid too. Just because you have nothing to lose now as a student doesn't mean your actions will not impact your future.

How do I prepare to raise the money from a VC for the first time?

First, try to fund it yourself or ask friends and family. Don't look for external funding until you're absolutely ready for it. Before you go to a VC you need to be clear about what your product is; not just from a technical perspective, but also from a market perspective. Develop a prototype before, otherwise, it will be hard to get any traction. Remember, your product is not just a technology. You need to be clear about what your product is. What's the total market size? What's the serviceable market? How big will your market share be? Who will be your customers? Be ready to justify those numbers. Make sure your corporate documentation is clean. Do you have a CAP table? Who owns what? What's the valuation? Be prepared to answer this question: "You want my money? How much do I get back?" Get references from customers for your due diligence documents, references that your investor can contact.

Second, you need to approach investors methodically from the very beginning. Have a professionally prepared due diligence packet ready for the VC that contains all your important documents, business plan, and financials. You should have that available so that when the VC asks for it, you're prepared to hand it over.

Finally, when considering VC money, don't be greedy. I know it's tempting to want a million dollars for a start-up, but ideally, you should be able to look beyond and into the value that the VC brings to your startup. An ideal VC investment will not just bring money but also name, validation, and connections.

How do you correctly determine the value of your company when talking to a VC?

In my opinion, this is a question for later. Don't evaluate yourself too early. Don't say that you have a slide deck, so your company is worth $5 million. I'll be the first to admit that I made exactly that mistake. I said that we have this great product, we have the market, the expertise, the customer contacts, and the due diligence. Therefore, it follows that we are a $5 million company. Big mistake. Wait until you have a prototype, products, or samples in the customer's hands. Only then you can have a meaningful discussion.

Take, for example, the U. S. housing market. In this market there are appraisal reports. The appraisal report indicates how much your house is worth compared to other similar houses in your neighborhood. Is that appraisal value the value of your house? No! The value of your house is what someone is willing to pay for it. Suppose you already have an offer of ten million dollars. In that case, you don't care what mathematical formula was used to derive your valuation. That offer alone just won the game against the formula. But do not try to do this too early.

How to choose the right VC fund?

Let's say one VC has ten funds. As an entrepreneur, you might say, "This company is a big VC company, it has ten funds. Let me see which one of them I can get." This is not the correct way of looking at it. You must look at the stage of each of the funds. Is it fully subscribed or are the funds fully used up or close to being used up? What is the charter of each fund? Is it for an early-stage company, a mid-stage company, a late-stage company, or a pre-IPO company? Is it for biotech, synthetic foods, software, or cyber-security? Unless you find the fund with the right charter and enough money, they will not be able to, nor want to, invest money in your company.

Let's say you find a fund that's for early-stage start-ups in your industry. Great, you found the right fund. Not quite. Suppose most of the companies in the portfolio are losing money. What happens? They may decide to change the early stage mandate to a late-stage mandate. This way the general partners can make money for the fund and keep the limited partners happy. The general partners will get green lights from the limited partners to change that mandate. However, the change in mandate may never show up on their website, so you won't be aware of the change. Make sure that general partners can help you open doors for you with the customer base. Remember, it's never just about the money.

Are there other sources of funding?

Suppose you aspire to run a company by yourself, keeping the profits in your pocket, without dealing with the public securities market. In that case, commercial loans are a good option. Most commercial loans, at least in the United States, want collateral from the business, not personal collateral, but things like your account receivables, equipment, or hard assets. For example, say you need $250,000 for operations and you have account receivables in the range of $300,000 – $400,000 and other assets that can be easily liquidated, my suggestion is to get a loan and forget the VCs. With the loan, you keep all the equity in your pocket, and you are not diluting your stock. To go this route, recognize that you need to have accounts receivable and at least two years of operating history which shows actual revenue for at least the past two years.

Another source of funding is strategic partners. Suppose you have a supplier, and he is interested in investing in your company. The person-in-charge of the business says, "I can't give you the money and I don't want equity, but I can give you an equipment lease for free or deferred payments for two years." He offers this option because if he wants to get equity, he needs to get his board involved. If the board is not involved the decision can be made much easier and much faster. Remember that financing is not always about money. If you must buy equipment that costs a million dollars and someone gives it to you instead, that's great too.

How do I work with international investors?

International investors may be governed by their local laws and may come with a different set of requirements. As a result, you need to recognize such a situation and be flexible when dealing with them. For example, I had a case where an international investment fund told me that it's easier for them to get the money, out of the country, in the form of a convertible bond.

How much should I budget for lawyers' services in an early stage start-up?

The short answer is, it depends. What is your product? What is your industry? For example, a medical device needs to go through an FDA clearance if it uses new hardware, which can be expensive.

Starting a corporation with a single class of shares and a board of directors should cost anywhere from five thousand to ten thousand dollars. Anything else beyond that, like employment contracts, consulting agreements with NDAs, leasing of buildings and renting space can cost anywhere from ten thousand dollars to fifty thousand dollars.

Circling back to shares, how much equity or how many shares should a founder offer when hiring a high-powered CEO?

This is a common question and much of the answer depends on the value that an individual brings to the company. Is that person there only for operations or do they do more than that? Do they bring in funding, open doors to new markets, provide skills the current team lacks? It also depends on what stages of operation the company is in. As a founder, you may aspire to become the next Bill Gates or the next Mark Zuckerberg but take your time; you have a lot to consider.

A Start-Up Building Tool-Box

Interview 2

A Successful Pitch

Nitin Vaish

Head of Energy and Transportation
Department at BootUp Ventures

Written by Siegfried Balleis, Jonas Schlund and Sophie Nehrig

"When you stand in front of any potential investor, you should express emotionally what's the vision of your company."

— Nitin Vaish

Nitin Vaish has worked in the energy and transportation sector with leading growth and incubation of new technology-focused businesses and as an executive. He holds an undergraduate degree from IIT Bombay and graduate degrees from Northwestern University and MIT Sloan School of Management. Over the years he's held many strategy leadership roles at various companies such as SunPower, EV Energy Storage Business at Celanese, and Bloom Energy. He now leads the Energy and Transportation department at BootUp Ventures, a Silicon Valley entrepreneurship ecosystem.

During his interview, Vaish draws on his extensive experience with startups, gives us valuable insights into the world of venture capital, and the common mistakes that entrepreneurs make. He answers the critical question of what makes a perfect pitch and how to prepare for a big presentation. Having the solution to a problem alone is often not enough. If you want to be successful, then you must be quicker than the others. In today's economy the following applies: It's not the Goliaths that devour the Davids; but, it's the start-up speed that makes the Goliaths of yesterday irrelevant.

He describes the emerging mega-markets in the transportation industry while also revealing the challenges and potential behind electric vehicles, autonomous vehicles, and the vastly growing shared mobility sector.

What roles do you play with the various companies you are involved in?

I have two primary complementary roles, the first one being working with investors. I primarily focus on technology sectors such as energy, transportation, and agriculture. This also includes sector deep-dives for an informed investment thesis, diligence, and providing support to companies post-investment. My second role is on the start-up side. I work with the CEOs and founding teams on various aspects of business that are critical for their company growth. While no two start-ups are alike, these engagements usually include growth strategy, fund-raising, and business development.

What is IIT Startups and what role do you play there?

IIT Startups is a non-profit organization that launched in 2018 to help start-ups founded by IIT alumni. It utilizes IITains, one of the largest university diasporas in the U.S., and has risen to the number four institution globally with the number of unicorns founded by its alumni. Demo Day is an event where startups can present their products and services to investors. Approximately a dozen companies are selected in this four-month accelerator program on Demo Day. As a part of the leadership team, I mentor start-ups in our cohorts across all aspects of company building and readiness. The goal is to have companies succeed not just at Demo Day, but beyond that. Several of the companies I've mentored have successfully raised institutional venture rounds subsequently.

Why is it important to guide the entrepreneurs from a business perspective upfront?

Seven out of ten start-up companies will fail. You have to ask yourself if you should get involved in this and what skills are needed. Although founders might have some domain expertise, it's important to know how to complement their strengths with someone who can provide business support and customer connectivity.

Unlike those working in a large corporation, where one might have some form of a safety net, people involved in entrepreneurship are essentially on their own. Because of this, it is crucial to bring in the right people, the right advisors, and the right mentors to help in building a solid foundation. There are accelerators, kick-starter venture funds, angel funds, and corporate venture funds that have become more widely available to entrepreneurs. Depending on your type of company and the stage it has reached, the optimal source for funding may vary.

What are the components that make up a pitch deck and what are the basic rules for creating a good pitch?

The key purpose of a pitch deck is not to answer all the questions the investors might have, but to describe who and what the company is. There are three primary aspects of the pitch deck: (1) the problem the company is solving, (2) why solving that problem is worthwhile, and (3) why this team is the one best suited for the job. There has to be extreme clarity about what problem the company is trying to solve because that is the core around which everything else revolves. As well as solving a problem there also must be a viable business proposition, such as whether or not the market size justifies it. Lastly and most importantly, the team composition is by far the number-one contributor to a company's success or failure. Being aligned with the mission means that the founding team is complementary and is best poised to succeed. You don't have to answer all the questions in the pitch deck. Remember that your primary focus should be on getting the audience interested enough to call in for the next meeting where they can ask you more detailed questions and understand the entirety of your start-up.

A good rule of thumb is to keep your pitch deck typically about ten pages long, or around a twenty-minute presentation where you present your team and what you are seeking in terms of funding. You must explain your personal philosophy because it is rooted in the core of what the company stands for. This should be followed by an additional thirty minutes devoted to questions. This method allows you to both synthesize the information and create interest and excitement.

How do you best identify the problem that needs to be solved?

It all starts with talking to people and ascertaining what their pain points are. Once you talk to enough people, you will begin to notice similarities. There are thousands of problems in the world, and your job is to discover which one you think you can tackle. If you start looking at people who are entrepreneurs, people who own companies, who are solving problems, the commonality you will find among them is inspiration. In the times we're living in there is a wealth of easily accessed information and networking opportunities available that, if you are driven, you will find people to help. It's not to say that entrepreneurship is everyone's cup of tea, but if that's what you choose, there are plenty of accessible tools that can help you create a solution to a problem.

We are in a special place here in Silicon Valley. Several large and well-known companies were formed or received funding from this area. I would even argue that what is happening here in the valley in terms of economic impact isn't only influential in terms of this country, but globally. It can't be compared to any other place in the world and is a huge driver both of jobs and employment.

How can I prepare my team for a business presentation in front of potential partners?

You can tell within the first twenty seconds after entering a room whether you have good team chemistry or not. This is important to keep in mind because the moment you walk into an office you are instantly being judged. At the start you will walk into a large conference room with a table and chairs. The natural tendency is to sit down and talk about the presentation, but it is best to stand. If you have a technical co-founder and a business co-founder, each person must be well prepared to present his or her own section, all making use of their individual presentation strengths.

The start-up space is a crowded one, especially in the world of software. There are hundreds of companies entering the race with the same idea. Be ready to answer basic questions, such as why you exist, why you're doing what you're doing and how you're doing it. You need to display your own "blue ocean" and explain why it is something that's worth getting involved in. Like everything else in life, you need to put your thoughts together and practice, practice, practice.

Do your research beforehand. Typically, there is a lead sponsor whom the team may have reached out to at the start. Work with that sponsor and ask him who will be at the meeting. Will it be the entire partnership? If so, what are their backgrounds? What areas might they invest in and what type of companies are they most interested in? What are their pet peeves? Are there certain aspects that should be emphasized more than others? This type of information will give you a clearer idea about what working with them might be like. Too many people forget about these steps, but they are essential for a beneficial outcome to the meeting. Remember that not every venture fund will be right for you and your team!

What do I need to cover in terms of financials during a partner meeting?

You need to prepare a simple high-level view of how the revenues will grow and how margins may evolve. You also need to explain your projected money burn-rate, the milestones you intend to reach, and how you intend to use your funds. All these things should be spelled out clearly.

What should I include in the presentation to leave a good first impression?

Use clean graphics and keep bullet points simple so you can confidently present, not just read off the slides. If you're not good at putting together presentations, there are plenty of companies that offer this kind of help for start-ups. You engage them for a nominal fee and they help polish the slide deck. They can really elevate the message that you want to communicate.

Make sure to include a slide about the team, providing key information about the founders, their pictures, and the logos of their companies or their universities. Put yourself in the shoes of the investors; they don't want to be bombarded with information. I've seen a spectrum of slides from people trying to list everybody in their team, even listing their experiences as far back as high school. This is an overkill of information. Keep it simple!

What must I consider when creating an effective "go to market" strategy?

When you go to the market with your product it is more about your channel strategy, your plan for moving your product or service through the commerce chain to the end-user. You have to find the right channel strategy for your company. This enables you to have that vision laid out in front of you when you make your presentation. In the case of a lemonade stand, the company grows beyond just standing out in front of a house with a jar of lemonade and a few cups. Do they want to expand their business? Are they franchising? How can they acquire more customers? Will they utilize word-of-mouth or ads on social media? That's why I strongly believe that going back to the business plan and doing thorough research early on is critical.

What measures can I take when trying to be a part of the success rate?

When the barriers to a market are low, many companies look into the potential market. For example, there are hundreds of companies working on sensors for self-driving cars. If you are starting a company in this space, the question becomes how your company is different and that question remains, even after you receive funding or find your first customers.

To increase your odds of becoming part of the success rate, you must ensure that you are solving a truly relevant consumer problem. Talking to potential buyers will give you a clearer sense of the problem. It's worth developing a prototype to receive real market feedback before you pitch your business plan because having that feedback refines your assumptions. After you know that, you can begin to ask yourself a set of key questions, such as how big the market is and how your team can best capture it. These questions need to be discussed with your team of people who are capable of working together because if the team isn't efficient, the chance of receiving funding is practically zero. Work hard on getting the right team in place very early on so that you can go after big market opportunities armed with the right solutions.

What are the important factors involved in achieving a successful start-up?

Customer experience and customer satisfaction become even more critical when the industry is more mature. Everyone is trying to grow rapidly, and when the market matures, economics will play out. Companies that provide better customer experience will often outlive companies with cost leadership.

Now more than ever, people want flexibility and better customer experience. In the case of transportation, public transportation systems were encouraged in earlier decades, but there has recently been a shift toward individual mobility. We see these kinds of rapid changes all over the world: E-Scooters in San Francisco, ride-sharing in Europe, bike lanes in big cities, and other equivalents all around the globe.

What are the challenges in the transportation sector worldwide?

In the U.S. almost forty thousand people are killed every year in vehicle accidents, and that number continues to rise. Although there is no conclusive reason, many indicators are pointing to the use of phones while driving.

Cars are used only five percent of the time each day, mostly while driving to and from work or school. The remaining ninety-five percent of the time, the car is parked. I don't think there is anything else in our life that is as under-utilized as the car. Fortunately, with Uber and Lyft, car-sharing is becoming more popular, with ever-increasing usage rates. If you look at large cities globally, roughly a third of the area is devoted to roads. And just like cars, those roads are not efficiently used, but we're devoting a huge amount of landmass just to take care of these seldom-used cars.

Why are the prices for shared mobility continuing to decrease?

A car is generally used five percent of the time, when you use that same car for fifty percent of the time, the amortization cost spreads across ten times more mileage. When you use that asset ten times more, the economics naturally drive the costs down. With self-driving cars, the cost to the driver will vanish. There is less need for maintenance in electric vehicles, while they have a much longer life in terms of mileage. There are electric vehicles now, like Tesla Model S, that can go up to half a million miles and stay at more than ninety-five percent of the battery capacity. This makes it easier to allocate the cost faster compared to actually owning the car.

What forms of transportation, apart from autonomous vehicles, will become important in solving the problem of transportation?

There are companies working on a shared model for flight travel specializing in short commutes, such as from San Jose to San Francisco. The cost is expected to be even lower than what people pay for an Uber ride. We also have e-scooters and e-bikes, which I think are more disruptive. What's beautiful about this option is if you look at your typical average commute you soon realize that bikes could do the job just fine. Despite traffic conjunction, we still drive ourselves because we are so used to owning a car.

If we're talking about a short distance, bikes and scooters are a better solution, especially in congested areas. We even saw car trips of zero to three kilometers vanish when bikes were on their sharing platform. Many companies are constructing a model where they provide different solutions in terms of services and products for individuals, such as connecting local trains, scooters, bikes, and cars.

What are the major factors leading to a change in the transportation sector?

There are many factors built around technology, especially the rapidly decreasing costs of lithium batteries, which have dropped seventy percent in the last five years. Beyond that, cars are evolving from being just a hunk of metal and electronics into something more akin to a computer platform on wheels. In fact, the number of lines of code in a typical vehicle is around one hundred fifty million and is getting more complex as these vehicles become more automated.

How does the rapid evolution of computing influence change in transportation?

You may have heard of Moore's Law: The number of transistors in each surface area doubles roughly every sixteen months. That has been an ongoing process since the '70s, and about six or seven years ago, this went beyond central processing units. With companies like Nvidia, there is a need for new computer architecture for computing to be done in real-time. Graphical processor units (GPU) have become a central platform for intelligence, and the learning rate on these GPUs is even steeper than CPUs.

Nvidia has become a de-facto platform for automation in vehicles. Some companies are coming in at different layers of optimization, whether it is around edge computers or different neural networks. This ecosystem, with both established players and a very healthy ecosystem of start-ups around computing platforms, is very interesting to note.

How have machine-learning algorithms, which can be used for AVs, evolved in the recent past?

In the span of five years we have created algorithms that are better at predicting and classifying images than humans. As these vehicles become more automated, you need to be able to detect what is on the road, what a person's intention may be, and what their next step will be. Are they stepping on to the road or are they just moving around a bit? Having the ability to build that intelligence and make predictions, based on a software standpoint is an incredible thing.

What does connectivity mean in this context? How does it help, what are the challenges, and what are the current developments?

Connectivity goes by different names: vehicle-to-vehicle, vehicle-to-infrastructure, or vehicle-to-almost everything. All the data is coming from different sensors in the environment around the vehicle. A typical level-four autonomous vehicle is a vehicle that can drive on its own without human intervention, in a very well-defined geographical area, and generates about four terabytes of data per vehicle per day. The largest fleet of self-driving vehicles in the U.S. is by Waymo, whose vehicles are in hundreds of units, with a total global fleet of over one billion vehicles.

How do you see electrification playing out in the Auto sector?

VW is investing twenty-five billion dollars to launch twenty different models by 2025. Ford has a whole program around electrification. GM came out vocally about going all-electric and the Japanese are doing the same thing. OEMs are also making this shift because it makes economic sense. The cost of electric vehicles has come down rapidly, especially from the battery's standpoint. The case for buying electric vehicles compared to gasoline or diesel will be unquestionable; the cost parity of EV versus any others will cross over by 2021. If you begin thinking about these things in a fleet environment, it might happen even sooner because of asset utilization which is much higher. Bloomberg's forecast is more bullish, with almost half a billion vehicles being electric by 2040. Just to put that in context, the global fleet of vehicles is typically over one billion cars and it takes twelve years for all of the cars to turn over to electric. We are in 2019, so in roughly two turnovers, more than half the fleet will be electric globally.

In almost thirty states in the U.S., a truck driver is seen as having one of the most unfair jobs. Trucks are the backbone of goods-hauling from point A to point B. E-commerce, logistics, and distribution are all most often fulfilled by trucks. Many factors are unfolding around trucking as a platform, and companies are working on how to get these truck units more coupled. When this happens, the fuel economy for both vehicles goes up. At the same time, there are now some technologies able to make the trucks more automated and connected. Some companies are already doing this on the road, and soon the cost of transporting goods from point A to point B will be cut almost in half.

How do you see shared mobility playing out?

Using shared mobility is up to ninety percent cheaper than owning one's own vehicle. If you live in a large city like San Jose or San Francisco, the need for owning a personal car will be less and less. One of the most cherished moments for U.S. high school graduates used to be getting their driver's license, but we are often seeing them often not even apply for their license anymore because people are now used to accessing mobility more as a service. If you are an OEM, tier 1 supplier, or a fleet owner, what does this mean to your business? How you deal with it becomes a make-or-break situation.

How do you see the COVID-19 pandemic impacting startups in Silicon Valley? Do you see areas emerging that will lead to a new wave of startups?

The current COVID-19 pandemic will structurally change several industries and investment landscapes. The short-term sentiment, from an investor standpoint, is to ensure that their portfolio companies survive, as the time horizon for "the "new normal" is as yet unknown, significant efforts focus on tactical operational rigor. At the same time, the current situation is also presenting promising investment opportunities across multiple sectors. Some of these include automation, healthcare, and enterprise software. There is no good time to start a company, but the present situation presents incredible opportunities for

A Start-Up Building Tool-Box
Interview 3

The Essence of Innovation

Mike Todasco

Senior Director of Innovation at PayPal

Written by Fabian Sperling, André Hochreiter and Dominique Schröder

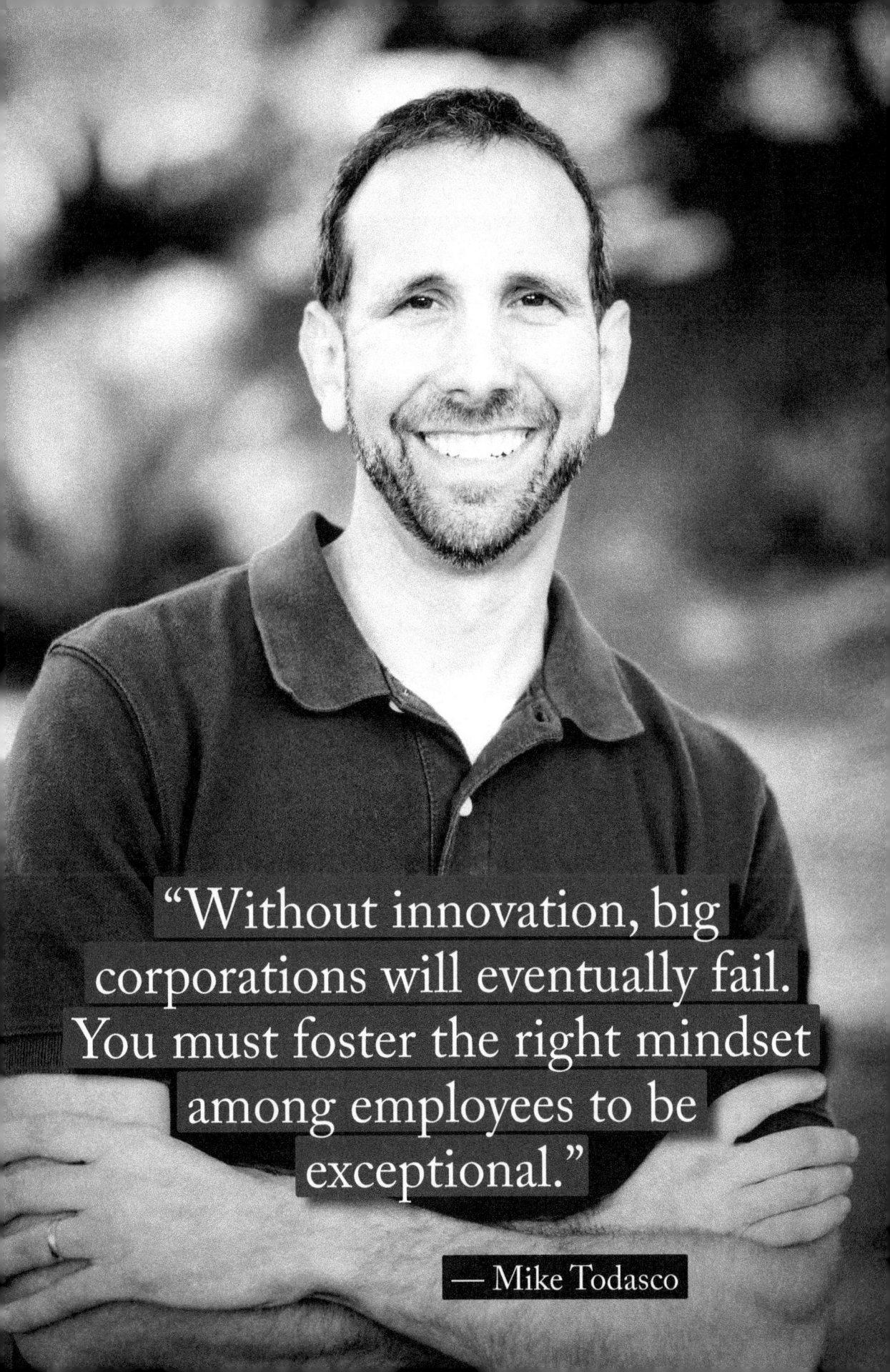

"Without innovation, big corporations will eventually fail. You must foster the right mindset among employees to be exceptional."

— Mike Todasco

Mike Todasco is the senior director of innovation at PayPal. He began his career at PayPal working in product management, product marketing, product launch, and product analytics roles. Today, he is responsible for increasing the creative output of employees across the company. Before joining PayPal, he was the founder and CEO of the eCommerce marketplace, Sketch Maven. Mike also spent over four years as the director of strategy, heading up mergers & acquisitions and strategic planning at NewPage, a portfolio company of the private equity firm, Cerberus Capital. He has an MBA from the University of California at Berkeley, Haas School of Business, and a BS in finance from the University of Illinois. Since 2013 Mike has filed over 100 U.S. patents covering payments, online and offline commerce, beacon/BLE technologies, biometrics, and many other areas.

M ike discusses his role at PayPal, the mega growth they have experienced over the years, and the differentiators that allowed this growth. PayPal's biggest competitive advantage is their ability to innovate. He discusses the creation of an innovation eco-system to ever-changing requirements and competition. He shares innovative methods on how to keep employees engaged in the innovation process, how to keep them motivated, and how to adapt to the competition. He also gives us a glimpse into the future of the industry, when talking about the role of AI and the challenges of data protection and cybersecurity. He discusses the threat of cyber-attacks, how PayPal protects against them, and the enormous potential behind blockchain artificial intelligence and augmented reality. Mike also gives us a glimpse into the future of this rapidly changing industry.

What tools does PayPal use to drive innovation? And what are some of your focus areas?

We have innovation labs in San Jose, Scottsdale, India, Singapore, and most recently in Shanghai. These labs focus on internal innovation; largely looking at new technologies in areas like augmented reality, robots, and blockchain. The way we do it is different compared to many other companies; it's inclusive. We are very different compared to the rest of the world of FinTech and Tech companies in general. We are a two hundred billion-dollar company in market capitalization, and the focus of innovation is not distributed on a centralized R&D department. This makes us unique in our industry.

We do innovation very differently, believing that anyone can innovate and orchestrate opportunities within our company. For example, an informal twenty percent time rule and the global innovation tournament. When I meet new employees at PayPal, which I do every week, I tell them innovation is not my responsibility, it is your responsibility, and we truly mean that at PayPal. I know a lot of other companies say that, but we truly practice what we preach. Our innovation team is comprised of me and passionate employee volunteers. This is intended to inspire innovation throughout the company.

Some of our focus areas are augmented reality, blockchain, and robots. We do things that we believe have a great potential for growth within the next three to ten years. We are currently exploring areas in quantum computing. The area of innovation must be intriguing.

People should happily be able to turn down a night of Game of Thrones for robot hacking. Those are the areas we chose, built prototypes for, and show to our customers.

How do you involve employees in innovation?

A big piece of our charter is to engage our 20,000+ PayPal employees and enable them to become great innovators. It doesn't matter if they're an engineer, a designer, an accountant, or a lawyer; we want to give them the tools, training, and opportunity to work on future platforms, exposing them and opening their minds, so that we can build a great product for the platform of the future.

A lot of innovation takes place locally and we've set up physical innovation labs over the years. While we do have digital tools such as the suggestion box, we also have teams of innovation ambassadors who are in all our major offices around the globe. They do similar things to what we do at our innovation labs, just on a slightly smaller scale. We bring in speakers, demonstrate new technologies and products, hold brainstorm sessions, whatever the local needs and desires might be, to engage the community, get them excited, and get them thinking further down the road. We also partner with universities and have amazing speakers coming to our campuses while still focusing on our global ambassadors' program.

What incentives are there for employees to engage in innovation?

Awards, trophies, and all the incentives you got for being in the chess club or the football club when you were twelve years old still matter when you're an adult. This is not only a millennials thing; it's something that persists for us all as human beings. One of the things we built is a blockchain-based innovation token platform, which is a reward system for employees. Within the walls of PayPal, these things have great value. When you do anything innovative within the company, such as participating in a hackathon, you can earn more of these tokens.

Another popular prize is a kickboxing session with our CEO. I have a limited budget compared to other departments, so we try to find inexpensive yet innovative ways to motivate our employees.

When did you start with PayPal? What has changed since then?

I have been with PayPal for nine years. This, in the world of payments, is an eternity. I was on the mobile team when I first started out and we had approximately seven hundred fifty million dollars of mobile transactions – we do hundreds of billions of dollars today.

When merchants decide to add the PayPal button as an option for payment, it indicates a trust, as well as a desire to reach more consumers. Many banks and tech companies are trying to enter our world, a world we've been living in for the last twenty years.

A great example of change during my time here is PayPal Working Capital which is a merchant product we launched a few years ago. We give loans to our merchants, based on their sales history and other factors. By doing so we see your transactions and that gives us an idea of what your business operations are like. This helps us understand your ups and downs. A small percentage of every transaction will go towards paying off the loan. These are the kinds of services we can offer because we have insight into payments and where the funds are flowing to.

What differentiates PayPal from other similar payment systems?

Differentiation is a big focus for us. There are two sides to our marketplace. We serve the consumers and we serve the merchants. An example of one of the most successful products is PayPal One-Touch which was launched a few years ago. Once you enable One Touch on your mobile phone, we put this long-lasting cookie on it that is constantly monitored to ensure identity security. It provides you with easier access to your account by eliminating the need to constantly log into your PayPal accounts. We make it easy for you to keep account information securely stored, over forty percent of our transactions are now done on mobile devices. This is something that's very much tied to our technology prowess and how we're able to manage risk as a company.

We are continuously improving the merchant's side as well, especially the merchant analytics. We aim to bring more data and analytics to the merchant's experience and give them more insights into the types of payments and how customers use them in their transactions. Although we do serve large global merchants that have their own analytic teams, we're here to support small and medium-sized businesses as well. I was a PayPal merchant myself before I joined the PayPal team. I didn't have any full-blown analytics teams behind me then, but as I worked with PayPal, I came to see the importance of the many tools we provide to those merchants and making our service a lot more valuable to them.

Finally, the concept of innovation; coming up with new products and creating better experiences. Having both buyer and merchant protection, while also managing risks, which is what we are world-class at. Identity security is the core of online payments because you cannot see the person face to face. Electronic transactions are much riskier and reducing that risk is the kind of service we provide as a company. We have shifted our strategy from being just a button to becoming the operating system for payments around the world.

What is the relationship between PayPal and new players like Google Pay, Apple Pay, and other similar platforms?

If you are a merchant in the United States, you can place any of those buttons such as Visa, PayPal, Google Pay, or Apple Pay onto your website. Eighty percent of the top five hundred retailers in the United States have PayPal on their website.

Some companies come from a legacy, which refers to the first movers in that field. PayPal is now twenty years old, which makes us ancient in the online banking business. When Apple Pay launched about four or five years ago, who do you think was the preferred transaction on the Apple Pay network? It was PayPal and our subsidiary, Braintree. Through Braintree, we enabled any of those pay-out options on any of our merchant's websites. We enabled this because we wanted to make sure that if someone wants to use Apple Pay, MasterCard, or something else, they easily can. It is all becoming integrated. You can use PayPal within your Samsung Pay or Google Pay. I use Google Pay that is funded by my PayPal account.

When asked about who our competitors are, we always give them the same answer; cash. So much of the world is still cash-based, there's so much room for growth for us overall.

How does PayPal keep up with consumers' current interest such as the Apple credit card?

It's a great card, tightly intertwined with Apple Pay in order to keep consumers within the Apple ecosystem. One of our consumer favorites is a product in the United States called Venmo. It provides a peer-to-peer experience where you can see not only all your transactions but your friend's transactions as well. Venmo is used primarily by Millennials and Generation Z, so there are a lot more emojis and stickers on the feeds, which is part of the Venmo experience. People who use Venmo are passionate about it because it is the first-time people over the age of thirty-five are exposing all their payments within their entire network. We are doing more payment volume on Venmo than with any of our other customers and it is still only based in the United States. We have started doing the monetization of Venmo, so in the United States, you can fund Uber rides through Venmo.

Now more than ever, PayPal is a portfolio of companies, although not all of them are consumer-facing. We need to create more experiences like Venmo if we want to compete with the Apples of the world.

We acquired Venmo in 2013. I remember having a discussion in 2012 about Venmo because it was becoming popular at Stanford University. Venmo was showing up around different campuses and was slowly gaining in popularity. A few people who were recognized as thought-leaders within the tech community began using it and that had a huge network effect, boosting Venmo's popularity.

What are your primary security measures given that many hackers attempt to attack PayPal?

I'm sure there are a lot of people trying to hack into PayPal as we speak. That's where the money is, right? Here's the thing though; we are damn good at security. If there was a mass data breach at a hardware store, would that change what you think of the store? Are you thinking "I go there because they take care of my financial credential?" No, you go there to buy a hammer and you will go there the next time for paint. The point is, you will continue to shop there. For PayPal, it's all about security and privacy. If we are breached, it's game over; that's it. About one-third of our company is solely focused on compliance, risk, or fraud. After we initially launch a new product, the losses go through the roof. This is because the first people, after our employees, who use the product are the bad guys. This is a routine thing that happens in FinTech when you launch a new product, and you need to manage this as best as you can.

What about Artificial Intelligence (AI) at PayPal?

I think it's most influential within the area of risk management. Most of the ideas and products that we come up with at PayPal begin with risk factors because that's where we need to stay ahead. If we're not innovating, the bad guys are innovating. That really keeps the company on its toes and is another driver of innovation. It is important even in simple things like chatbots or the legal world. We're starting to look at how we can integrate AI and machine learning to do contracting more effectively within the company. I believe there are a lot of ways that this can begin to emerge in our company.

When imagining an augmented reality in the world of payment platforms, I imagine taking out my phone, beaming a running shoe or a bicycle, and saying, "I want this," and PayPal handles the rest of the transaction. Is that correct?

Why not? That's the beauty of augmented reality, especially as the hardware gets better. Right now, it's mostly on the phone, but as hardware companies produce more glasses-based form factors it's going to become more common. PayPal is going to be a part of that landscape and will enable payments to people and businesses in many ways.

Do the innovation themes, such as blockchain and augmented reality, come from top management or bottom-up?

To be completely honest, it's both top-down and bottom-up. We work with corporate strategy teams and leadership to try and identify what platforms are emerging in the market and where we see PayPal being able to play a role two to six years into the future. Where do we want to tool up as a company within our own skill sets? But there's also an organic interest that emerges. Blockchain is a great example. We have a lot of people in the company who are passionate and excited about the opportunities and what we can do within blockchain. I think a lot of people raise their hands to volunteer and come up with new ideas in this field because of this excitement and challenge. So, it really comes from both directions.

Some employees are sponsored by an executive who wants to build something that does "x", and therefore this project will have its own team. I can give just as many, if not more, examples of those grassroots projects you just mentioned. "Hey, wouldn't it be great if we could get involved in this or that type of experience?" If you can recruit enough passionate people, we then give you the support, the structure, and the exposure within the company, along with all the necessary tools to help you succeed. I constantly remind new hires that they are in charge of innovation and I know they will become the next generation of great innovators.

We are human beings and by nature, we're innovative. The incentives you set up and the support you give makes innovation happen. It may be something that has to be implemented in a large established company, which might not already have that innovative spirit. I'm reading a book called Loonshots by Safi Bahcall. One of the points the author discusses is the importance of innovation, which should be exemplified by management. If you don't have executives who are talking about this all the time, not just the CEO, then it is never going to happen. There are structural changes that must happen within the company.

What about innovative ideas that are not aligned with the PayPal road map?

People innovate in many ways. Some come to our speaker events, some want to learn about new technologies, some brainstorm, some do all of these, and some do none of them. I'd say that approximately twenty-five percent of our employees participate, and the rest do not. We want to improve our ratio, but we will never force employees to attend, as that could cause a negative reaction.

If someone creates something brilliant with robots but it doesn't really fit into the road map, we have our own venture fund that holds millions of dollars. It could inspire something else down the line. You're never going to know if something has value unless you're willing to give it a fair try!

A Start-Up Building Tool-Box

Interview 4

Innovation and Patents will set you Free

Gurtej Sandhu

Senior Fellow and Vice President
at Micron Technology

Written by Ákos Balász

"Innovation is a bit like being on a zipline. You can't control the speed or intensity, but you can control your direction forward."

— Gurtej Sandhu

Gurtej Sandhu is a Senior Fellow and Vice President at Micron Technology. With over 1,300 patents to his credit, Dr. Sandhu is recognized as the seventh-most prolific inventor, based on the number of U.S. utility patents granted. In his current role, Dr. Sandhu is responsible for Micron's end-to-end R&D technology roadmap. The scope includes driving cross-functional alignment across various departments and business units to proactively identify technology gaps. It also includes managing the engineering organizational resources and executing innovative technology solutions for future memory scaling. His responsibilities include leading several internal project teams worldwide and managing interactions with research consortia around the world.

Dr. Sandhu received his degree in electrical engineering from the Indian Institute of Technology, New Delhi, and his Ph.D. in physics from the University of North Carolina, Chapel Hill. Dr. Sandhu is also a Fellow of IEEE and in 2018, he received the IEEE Andrew S. Grove Award for outstanding contributions to silicon CMOS process technology that enables DRAM and NAND memory chip scaling.

G urtej Sandhu talks about the world of technology including proactively identifying technology gaps and managing the engineering organization to resource and execute on developing innovative technology solutions.

What made you want to work for Micron?

At the time I was pretty unsure of what to do and I thought the best person to ask would be my professor who had worked at IBM before becoming a faculty member. He'd been giving me advice for years. Outside of your parents, your teachers are the ones who know you the best. I told him that I liked the spirit at Micron, I just didn't know if they were going to survive. My professor said "If you go to a big company, they will put you into a box and you aren't built for a box. On the other hand, you want to achieve great things and create impact, then Micron is certainly the right environment for that."

Can you tell us a little more about Micron?

Micron was founded in 1978 by twin brothers Wand and Joe Parkinson. They were engineers and lawyers from Stanford and Harvard. They got into the business when companies were going bankrupt, and the competitive environment was so bad that even Intel had dropped out. That is when these guys decided to make chips. It was a tough environment and the company knew that in order to keep the costs low they had to make small chips. With small chips you can have more chips on one wafer thereby reducing cost and increasing revenue. Although Micron was like the 15th company to enter this space, over time they became a top memory chip supplier; thanks to their many new technological advances and cost reductions. Micron knew that the only way to do all this was through aggressive technology development. As a technology engineer fresh out of grad school, this was music to my ears.

We often hear the advice that you should look around for a new company after 3-5 years. What made you stay at Micron for so long?

One thing I learned while in Boise was that location matters to a lot of people. For me, the location wasn't a problem. The important thing was having a job that I truly enjoyed.

At a minimum, an employee is expected to work forty hours a week, the largest chunk of their lives. What do two weekend days matter if you aren't enjoying the other five days of the week?

Micron was a tough environment. They needed to churn out innovation after innovation at high speed. Since I'm someone who likes to solve problems by creating technological innovation, my work was very much appreciated. And I felt honored that they offered me such a challenging environment. Considering all that, why would I want to leave?

How did starting in Boise instead of the Silicon Valley affect your innovation process? Do you have any advice for people starting out in the same environment you did?

Being in Idaho gave us the advantage of isolation. People are always giving or trying to give you advice, even if they often don't fully understand what they're talking about. But it turns out that having ambition while constantly being told that you can't do something is counterproductive. We tried many ideas and some of them didn't work. My advice is to have a strong conviction and consider your ideas based on their merits. I am not suggesting being stubborn, but don't let yourself be too easily swayed. Consensus is one way of saying "no" to innovation. By definition, if there is consensus, there is often no innovation. Innovation involves accepting some uncertainty, and that's not possible if your back is up against the wall. Take steps forward; otherwise, the competition will take them for you.

You may wonder if innovation is unique to a certain region. The answer is no. Innovation is as old as history. Think of stone-age tools or the wheel. Over time, the number of innovations has increased exponentially. While not all innovations have a positive impact, they do all have some impact. Without it, no one would care about it much. Innovation increases connectivity in the world, and the transfer of information accelerates the pace of innovation.

How does the transfer of information/ interconnectedness accelerate the pace of innovation and technology?

We as a species are far less developed in many physical aspects than other species. That is why it was necessary to become smarter. Once we overcame our fear of fire, we learned to control and use it. Just learning that provided us with a tremendous benefit. People first started to gather around these fires as protection from predators. This inherently improved our communication, both socially and through language skills. We improved our methods of passing on information from one generation to the other. Fire improved our social connectivity and helped us survive. The reason that homo-sapiens survived and other species didn't is that we were able to work effectively in large groups. We seem to be programmed to do that.

We have come a long way from gathering around fires. Since the mid-90s the latest social connectivity innovation has been the Internet. For the first time in history everyone in the world was interconnected and sharing information has never been easier. The pace of innovation goes up when our ability to collaborate is improved. Some of the innovations actually serve as catalysts that spur an even faster rate of innovation. The number of patents granted has just exploded since the Internet came along. The pace of innovation has increased exponentially and the time it takes to adapt to an innovation and make an impact on society has decreased considerably. For example, inside a phone is something called a NAND flash chip. This necessary technology was not available for a long time, at least it wasn't available in terms of cost-effectiveness. Steve Jobs and Apple made this technology affordable and now it has become the de facto standard for our phones. Almost every teenager in the U.S. has a smart phone now, and this will result in even faster innovation.

What is Moore's law and what's its impact on memory chips?

NAND chips didn't exist before the early 2000s. We call these technologies linear technologies because they are in the same lane and you just keep shrinking the chip. We knew that in about six years this technology would have nowhere to go because of the limitations of physics. We had to quickly come up with something different. Moore's law which was named after Gordon Moore, one of the founders at IBM states that the cost per unit has decreased a million times over the last few decades. This effect of Moore's law of scaling is slowing down and we cannot sustain that, so now we have to innovate in different ways. Over time, the transistors on the chip went from a simple planar structure to a more complex multi-level 3D structure. They have become smaller but taller, just as a city grows vertically with high-rise skyscrapers. I called these nano-mems and we are building structures on nano millimeter scale. There are a lot of innovations that we need now. We collectively call these more-than-Moore-innovations. Life after Moore's law simply has to happen

Could you shed light on the innovations in memory chip technology?

Multiple fields need memory chip technology. It all started with the PCs but now with the emergence of IoT, there is a constant increase in the need for memory chips. Just look at the cars; older cars were reliant on chips for their entertainment systems. Today they can't even function without a chip because chips control everything. This is a huge industry, with many companies building the same chips that go into these devices.

We have two types of devices: memory devices and logic devices. In 2010, 84% of all devices produced were memory devices. However, even logic devices have a memory component, so ultimately 99.99% of all devices may be built for memory storage. This is the effect that memory chips have on our time since we are storing enormous amounts of data. For example, a self-driving car needs a logic device to do the function, but they also need enormous amounts of memory capacity to make it function. So, in order to build a new technology, you have to provide it with the right amount of memory.

Another avenue for innovation began with the era of artificial intelligence. While language processing is getting better, one of the biggest challenges we are still facing is in the domain of computing power and in moving data fast. For the past many years, we've been approaching computers the same way: here's your computer chip, here's your processor chip, here's your memory chip. Now make it work. However, this approach is outdated, and innovation has to happen to sustain this business. We must co-mingle those functions and do some computing on the memory chip meaning a new way to do processing is needed.

Over time we began utilizing more and more of the elements on the periodic table to build chips. We realize that in order to sustain cost scaling we needed to add new materials. If you look at all of the elements, the only things missing in making the chips are gases and radioactive material, and they can be quite dangerous. My prediction is that we have reached the limit.

How do we get past the current bottlenecks?

We have looked at every other possible option out there, so this is where the innovation part comes in. How do you do things differently? We still need solutions, but how do you go about getting them? We can't always revert to the old ways, so the question now becomes "Can you use innovative ways to predict novel mechanisms in physics?" We found new opportunities with two-dimensional materials, but we do want to be smart about discovering new materials to connect them to the new applications. We want to be able to model these things on a computer since you can discover new materials by designing their traits. Overall, in terms of innovation and memory, the opportunities are even bigger now. We can't just look at one material or one device. We must look at the entire spectrum of how memory is used in society. How can we be innovative about using it, coming up with new market spaces, and new ways to compute things? So many opportunities exist!

One can usually expect there will be technical challenges, but there are also business challenges as well as the challenges of writing software. Software is built on layers. This makes editing difficult because you need to depend on the people who built the software before you. You have to re-engineer software all the way from start to finish in order to enable new ways of computing. I hope that students, such as those working in fields of IoT, will enable some of these machines.

If you are an engineer, be careful! No amount of good engineering can overcome the fundamental laws of physics. Don't waste your time doing things that aren't possible. Physics dictates that you cannot have a charge based memory chip which can retain information for 10 years and still be fast. You will never have a fast device that will retain information forever based on common physics. That does not mean you give up. Look at other mechanisms, begin to explore moving atoms, and observe how they work.

Where does the innovation process start?

If you are thinking of ideas and innovations, first try to figure out who's going to use it, who's going to gain value from it, and how will it help society in general? It is extremely important to have ideas that work, but market research is also essential. You can have a great idea, but the problem is that often no one will pay attention to it. Society will only use those products that they like, need or want.

How do you see the world of memory storage unfolding?

The future market segment we are looking at is quantum computing. Customers are expecting us to anticipate how much data needs are going to increase. Harvard wanted to make computers out of DNA and all kinds of things. We tried to make polymers work and it was a colossal failure. The organic molecules are too fragile to make anything useful. But then we began talking to a chemist and physicist. We did calculations on the physics of DNA and found it worked for memory. Cells are multiplying in your body. You have DNA that has to be unstable while the cells are multiplying while you don't even realize it's happening. These long molecules, the DNA, fold and unfold, changing the capabilities of the molecule dramatically. Every time it splits into different cells there is the possibility of errors. If those errors were carried over, our lifespan would be about 24 hours. Fortunately, there is something called error correction that saves us. If a cell splits and there is a defect, it usually self-corrects. There is an amazing amount of activity going on in our bodies. That's how nature works. It's absolutely amazing!

There's actually a book of knowledge, an ancient Indian scripture written thousands of years ago. One of the interesting things about it is that it was written in an older but common street language so that everyone could read it. It features the word "manas" which means "memory" and there are nine different types of memories that are discussed in the book. There's a talk of memory inside a body and I instantly thought that one of them has to be the brain. But that wasn't it. They weren't talking about where we store information, but about where we insert a memory into our body. Characteristics such as facial features and skin tones are a memory, transferred from our forefathers; It's a memory your body has kept from previous generations. This book is over 5,000 years old, but it sounds a bit like the theory of evolution. There's another example we gain from biology. When we get sick, our bodies remember that event so that the next time we get sick it can protect us against that specific illness. Sounds very much like the immune system. My point is that even then we knew about the ways our bodies store information, how it used DNA to do it.

Information storage was recognized a long time ago. If we were to pull off making systems for DNA to store archival memory, we could store numbers for a hundred years; but that would only be possible when using one billion kilograms of silicon to replace one kilogram of DNA. That's the power of density when storing DNA. This isn't going to happen tomorrow, but it's an amazing possibility because the need to store DNA information is only going to grow from here.

Shifting gears to your journey of patents. How did you manage to get 1300 patents?

When I began my career, I didn't know what patents were. I just knew I had creative ideas. Patents are just me doing my job, coming up with ideas, and solving problems. Companies are the ones that need patents, so they told me that if I had good ideas, I should write them down and then go before some committee which would then decide whether to grant me a patent or not. The process was already there before I knew what it was. When going for a patent the key factor is to describe clearly what your idea is and who you believe will care about it. Do this all on one single page.

What is the relationship between innovation and technology?

At one point in my life, my college in Delhi was the only place that had an IBM computer. It was the most advanced machine I had ever seen. Since then, the phone you have in your pocket is 200 times more powerful than that computer was, and it's getting faster all the time. The most fascinating part of the computer system is the memory, and its size is constantly growing. We store a lot of information on these things without even giving it a thought. A 256 GB storage capacity that now costs about twenty dollars would have cost fourteen million dollars 40 years ago!

Innovation is a bit like being on a zipline. You can't control the speed or intensity, but you can control your direction forward. The pace of change is inexorable. You can't say that something will never happen because literally almost anything may eventually happen. Just make sure that it happens the right way. Take an active role in shaping the outcome. In a few years, a computer will have the capabilities of the human brain, not in terms of being able to do everything but in terms of its raw computing power. At this rate, we will have computers with the power of all the human brains on the planet combined. Still, the question remains: What are we going to do with this power?

Innovation by itself is not enough and neither is technology. You have to connect these to something useful, whether in terms of cost or performance. You have to identify what the market wants, what your technology can do, and how to keep your costs low. When it comes to memory, we didn't need innovation on just performance; we needed cost reduction.

In the early days, no one cared much about the memory; it was all about increasing the processing power. Now, every chip has a NAND flash memory that not only enables phones but the cloud hardware as well. If NAND chips stop existing tomorrow, life as we know it would cease to exist. It's that powerful. It's a huge market that requires a lot of creative solutions to sustain the success of a company.

Innovation Outposts and Smart Buildings

Ram Sriram

Vice President of Business Innovation for the Silicon Valley Business Innovation Group at FXPAL & Founder of NEXPRISE

Written by Holger Hackstein, Matthias Lochmann, Christian Grenz

"Addressing the pain point of the customer produces a perfect product-market fit. If you can achieve that, the main battle is over; the rest of it is mechanical."

— Ram Sriram

Ram Sriram is the founding member and Vice President of Business Innovation for the Silicon Valley Business Innovation Group at FXPAL. He has over twenty years of experience as a software technology executive in both public companies and venture-funded start-ups. He has held senior executive roles in R&D, product marketing & management, business strategy, and business development. His leadership style and entrepreneurial drive, and his deep understanding of the market and technology, has made him highly successful at creating new business opportunities, growing companies, and turning around struggling businesses. Ram holds a master's degree in Computer Science from The University of Tulsa.

I n this interview, Ram emphasizes the importance of innovation outposts and why companies of any size need to tap into the innovations happening in Silicon Valley. He discusses how these outposts help companies keep their competitive advantage and remain relevant in the highly dynamic world we live in. In the second part, Ram provides a breakdown of IoT, the technology that has enabled the fourth industrial revolution, and its application in smart facilities. He explains the unlimited market potential behind this technology and how it ties into various industries, and the benefits people can reap from this correlation.

What is the foundation of a successful start-up in Silicon Valley?

It doesn't matter if you're in Silicon Valley or anywhere else in the world. This principle is universal. It's called a "value proposition". To place an attractive product, you need to focus on resolving a significant problem – a the pain point – for the customers. This is your value proposition and the most important factor in your success. Addressing the pain point of the customer produces a perfect product-market fit. If you can achieve that, the crucial battle is over; the rest of it is "mechanical" in terms of what needs to be done, like managing your supply chain and choosing the right distribution channels.

Silicon Valley has been a leader in most start-up metrics. The region hosts twenty thousand active start-ups employing approximately two million people. A third of the global early-stage investments are made here in Silicon Valley. It is interesting to note that about fifty billion dollars are put into start-ups or early-stage companies annually in Silicon Valley.

Why do companies create Innovations Hubs?

Large companies rarely create disruptive new products and opportunities because their focus is on utilizing their talent to improve existing products. They need a whole different business model, an entirely fresh approach, and a mindset to innovate. Many therefore use innovation hubs and outposts in innovation ecosystems to drive new products into new markets relatively quickly and cost-effectively.

Why do innovation hubs work? What have we seen come out of them?

Innovation hubs are not connected to the existing business model or structure; they have complete freedom to do new things that can disrupt the status quo. It's extremely important to create this field of experimentation and to enhance out-of-the-box thinking.

As an example, the taxi industry was globally monopolistic and state-regulated, one that was waiting to be innovated. Along came Uber, which enabled every car to be a taxi, every driver to become a taxi driver, and thereby created new employment opportunities. They significantly enhanced the taxi experience while reducing costs and wait times. It addressed severe customer pain points and had a viral effect. This shared innovation model was taken by Airbnb into the hotel sector, inspired food deliveries such as DoorDash and Postmates and a whole range of other companies.

The traditional automotive industry is going through a major transition, especially in Germany. How do big companies make sure they stay competitive in the highly volatile global economy?

More than fifty percent of big companies have innovation outposts in Silicon Valley – companies ranging from financial to automotive to life sciences. Given the rapid advancement of driver assistance technologies especially in the U.S., it's important for automotive companies to be a part of the latest breakthroughs, work with leading-edge technology start-ups, and attract the top talent. Audi just recently launched their first office in San Jose to enhance their competencies in advanced driver-assistance systems (ADAS); BMW built their innovation outpost in the heart of Silicon Valley already more than twenty years ago.

If you look at the trend, many global companies are setting up innovation centers or incubators around the world. Companies use blossoming ecosystems to help refine their ideas. We see that happening worldwide, in Shenzhen, Tel Aviv, Berlin, yet mainly here in Silicon Valley.

What makes Silicon Valley an attractive option for innovation outposts?

Silicon Valley perfected the game of the innovation cycle. When you look at it, there's a great ecosystem consisting of resources like National Universities, National Labs, private

Universities like Stanford, Berkeley, UCSF, and so on. There is an enormous corporate ecosystem here as well and when you couple these with mentors, business angels, venture capitalists, you now have the magic formula to build successful businesses. Every year almost twenty thousand new ideas or companies come out of Silicon Valley.

Living and working in an innovation ecosystem such as Silicon Valley while having an open mindset for partnering with other start-ups in the field you are interested in is the cornerstone of any success. Of course, in any entrepreneurial ecosystem, not everyone is successful, and approximately only ten percent reach the next phase. It usually takes a seven to ten-year trip before a new business reaches the big leagues.

What are the characteristics of innovative companies?

Innovative companies focus on two main types of innovation: sustainable and disruptive. Most existing companies are good at sustaining innovation by making functional improvements and creating the next generation, model, or version of a product or service. It's usually done by internal groups within the company whose thinking is based on "I need this feature, I will add this feature to the product, and I will sell it for premium."

By contrast, disruptive innovation discovers not only new products but products with a whole new business model. Again, let's look at Uber. It essentially focused on transportation, which is the taxi industry, but at the same time, it's an entirely different business model. It's not about the taxi industry trying to develop new features or product ideas, but about software entrepreneurs disrupting the taxi ecosystem.

Can you give an example of a larger company investing in a start-up for innovative purposes?

Flextronics (FLEX), the world's third-largest electronics company, and Fitbit, a world market leader for fitness tracking devices, are an interesting example. Did you know that Fitbit came out of FLEX? Fitbit once consisted of just a handful of FLEX-employees with a highly entrepreneurial spirit. Without any resources to create a hand wrist tracking device, they created a start-up "Fitbit" within an incubator. This allowed Flextronics to do all kinds of innovative manufacturing and prototyping. Flextronics took a small equity stake in the Fitbit and then provided them a full range of design, engineering, and large-scale manufacturing resources. Flextronics, therefore, explored entirely new opportunities through strategic linkage and they did it because they were dependent on another company to innovate.

These days, networking and support for start-ups have become an attractive way for many tech companies in Silicon Valley to invest in new technologies and market trends. This type of investment has become an important pillar of strategic investments. As a second example, Intel has its incubator and accelerator teams in-house. They continuously bring in start-ups to work with them. Once Intel sees highly valuable market potential in any of these start-ups, they bring in their own experiences and work out this new star. It's about an outside-in mindset, to bring external ideas in.

Is failure important to success?

You have to distinguish between failure while innovating and failure to innovate. There's a subtle nuance; innovation inevitably involves failures, but that doesn't mean you should stop innovating. The fastest way to innovate necessarily includes an abundance of failures because that means you are taking risks and working hard. There are successful leaders in the world like Apple and Google that have failed. Google tried to replace Facebook as a social network and failed spectacularly. Microsoft's Windows Phone was a failure. Web TV is a failure. Amazon's Fire Phone was a failure. They all failed and learned from it.

At every point in the start-up phase, including the opportunity discovery phase, validation is crucial. Talk to potential customers, not ten but hundreds. Be honest and admit you've reached an impasse. Do not try to make a caterpillar into a super caterpillar, make it even bigger or faster. You want to produce a butterfly. To be successful, you need a good sense of market growth and disruptive market opportunities. Furthermore, keep your VC in a close loop and push for feedback and support.

What is the success rate of VC-funded companies?

Most people talk about a hit rate of ten percent, but the chances of success are one in a hundred. It's a hard business, even with all the backing of venture capitalists and other kinds of seed capital. Stanford generates a lot of patents, but only a few make monies like the Google search algorithm. You need to figure out how to convert the patent into multiple portfolio companies or portfolio products, so some of them will succeed.

What is a Smart Facility and what is its potential?

A smart facility could be a building, campus, city, or broader entity. Smart facilities leverage IoT technologies with sensors, actuators, analytics, and other items to monitor and manage various aspects of these facilities. Some of the aspects that are monitored are lighting, processes, security, and people. You may get continuous returns on your investment by saving energy in your facilities, or you increase order volume and revenue significantly if you can boost efficiency amongst your workforce.

Why do companies invest in Smart Facilities?

Making buildings and infrastructure more efficient is nothing more than a drop in the ocean. In the end, it's all about improving your business performance. The question that needs to be addressed is: "How do you make your employees more productive?" – That is what business performance is all about. People complain that the inside temperature hinders their productivity because they are uncomfortable and can't focus. By adjusting the temperature using IoT and the sensors in the building, we can generate a comfortable environment and thereby increase productivity. Current thinking is focused on making buildings and facilities more efficient, but it's important to understand that it's about the people and how to make them more productive.

IoT is a three hundred billion dollars plus market, so it's key to think about business opportunities in that field. IoT is the underlying technology required to drive these so-called smart spaces or smart facilities. It may still take five to ten years until we see large scale deployment of IoT in any kind of facility. However, already Amazon is disrupting this market in terms of getting the efficiency to levels where others have to scramble to keep up. There are fantastic opportunities here and tremendous disruptions happening by combining IoT with machine learning and A.I.

Give us some examples where IoT-powered offices have improved their employee's productivity?

Office employees spend a lot of time hunting for conference rooms. Often, they stop what they're doing, just to schedule a vacant conference room – hilarious, and highly inefficient. This hinders productivity. Location services make this a thing of the past. During a meeting, a sign above the door turns red, and after the meeting turns green. There would be a real-time feed of the availability of a conference room, as opposed to manually looking at the schedule calendar. Another interesting application is hot desking. In this situation, you don't have a designated office cubicle or office room – you just take any available space. As soon as you sit in the space and plug in your computer, it immediately signals that the spot is no longer vacant. This concept is becoming very popular these days, particularly in banks, as they are trying to downsize their real estate footprint. They can consolidate ten buildings into five and reduce their massive space overhead.

Are there obstacles we might encounter in the process of switching to smart facilities?

One area we need to think about is hardware. People are trying to build very vertical siloed applications in terms of how the hardware talks to the software. It is crucial however to build an open architecture because the hardware side is being disrupted. When companies invest in sensor hardware, and two years later something new comes up, they are forced to rebuild the application because it doesn't work with the new device. The solution is to create a neutral middleware that can talk to all kinds of hardware in a standardized way.

Do you foresee any other future trends?

One trend is what we call wireless mesh lighting. Many lighting companies, such as Acuity want to position themselves to be the new iPhone of building lights. LED lighting is equipped with sensors, which are connected across the building to create a mesh network. Thus, you can measure various aspects such as temperature, pressure, carbon dioxide, and carbon monoxide.

Something is interesting about the environment inside buildings. When you are in a conference room, you may feel somewhat hot and become sleepy. Do you know why? A study reports that because of the closed nature of conference rooms, proper ventilation is not possible. This causes a higher concentration of carbon dioxide in the room, which makes you sleepy. Having sensors in conference rooms that measure those kinds of particles and act upon that data improves productivity. This mesh network with tiny packaged sensors, embedded in the lighting, can measure ten to twelve different indicators at once. These indicators are fed into the cloud where the information is used to control air quality.

How can IoT improve human efficiency in manufacturing?

Smart manufacturing is an area with huge opportunities. You have machinery which is very expensive to operate, and safety is a big issue. Billions of dollars are lost because of injuries in terms of healthcare bills, lawsuits, and various other things in the U.S. The safety perspective is driving manufacturing and warehouses to install sensors in machinery and equipment.

Another question that's currently being addressed is how to track people's hand movements. In the assembly line, people's efficiency is different because some work faster than others. It is a big challenge to make everyone on the assembly line get to the same level of efficiency. Tracking people's hands and movements could be used for both efficiencies as well as safety. Systems are being deployed, but not yet industrialized.

How can IoT be used to improve the safety and security of the workplace?

Tracking people for security has become an issue in a lot of companies. People walk in, they register with the front desk, walk around, and you can't trace them. In some cases, they may be able to access a restricted area containing sensitive information. With a smartphone in their pocket or a provided wristband, we could monitor their location through the building and ensure they are where they should be.

I came across a situation where people who are working late, such as janitors, have an accident and nobody knows what happened to them. Using these sensors, we can monitor if people are not moving, if they're stuck in a room or location, or if they are somewhere for an extended amount of time. Appropriate people are notified who then respond and save human lives.

How is IoT utilized in retail?

Amazon has completely automated stores where, as soon as you pick up the item and put it in your basket, it's checked out. You don't need to do anything; you just walk out with your items and Amazon will charge your credit card. It's touchless with no check-out counters – the sensors automate everything. In fact, they are working on all kinds of technologies that allow large-scale operations such as grocery stores to be completely automated. With the sensors, you can precisely track what the customers are doing, and what items they're picking up to keep – or reject and put back into the shelf. There's a revolution on the horizon in retail because of the margins and other factors involved. It is an excellent area for automating and reducing the cost.

Many grocery stores have specific items placed next to other items because when you're buying one, there is a good chance you'll also buy the other one. Retail companies are conducting analytics to understand where to position the products within the store itself. They're trying to optimize retail to avoid stock-outs and deploy sensors to track goods. Automated stocking is one of the big problems people are trying to solve and it could be handled by smart robots in the future. Through all these retail analytics you can do layered optimization and understand the traffic patterns of the customers which finally allows you to conduct proper merchandising and marketing.

Are there IoT applications in other areas of the supply chain in between manufacturing and retail?

Smart warehouses and smart transport are gaining traction. There's a lot of automation happening in the warehouses and distribution centers; e-commerce is a driving factor for that, so it's critical to bring costs down. There's a tremendous amount of investments in the Amazons of the world and various other warehouse-based companies. The transportation methods of goods from warehouses to distribution centers and eventually to the retail stores offer great investment opportunities. The idea is if you start deploying IoT technologies in all these locations and connect them to what I call smart interconnected spaces you will increase the efficiency dramatically.

Amazon is leading the way in terms of warehouses and distributions. If you want to know what's coming, investigate patent filings. Amazon is working on patents on a dispensing system that monitors whether workers are putting their hands in the right places. You could help workers by tracking their hands and guiding them to the right bin to cut down the amount of time spent searching for parts. Amazon is working on many patents from an efficiency point of view because they understand that efficiency improvement could result in massive cost savings.

How can hospitals take advantage of IoT devices, like smart sensors, and robots to improve health and security?

New hospitals being constructed these days get accessorized with sensors to optimize building performance and speed up procedures and operations. A potential application is infant security. A big issue in the U.S. is that babies are being kidnapped from hospitals. You can install geo fencing around the hospitals and put tags on the children's wristbands to ensure the infants are secure. If they are taken past the geo-fence without approval, the alarm is triggered, and various people can respond to the situation. Patient wander management is another application that can assist with security and health. People with certain mental issues and diseases often wander around and get lost.

We did a pilot in a hospital and were able to improve the number of patients who can be processed using sensor technologies by almost thirty-five percent. Large improvements can be achieved in terms of how we track and manage the flow of patients.

Robots can be used to deliver food and accessories such as linens, blankets, and towels for patients. Through a sensor system installed throughout the paths robots are taking, they would navigate securely within the hospital. Vision systems and light radars are expensive; however, using ultrasonic or infrared sensors, robots can properly guide themselves to the right destinations. In fact, if you go to UCSF, and maybe to a couple of other Californian hospitals, all food delivery to the patients is done by robots. Patients order food on the iPad from their bed, the information is sent to the staff, and within ten to twenty minutes, the food robot arrives. There is significantly less danger of contamination since the food is untouched by any of the staff members.

Are there any other areas where IoT being used?

In hospitals smart parking guidance is being used in parking garages. If you go to some of the big hospitals in the U.S., it is difficult to find a parking space – it can easily take you fifteen to twenty minutes. This delays your appointment, which cascades down and reduces the efficiency of the hospital.

IoT is used to guide you to the next vacant spot. Typically, in the case of underground parking or parking garages, there is a sensor located above each parking spot. If a spot is vacant the sensor is green; if occupied, the sensor is red. At the end of each aisle and on every level of the parking structure is a digital sign located on the ceiling displaying how many parking spots are available in that row. This allows traffic to flow efficiently and people to spend less time searching for a parking spot. Imagine how much time that would save. Just think of all the things that people can invent and solve when they do not have to spend hours searching for parking. It is quite exciting.

Part III

Mega Growth, Mega Markets

Emerging Mega Markets

Meyya Meyyappan

Chief Scientist for Exploration Technology
at NASA's Ames Research Center

Written by Anatoli Kalysch

"Nanotechnology is the technology of the 21st Century, and there is no question about it."

— Meyya Meyyappan

Dr. Meyyappan is the chief scientist for Exploration Technology at NASA's Ames Research Center in California's Silicon Valley. He served as the director of the Center for Nanotechnology at Ames until June 2006. Dr. Meyyappan is the founding member of the Interagency Working Group on Nanotechnology (IWGN) established by the Office of Science and Technology Policy in Washington, D.C. The IWGN is responsible for developing the National Nanotechnology Initiative. He has authored and co-authored more than four hundred articles in peer-reviewed journals, conducted more than two hundred and fifty seminars at universities, and presented more than two hundred fifty Invited/Keynote/Plenary Talks on nanotechnology subjects around the world. His research interests include carbon nanotubes, graphene, and various inorganic nanowires, their growth and characterization, application development in chemical and biosensors, instrumentation, electronics, and optoelectronics. Dr. Meyyappan holds a bachelor's degree from Madras University, India, a master's degree from Aston University, Birmingham, U.K., and a doctorate from Clarkson University, Potsdam, N.Y.

In this interview, Dr. Meyyappan shares his insights on a wide variety of topics ranging from neuromorphic computing to the world of nanotechnology. He helps us understand the reason behind their extreme market growth potential by explaining the applications of these technologies on various products like biosensors, printed sensors, and the multi-hundred-billion-dollar industry that is rapidly gaining a strong presence: individualized medicine. Dr. Meyyappan brings up terahertz imaging as a potential enabler of a new age for medical imaging and a disruption in the healthcare sector. He depicts a future where programmable materials will allow us to harness the power of triboelectricity to charge our everyday consumer electronics, such as smartwatches. In the future, according to Dr. Meyyappan, even the problem of scarcity of freshwater in certain regions could be solved through the use of nanotechnology and its ability to create selective membranes, making ocean water desalination much more affordable and available.

What are some upcoming innovations in the world of e-computing?

Classical computing is a well-researched topic. Therefore, people are increasingly looking to alternative forms of computing to enhance conventional solutions. One innovation gaining attention is quantum computing (QC). However, I'm not going to focus on QC but will be discussing neuromorphic computing (NC) which is becoming very practical.

In NC, we are attempting to imitate the biological neural system to create a computer. This is quite challenging since it requires an understanding of biology, physics, mathematics, computer science, and electrical engineering to make such a system work. The benefits could far outweigh the challenges, as it could open the doors to highly efficient and effective enhancements to our current computer systems. This means smarter AI, more energy-efficient systems, and possibly multi-purpose systems we haven't yet imagined. To ensure the practicality of such an NC-based system, we are currently considering two possible alternatives. The first would make it available faster but could possibly compromise performance in the long run; the other could lead to a better performing system but would take longer to achieve.

If neuromorphic computing is such a game-changer, why not opt for the short-term approach and reap the benefits sooner rather than later?

With the short-term approach, we would utilize known devices, mostly silicon-based, which is quite close to how computing works today. Silicon-based mechanisms have been researched very well, and we have a relatively good understanding of the potentials and limitations of these systems, such as spatial constraints between transistors. This makes working with them quite comfortable. On the other hand, the time of Moore's Law is slowly coming to an end, with limited game-changing efficiencies and improvements possible along the way. This could result in performance limitations soon enough for neuromorphic computing systems, and we need to be aware of this if we continue down this path.

The second approach is to build on non-silicon-based devices. This means lengthy research before the devices could become practical, but would ultimately reap extraordinary performance gains. For example, Hewlett Packard used oxide-based materials such as titanium oxide, to create an electronic circuit called a memristor. A memristor is a conjunction of two components of memory and one of the best performing artificial neurons to date. This could outperform a silicon-based device and, with more research, create extraordinary systems. Why don't we use them already in our day-to-day computing? As it turns out, mass-producing these neurons, at least for now, is a massive challenge because of the spatial constraints on the microscopic level they require in order to be built. Solving this would mean incredibly low-energy consumption for our future computing prowess. In the long run, this could bring great rewards and should be pursued.

Please give us a brief description of what defines nanotechnology.

A nanometer is a billionth of a meter. To put this in perspective, a human hair measures 10,000 nanometers and DNA measures only 2.5 nanometers. This means that one nanometer is taking ten hydrogen atoms and placing them right next to each other. Nanotechnology involves creating useful products by manipulating matter. It is not a matter of simply making products small, which is what IBM, Intel, and TSMC have done. We are talking about manipulating matter and taking advantage of unique properties by going to the nanoscale. The object to be created could be nano or it could be even micro or macro. For instance, you can assemble nanocomposites and construct an aircraft.

An interesting fact is that properties at the nanoscale are different from macro-scale properties. The reason properties change when you go from bulk scale to nanoscale is that nanomaterials have a large surface area for a given body. If you take a 30-nanometer iron particle, approximately five percent of its atoms are on the surface, with most of the atoms located inside. The atoms inside are bound with their neighbors, and they're happy. On the other hand, the atoms sitting outside are exposed, restless, and active. When you downsize, the number of atoms that are inside become smaller, while the fraction of atoms on the outside increases. Therefore, when you go to the nanoscale, properties change.

A simple example is the melting point. A gold bar melts at around 1,064 degrees Fahrenheit. On the other hand, five-nanometer gold particles melt 200-300 degrees sooner, at a lower temperature.

How is nanotechnology applied in day-to-day life?

Nanomaterials have a large surface area for a given volume. The surface to volume ratio of particles is of importance in many common products, like cement, fertilizer, table salt, sugar, detergent, coffee, anything of that sort, and not-so-obvious products such as paint, toothpaste, lipstick, chewing gum, and even slick magazine covers. These all have fine particles. The surface covering automobile tires doesn't consist only of rubber; they use nano-silica powder to keep the rubber from unraveling. That's one of the reasons that tires now are better than those we used thirty to fifty years ago.

Take, for example, peanut butter. We have two types, crunchy and creamy. The difference between crunchy and creamy is the particle size of the peanuts. Medical tablets, vitamins, and painkillers can be released in a timely manner because the dissolve-time in the stomach acid is dependent on the particle size. As you can see, there are a lot of products we use in our daily life where the effectiveness is greater using nanotechnology.

How does nanotechnology impact computing and communication?

Throughout the past two decades, we have witnessed the growth of personal computing, with most people now owning a laptop. The future will involve ubiquitous computing, where there are thousands of computers, or chips, embedded in everything we use. We currently have chips embedded in cars and smartphones and so on. Pretty soon we might have chips embedded in the walls, chairs, clothing, or light switches. This is essentially connecting things, which explains the new phrase, the Internet of Things (IoT). This is a multi-hundred-billion-dollar industry we see is on the horizon. IoT will require software enabling multi-connection and an abundance of hardware. Whether it is sensors or actuators, they must be both small and flexible. Silicon may not rule IoT, because IoT may require cheaper and more flexible materials than silicon can provide.

At NASA Ames, we decided to resurrect the vacuum tube. You might think that's crazy, but hear me out: the problem with vacuum tubes back in the day was that they broke easily, were bulky, and consumed a huge amount of power. This is why they disappeared. The integrated circuits were able to beat them very easily on every point. However, despite the disadvantages of vacuum tubes, they did have two distinct and undeniable advantages. Firstly, the vacuum tube out-performs integrated circuits from a speed point of view because the electrons travel faster in a vacuum. Integrated circuits are made of a material like silicon and gallium arsenide and if there is material, the electrons will collide with it. Every time an electron experiences collision with the material, it will slow down. A vacuum has no material; it is the absence of material. If there is nothing, then there will be nothing to collide with. The electron speed is theoretically the fastest you can move from point A to point B. Vacuum-based solutions will always be superior in that regard.

The second advantage is that there's no need to worry about radiation. This is extremely important, particularly for military or space exploration. Whenever the military or NASA uses electronics, they must wrap them up in a way that prevents radiation exposure to such things as gamma radiation, alpha particles, and all other space radiation. Wrapping it will make the device bulky and heavy. Vacuum tubes are immune to radiation.

The innovation here is to bring back vacuum tubes but to re-innovate them to remove disadvantages. When you try to combine the best of old technology with modern technology, the potential is better than some of the newer exotic developments.

What is your take on printing sensors?

The printing sensor started a few years ago and is called printed electronics. There are printers slightly different from your common printer that allow you to print these devices directly on flexible substrates like paper, textiles, plastic, or metal files. Printing is fast, it's inexpensive, and there is no need for clean-room fabrication, which means you no longer need a billion-dollar lab. If you are printing on paper, it could be a disposable sensor for one-time use. This is ideal for many medical applications; you don't want to have cross-contamination, so you don't recycle. This creates a need for disposable sensors using paper and such materials, which are cheaper but are still a green technology, with low-power use. Most important is that the technology is adaptable to the needs of third world countries.

Which country is most progressively working on printed electronics?

I was astonished when I went to Finland a few years ago. It's a country of four million people, and there were many companies and universities involved in working on paper-related technology. If you adjust for the population, I believe Finland is number one in the world, and I asked them why so many people work in that field. They said, "When you think of Finland, you think of Nokia, but our largest export is paper raw materials and related products. At the same time, people are writing and printing less. If things don't change, we will be out of business soon. We need to brainstorm about clever ways of using paper for higher-finished products. That's why so many of us are working on printed electronics." They produce what is called a nano structured paper, with properties controlled in the process.

What are the current limitations to printing biosensors and what is the research focused on?

The printing processes can't manufacture the sensors yet. This is the future we are moving towards, but I cannot tell how soon we will arrive at that point. From a technical point of view, the kind of detection limit and sensitivity you know from the conventional micro-fabricated sensors are reachable. The idea is that these sensors, whether they are printed or micro-fabricated, should be cheap due to the limitation of its one-time use disposable applications or other demands of the IoT.

What nano developments do you foresee in the medical field?

What is becoming a critical use case for nanotubes is a sensor-based approach, such as having sensors able to cover an extensive range of the electromagnetic spectrum and terahertz imaging. This is slowly gaining more attention, but the current systems are far too clunky; they are usually the size of a pool table or even larger. If terahertz imaging could be made practical in a sensor or a scanner, this could usher in a whole new age of medical imaging and would be a disruption in the healthcare sector.

Current approaches such as X-rays or CT scans give off ionizing radiation. As we all know this is a health hazard because, over time, this radiation can cause cancer. However, this danger would be a thing of the past with terahertz imaging because no ionizing radiation is emitted. This would make our health care safer and have an impact on several areas of our lives.

Soon we will have biosensors with the ability to analyze various fluids automatically. A lab is required to do this nowadays. Biosensors are small, lightweight, have low carbon consumption and, as with minimal need for human processing. They will have negligible "false alarms". Best of all is that by performing the analysis yourself, you retain control over who receives your data. Biosensors could monitor various chemicals in your body and help with diagnosis and treatment of various diseases by displaying spikes in certain compounds in the bloodstream.

Human genome sequencing required tens of billions of dollars and an extensive amount of time in the early days of its development. There are now companies that can sequence your genome in a couple of hours, for a cost of around one hundred dollars. This is all moving us toward more individualized medicine.

Medicine today, both diagnostics and therapeutics, is based on statistics. The statistics are based on information from various people. If you happen to be in Norway, a homogeneous population with local statistics, your statistics will be meaningful. What if you take such homogeneous statistics and apply them to a place like the San Francisco Bay Area? Those statistics don't work, the results are not generalizable. Here is where individualized medicine comes in. Personalized diagnostic based on your genetic makeup as well as therapeutics.

What impact do you see in manufacturing?

We try to assemble from the bottom up, not only the large technologies but the materials themselves. This allows us to produce lighter, stronger, and more easily programmable materials. By programmable I mean the programming of the properties of the material. A few people around the world have been researching self-healing materials, where the inspiration comes from the skin. A good example would be the lotus effect, which enables materials with self-cleaning surfaces. A German University has played a significant role in its development. The idea is to incorporate the self-cleaning surface into automobile glass.

What are the applications in the energy area?

Think of the development of lightbulbs over the last few years. The filament bulb, which wastes ninety percent of its energy, has been replaced with the solid-state bulb, which is far more energy-efficient. Many research groups are working on making them as afford-able as possible to hasten the disappearance of filament bulbs. When you think of ener-gy production, you should have mechanical energy harvesting in mind. Wearable devices that use 1-100mW could easily be charged by your movements, known as Triboelectricity. A smartphone or smartwatch could be charged in your pocket or your hand while you're moving.

Triboelectricity is a large field that many are tapping into. For example, in the winter-time, you will sometimes put your hand on a doorknob and get a little electric shock. Those shocks can get up to kilowatts and can occur on any contact with different surfaces. This is an unusual and interesting energy source now being studied by many people. The Chinese Government is spending a hundred million dollars to study its potential uses.

How does nanotechnology impact concerns about clean drinking water?

It's one very important problem to solve, but it's only one part of the question of sustain-ability in the future. Water availability itself is also a pressing concern. Nearly a billion people lack access to clean drinking water. For instance, the Middle Eastern countries are already under extreme water stress and it's an increasingly pressing issue. Water resources are becoming more problematic because of the effects of climate change and continually decreasing rainfall, with many areas experiencing periodic droughts. We, humans, have managed to pollute virtually everything we touch. We must find new energy-efficient and cost-effective water purification technologies. Nanotechnologies are playing a major role in discovering selective membranes that have mechanical desalination. Oceans cover over seventy percent of the earth's surface and hold over ninety-seven percent of Earth's water supply. Currently, only a very small percentage of this resource is being refined into safe drinking water. The lower cost of desalination due to nanotechnological advances could greatly boost this percentage and would provide access to these water reserves in areas of great need.

Since we're discussing the impact of nanotechnologies on water, how does it impact agriculture?

People are beginning to install sensor networks that monitor soil conditions. The simplest things to monitor are pH values and nutrients. With sensors, you can specify how much water you need, allowing you to conserve water. This has quite a bit of funding in the United States, especially from the U.S. Department of Agriculture, to advance these technologies. Sensors are most important for monitoring food. We, as a global community, produce enough food to adequately feed every single human being on Earth, yet an enormous amount of this food is wasted, particularly in countries like India. India produces enough food to feed virtually everyone, but unfortunately, much of it goes to waste. We need sensors in the fields, we need them in the warehouses, in the distribution centers, and in the stores. We need sensors for the entire supply chain in order to accurately monitor this precious resource, our food.

What do you think about energy storage technologies, particularly hydrogen storage?

According to the U.S. Department of Energy, the current requirement for hydrogen storage is about seven percent. What carbon nanotubes can store is not enough for application, so people are now researching numerous other materials. I believe there's too much focus on hydrogen. We should try to discover if methane can be stored. Why? Because methane is a compressed natural gas, and if you look at busses in Europe, for example, they are using CNG in cylinders as a storage method. Improving that storage is low-hanging fruit. In my opinion, first, remove those limitations with CNG before jumping into better devices.

How far along are we on the path toward the future you've been describing?

Merrill Lynch studied every major revolution mankind has experienced, starting with the textile revolution, then the rise of the automobile, computers, and finally technology. They found that it takes approximately 20-25 years for the technology to be set up. It becomes prevalent for the next 70-80 years and then finally it becomes a commodity. We will be milking computers up until about 2025, and from then on nobody is going to be paying much attention to computer technology. Computers will still be around, just like the rail-road is still around. If you take the same development structure and apply it to nanotech-nology, it should be taking off by about 2025, and eventually will become a commodity by 2080. No question about it, it will become the technology of the 21st century.

Why will nanotechnology be the technology of the twenty-first century?

As an enabling technology, it's going to have its fingerprint in every industry, every sector, including the emerging IoT. Everything today has two sides, the hardware side and the software side. The software side is obvious. It is dominated by big names like Google, Microsoft, Facebook, Twitter, and so on. Software is important because without software this phone would be a paperweight. But you need the hardware to advance to make things smaller and more affordable. Hardware development will be controlled and taken over by the nano components. You can see that from the investments in virtually every country in the world.

What about the science fiction technologies such as little machines that patrol your body and repair damage? Are you working on such technologies at NASA?

Well, if you are an individual who has a billion dollars and you assemble a crew to work on whatever you wish, you can probably do it. But that's not the way the world works. You know whether it is a German Economic Ministry or U.S. Department of Defense, people who are funding have a timeline; they have specific goals. You can't just go out and do things that may or may not work out. In this natural selective process and the way we do business, people look for the low-hanging fruits. For that reason, some of your vision is and will remain science fiction, for now. But who knows? Maybe one day we'll actually get there. Even now, there are small groups working on these ideas, but I'd say they don't have the critical mass to make it a reality just yet.

What issues do hardware startups face in comparison to software when seeking investment from a VC?

There are a lot of start-ups right now, many with a wealth of good ideas and interesting approaches. The main challenge is to stay around long enough to become a serious player in the field. That's difficult for these hardware start-up companies. I'm going to give you my biased opinion. I've been in Silicon Valley for the last twenty-four years and I've observed how it operates. To me, these venture businesses are good at incubating software companies, but at this time we must deal with hardware startups. Many of the successful methods you use with software companies will not work equally well for hardware development; the latter needs other approaches and definitely longer timescales. The "One size fits all" approach won't work. The problem is that venture capitalists keep trying to force the same old tired model on every one of their startups, regardless of hardware or software and it just won't work.

The World of Blockchain

Ahmed Banafa

Cybersecurity Expert and Author, Professor for General Engineering at Charles W. Davidson College of Engineering at SJSU

Written by Spyridon G. Koustas, Marius Garzorz and Xenia Dolguschew

"Some people ask me, "How can I use blockchain for my industry?" I tell them that this is the wrong question to ask. First, you must understand what blockchain is. It's easy to apply once it's understood, but not the other way around."

— Ahmed Banafa

Ahmed Banafa has extensive experience in research, operations, and management, with a focus on IoT, blockchain, cybersecurity, and AI. He is a reviewer and a technical contributor to the publication of several technical books. Ahmed Banafa served on the faculty at several well-known universities and colleges, including the University of California at Berkeley, California State University-East Bay, San Jose State University, and the University of Massachusetts. He is the recipient of several awards, including the Distinguished Tenured Staff Award of 2013 and Instructor of the Year for 2013 and 2014, and holds a Certificate of Honor from the City and County of San Francisco. He was named as the number one tech voice to follow by LinkedIn in 2016, and his research is featured on many reputable sites and in magazines including Forbes, IEEE, and MIT Technology Review, and was interviewed by ABC, CBS, NBC, and Fox TV and various radio stations. Ahmed Banafa studied cybersecurity at Harvard University and is the author of "Secure and Smart Internet of Things, Using blockchain and Artificial Intelligence".

P rofessor Banafa talks about blockchain, a technology with the potential to redefine the cybersecurity and financial industries as we know them today. He explains the endless applications of blockchain for various uses – smart contracts, for example. Due to the recent boom-and-bust cycle of Bitcoin, cryptocurrencies became a much-discussed topic. Professor Banafa sheds light on this topic and how it relates to blockchain. We also ask him about the most researched areas in the world of technology: IoT and AI. As an expert on cybersecurity, he illustrates his opinion on GDPR and the importance of an overarching set of guidelines in the data security field.

What exactly is blockchain?

The best definition I have ever heard came from MIT professor and blockchain expert, Dr. Abel Sanchez. He defined blockchain as: cryptography plus human logic. Cryptography is the firewall we have encrypted, like SHA-256. The five elements comprising any blockchain are cryptography, peer-to-peer-networking, consensus mechanisms representing human logic, the ledger where you can record the list, and the validity rules.

Imagine there are thirty people trying to enter a room and that there is a door that requires a special card to open it. With the current centralized system, a person would swipe their card to get inside. Using blockchain, each of the thirty people would have a list with pictures of the people authorized to be in the room. So if somebody who was not on the list tried to come in,, they would start talking to each other, asking "Hey, can you please check to see if this person belongs here?" That synchronization is referred to as gossip protocol within the blockchain. Human logic is the list and the motion of everybody talking to each other. On top of the current system, we added human logic; consensus protocols and algorithms.

Can you tell us how a blockchain is initialized and what the content of a block is?

A blockchain is initialized with the genesis block; this is the foundation of the trading system and the prototype for other blocks within the blockchain. Each block has five elements: The index, the timestamp, the previous hash, the hash, and the data. When you change any of these elements, you will change the whole block, and then the previous and the following blocks will see that something has occurred. The beauty of blockchain is that the programming is not heavy, its power comes from the network. You must convince fifty-one percent of all blocks to be changed. This is where human logic comes into account.

What is the story behind blockchain technology?

Blockchain has its roots in the public-key cryptography, first demonstrated in 1970. It was used to uniquely identify the owner of an address as the only party authorized to modify the state associated with an account. In the late 1970s, the cryptographic hash functions and Merkle trees were invented and used to link transactions into verifiable chains. In 1993, proof of work was used to demonstrate that a non-trivial amount of computer time was devoted to generating a given Merkle tree. In 1994, a model for self-enforcing agreements called smart contracts was invented. Peer-to-peer file-sharing was introduced in 1999, which was used to disseminate a copy of data to an undefined number of network nodes.

We have reached a point where we can look back at how it all started because we have new resources and algorithms, we have the computing powers, the memory, and the skills. We have all these innovations and ideas. So we looked back and said: "let's use it in a new way."

What types of blockchains exist?

We have three types of blockchains: private/permissioned, public/permissionless, and hybrid/federated/consortium. Private blockchains are closed ecosystems within a company that can be accessed by those approved. Public blockchains allow anyone to access the data. Federated is a hybrid between public and private blockchains and are often ecosystems within multiple organizations. It depends on the application, but companies will never allow public blockchains due to loss of influence, even if it is deemed safe. There are different ways to use blockchain and they all differ in participation, ability to act as a node, energy consumption, security, speed, and trust level. Which one you use depends on your needs.

What kind of tracks are there and how are they important to Silicon Valley?

Blockchain is an important part of Silicon Valley and we have three tracks of blockchain, each one with its own ecosystem, its own players, and actors. The first one is the pure Research and Development (R&D) track which is conducted by universities, mainly large schools such as Stanford and Berkeley. This track is focused on understanding what it means to develop a blockchain-based system. The goal is investigation and learning, not necessarily delivering a working system.

The second track is the Immediate Business Benefit track. This track covers two bases; one is learning how to work with this promising technology and the other is delivering an actual system that can be deployed in a real business context. Many of these projects are intra-company projects.

The third track is the Long-Term Transformational Potential track. This is the track of visionaries who recognize the true value of blockchain-based networks, which means reinventing entire processes and industries as well as understanding how public-sector organizations function.

Some people ask me, "How can I use blockchain for my industry?" I tell them that this is the wrong question to ask. First, you must understand what blockchain is. It's easy to apply once it's understood, but not the other way around.

What role does blockchain play in the workforce?

Blockchain development is the number one skill listed on LinkedIn in 2019, but only 3.3% of companies worldwide have deployed blockchain as a product. According to the marketing life cycle, even though blockchain was implemented in 1966, it still hasn't gone beyond the growth stage. We are nearing a tipping point. Many prototypes have been built but blockchain technology has not yet been applied at scale, so the future remains uncertain. If you want to catch that wave, you can look to schools that are catching up in this field, like San Jose State University. Blockchain, robotics, and digital transformation are all essential to creating blockchain and you need experts from all these areas.

One important part of blockchains are "Smart Contracts". What makes them so special?

Smart Contracts were designed to send and receive money. The factors that make them special are the conditions you can attach to them. For example, if the owner does not check the account for two months, the money, the password, or the private key will be sent to someone else

If you are conducting business with someone and the GPS on their phone hasn't tracked them in the office for two weeks, , the money will be returned to the sender.If you want to make sure that I am actually giving a lecture, what kind of parameters would a smart contract have to verify that? My phone and laptop are here; with GPS you can locate that. My voice could be recorded, or cameras could verify my. If you'd have access to all of these parameters, you'd have proof of my presence.

Is it better to use smart contracts when using short term contracts?

Yes. Technology changes fast, so the accompanying impacts are better foreseeable in the short term. This is very important to consider. Nevertheless, there is a need for attorneys to discuss this on a juridical level. Ricardian contracts are used for this, they are written in plain text by attorneys and set at the top of smart contracts in order to deal with situations like this.

What challenges do we face with blockchains?

The first challenge is scalability. Visa and MasterCard have a minimum of twenty-four thousand transactions per second. The maximum we receive with blockchain is four thousand transactions per second (tps), or maybe three thousand tps with the use of IBM's solution. The next two challenges are the processing time problem and the processing power problem. Lastly, storage is a big issue. It may not be a problem now, but it may when, in the future, you have permanent copies requiring large storage space.

What are some of the blockchain regulations a company may face?

Regulation is another pressing issue. As an example, Bitcoin is not allowed in China. If there ever comes a time for regulations that the cryptocurrencies or the blockchains must follow, problems will certainly arise. Regulations sometimes hold back industries. Healthcare is a good example: there's a regulation in the U.S. called HIPAA, which is very strict about transference of information.

What is the correlation between blockchain and Bitcoin?

The public perception that blockchain is Bitcoin is not true. Bitcoin and the criminal perception of ransomware are an outcome of blockchain.

There was a ransomware called "WannaCry" that quickly grew globally. There was one common factor among all the computers that were attacked by it. All of them were using Windows XP, some people didn't upgrade to the newest version, providing an open door for ransomware. Cryptocurrencies also play a role in other criminal activities such as human trafficking. I know of specific cases within Homeland Security and the FBI. Another example is a hardware wallet from Europe called the "NANO". If you plug it in a certain way, it will erase everything, and your money will be gone.

When I make presentations on blockchain here in the valley, people sometimes say they don't want to hear anything about cryptocurrencies; they didn't attend the presentation to hear about cryptocurrencies. The problem is that we started with a bad name: "cryptocurrency", though the underlying technology is capable of much more. The technology itself is kind of a distributed ledger of which people have copies of their own. These copies sync with each other and verify the contained information in the blocks by using SHA 256 encryption.

Would you invest in Bitcoin?

My students ask me if they should invest in Bitcoin because their friends made a lot of money with it. I tell them not to touch it. It makes no sense. It went up to twenty-one thousand dollars for one Bitcoin and now it's just under four thousand dollars per Bitcoin. To be more precise, I asked if one of them would buy a car for five thousand dollars without first checking it out thoroughly. The answer, of course, was no. I went further and asked them to give me five thousand dollars for a hand-drawn car on a notepad. At this point, the light began to dawn on them about what I was saying, and they just gave up on Bitcoin. Right now, it's just a bunch of numbers.

How do you convince investors to invest in blockchain technology?

The blockchain market over the past eighteen months has been moving from an "explain this to me" PowerPoint phase to the "prove it to me" phase, using working conference room pilots. Enhance your business model with blockchain at a different level. Implement blockchain in different ways and, trust me, the venture capitalists (VCs) will love it.

The other important thing to talk about is how we can implement this concept. Blockchain has four cases to prove it is moving from pilot to application. The first method is verified data dissemination. Verify the data and information you are sending. The second method is via asset and product tracking. The third is asset transfer, and the final possibility is certified claims.

What is the correlation between blockchain, Internet of Things (IoT), Artificial Intelligence (AI), and cybersecurity? What opportunities do you see in those fields?

IoT, blockchain, AI, and cybersecurity are all interconnected. IoT feels, blockchain remembers, AI thinks, and cybersecurity protects. Each one of them is a field of promising research for startup companies, many of which decide to specialize in one or more of them. To pair IoT with blockchain is a safe model because the biggest problem for IoT is that it's too big, too complex, and has too many moving parts. There are four sections within IoT. First, the sensor. Second, the network. Third is the intelligence of the cloud, and fourth is the application. This prompts the question of how to protect them all. Each of these issues provides an opportunity for startups to research and solve.

How does the combination of blockchain, IoT, and AI work?

The interesting part is how we can combine blockchain, IoT, and AI. How can I verify that the sensor is sending the information and not changing that information? This is where we see the blockchain, AI, and IoT interact throughout the whole process. If you think about it from a business perspective, it opens up many opportunities for startups. Blockchain and AI meet exactly in the IoT territory. AI and blockchain will help the IoT to function better. Blockchain deals with security and AI deals with active and intelligent actions. This will help the IoT function better, and this is where I see them overlapping.

How is blockchain used in the pharmacy industry?

We have approximately seven to ten billion dollars of returned drugs and nobody will accept them because they are not sure if they're real or counterfeit. The question is, how can we prove they're real? There is a German company called SAP, that is working on a solution. SAP has an app that involves taking the information provided by the supply chain and sharing it using blockchain. The name of this app is advanced track and trust for pharma. They have a very nice dashboard that tracks all the information, even geographic location, based on the GPS of the product.

How is blockchain used on a state level?

Blockchain is already used in refugee camps in the country of Jordan. Children born there have no official ID, so their eyes, facial description, and fingerprints are scanned and used as their ID. Based on this form of identification, people are able to receive their food and the troublesome problem of faking IDs is eliminated.

How can we approach blockchain scalability?

There are many approaches to blockchain scalability. One of them is charting; this means you don't save the whole data set, just pieces. The other approach is proof of X, which is proof of the assignment. This means you will assign five hundred nodes out of ten thousand nodes to store the whole record, making the whole process move faster.

Do you think the EU GDPR (General Data Protection Regulation) poses a threat to upcoming companies that want to use blockchain in a more extensive way?

I wish we had an equivalent version of GDPR here in the U.S. because we are in really bad shape relating to something which I call SSP (safety, security, and privacy). Last week we heard Facebook announce that six hundred million passwords were saved in plain text. I will take fifteen percent off a grade if I see a single unencrypted password in a student's project. Many companies will tell you there's no chance of you getting a job with them when you do something like that.

In the EU GDPR there is something called "the right to be forgotten". How can something be erased that is widely distributed on a blockchain?

This is the reason you don't see Facebook, Google, or Twitter jumping rapidly into blockchain. Why? Because they know this can become a huge problem. Those companies have tremendous amounts of data, so it's a challenge. Blockchain is entering the growth phase, so there are many things besides this that must be dealt with before it reaches the point where everybody understands it and applications will become more common. We must make it clear that blockchain is in its deployment phase right now.

Can blockchains pose a threat to banks?

Banks are threatened because money can be sent directly, without centralization. The biggest organization that has patents of blockchain is Bank of America in the U.S. and the Chinese Republic Bank, looking internationally. They know they are going to be left behind if nothing happens. Venmo is the closest thing in that sector enabling peer-to-peer transactions.

In your book "Secure and Smart IoT", you suggest blockchain as a solution, can you elaborate more on that?

Blockchain offers new hope for IoT security for three reasons. First, blockchain is public. Everyone participating in the network can see the blocks and the transactions stored. Users can still have private keys to control transactions. Second, blockchain is decentralized, with no single authority that can approve the transactions, eliminating the Single Point of Failure (SPOF) weakness. Third, and most important, it's secure; the database can only be extended, and previous records cannot be changed.

Mega Growth, Mega Markets

Interview 3

The Power of Networking

Shubham Goel

Founder and CEO of Affinity

Written by Christoph Stoll and Holger Hackstein

"Make sure your customers absolutely love your products and your services. They should be raving about it to their friends over dinner and on social media platforms. Then you've got a true word-of-mouth engine started."

— Shubham Goel

At just 23, Shubham Goel is a rising star in the Silicon Valley tech scene. Shubham graduated from Stanford with a degree in computer science and engineering. While at Stanford, he became a partner in the Dorm Room Fund, the Bay Area VC that made investments in student-run start-ups. He then co-founded Affinity, a leading relationship intelligence platform. As an expert in artificial intelligence, Shubham believes in the power of computers and technology to help bring people together and forge deeper, more meaningful personal and professional relationships.

I n this interview, Shubham relates the difficulties he had to overcome when coming to Silicon Valley and how his international experiences, beginning in his hometown of Delhi, India, helped him along the way. He recalls the inspiring culture he encountered in Silicon Valley and how it encouraged him to pursue a career as an entrepreneur. He explains what Affinity is and the way it redefines inter-enterprise relationship management. Impressively, Shubham started a multimillion-dollar business while still a college student. We asked him to let us in on the secret to his early success; so, he explains to us how to generate ideas, turn those ideas into reality, how to scale them, and what key elements a new entrepreneur should be aware (and sometimes wary) of.

Shubham, tell us a little about your background, starting with where you grew up.

I was born in Surat, a city in the state of Gujarat, India. It is the fastest-growing city in the world in terms of GDP with an annual growth rate of ten percent primarily because ninety percent of the world's diamonds are polished there. Growing up, I lived in various Indian cities, including Nashik and Sesa. Sesa is a small city of approximately three hundred thousand people, a small population by Indian standards. My mother is from Sesa, and during my time spent there I learned what rural India is truly like. We eventually moved to Delhi, the capital city of India where I spent most of my time until I was nineteen years old. They were the most important and formative years for me in terms of how much I learned.

While in Delhi, I attended a large high school that had a thousand students in my senior class. One of the most important lessons I learned in school was that every person is different and everyone has their own interests, activities, and relationships. Many of my friends played the piano, some liked football, while I liked mathematics and programming. I realized that I wanted to focus on a specific area of mathematics, and I choose number theory. It was after completing a research project on a very specific area of number theory that I realized what research truly meant and how much patience is required in order to complete a project. I believe these were the most formative and motivational aspects of my high school experience.

How did you discover Silicon Valley and how did you manage to get here?

I spent a lot of time working on the computer. I wanted to know what people were doing with their computer science knowledge, and that led me to discover Silicon Valley. Based on my interest in mathematics and computer science, I was interested in attending the computer science program at Stanford. My parents were very supportive of my decision and helped me in every way possible. Fortunately, Stanford accepted me.

What kind of experience did you have a Stanford? What did you learn?

If I had to point to three things that I learned that had the greatest impact on me during my time at Stanford, they would be meeting interesting people, being open to new ideas, and getting out of my comfort zone, which was crucial to shaping my development at Stanford.

I was part of two student organizations. One was Stanford ACM, a group of interesting and like-minded people who wanted to build things, hack computers for fun, and become great engineers. The other was a community of entrepreneurial students who focused on organizing events geared towards starting a business. Joining these two communities gave me a chance to not only meet people who were fun to work with, but whose interesting mindsets helped make me more open to new ideas. The philosophy there was that if you worked hard on common commodities and became the best you could at it, you would eventually become successful. Innovation is not a core competency in Indian education, so being open to new ideas was a big change for me.

How did you get into the startup scene?

At the student group I met someone who I really enjoyed working with. We decided to live together the upcoming year so that we could work on projects together. We had so many interesting ideas and we just needed to figure out a way to apply those ideas.

In the Bay Area, there are summer incubators where you essentially sign up for a twelve-week program. They offer you an office space and some financial compensation. The Silicon Valley plan is pretty simple. If your ideas work and others like them and think they may eventually become profitable, you know you're doing well and are on the right path.

What was the incubator experience like for you?

We had the opportunity to work with an incubator and had a typical twelve-week-long "garage" experience. The original idea was to help high school students get into college. Four weeks into the program we realized we were not excited about it anymore. Not being excited about your original idea is okay, but it was still a hard pill to swallow, especially since we had been working on it for so long. We spent the next two weeks asking ourselves what we were going to do now and trying to figure out what other ideas we could come up with.

After six weeks we were at a point where we couldn't set up a company because we couldn't think of any interesting problems to solve. That was when we decided to spend the next six weeks learning more about what people do for a living and how we could improve their situations. The ability to switch ideas a third of the way into productivity, and all of our hard work, made me realize the value of the incubator program; it gave us the opportunity to do something completely new.

You threw away your original idea and started searching for a new one?

Yes! We went to one of the employees in the incubator and told her we didn't think we could start a company and explained our reasoning. We told her that in order to solve a problem we first needed to find a problem. Since we didn't know much about how the world worked, we figured a good place to start would be to learn about what people do for a living and how they feel about their work. We asked the incubator employee if she could introduce us to her friends that worked in various industries and talk to them about their roles. I was pleasantly surprised when she said: "Oh. Yes, that's fine. Don't worry. No company formation is easy. I'll introduce you to my friends."

We talked to people from various industries such as the financial world, selected VCs, private equity fund owners, real estate agents, investment trust owners, sales directors, start-up founders, business developers, engineers, and engineering managers. We wanted to make sure to ask them questions that would produce answers we could use, such as: "What do you do for a living? What skills and knowledge does it take to do your job? Help me understand what your role entails." We found that people love to talk about themselves and their jobs. These conversations often lasted a lot longer than the designated twenty minutes and people really opened up to us about their lives.

After many of these conversations we discovered the similarities in what people did and the fact that the majority of executive time is spent managing external relationships. Employees in an organization interact with others outside the company to build relationships and discover how to sell something. We found that managing these relationships was a big issue in all sectors. Thanks to incubator employee and her connections, we were able to identify new pain points and problems.

How did Affinity develop out of this "big issue?"

We believed that we could solve the challenge of managing relationships through a computer program, and that's how it all started. Within the first three months, we saw a real potential in this idea and took the giant leap of faith in starting a new company. My co-founder left Stanford and I quit my full-time job. It's kind of like a Hollywood movie where two entrepreneurs set out to see what's going on in the world and end up building a team to validate their ideas. That's exactly what my co-founder and I did. We tried to convince all our friends to join us in this crazy idea that we thought just might work, and we succeeded.

What did you learn from getting Affinity off the ground?

One take-away from our experience is that your network is much more powerful than most of us realize. Your network is probably the best source of information for your team and it inspires confidence because it shows how well you work or have worked with others on projects.

Another take-away is the need to have a few high-quality people instead of many mediocre teammates. It's important to set the team dynamics right. How well do you work together? How do you resolve problems together? It is imperative to get the smartest people to join you early on because they're harder to find later on in the collaborative process.

Last, I learned that the way colleagues interact with each other is extremely important to the success of your team. It is important that people understand each other and enjoy working together. We hadn't considered these factors early on, but we managed to hire the right people and it worked out. If I started another company, I would be far more thoughtful about this when hiring people.

What should someone focus on when they are initially getting their first few customers?

Make sure your customers absolutely love your product and your service. They should be raving about it to their friends over dinner and on social media platforms. When that happens, you get a true word-of-mouth engine started, which makes your business grow quickly. We put dedicated efforts in a stellar customer experience. People like buying things that their friends can't stop talking about. We really wanted to make it happen, so we also gave the stakeholders some equity and we gave people some advisory shares. We acquired our first five customers from our network and our investors' network. How does your product work and what do the customers love about your product?

In sales, business development, financial services, and recruiting, every dollar and material value that is exchanged typically comes down to your network. For most organizations, it is vital for them to understand and learn how to utilize their relationships. Companies spend forty billion dollars a year for systems that claim to help them use their connections. Unfortunately, these systems are inefficient and difficult to use due to the need to enter all data manually. They are also generally bad at mining hidden value in an organization's network. This is where Affinity comes in.

Our software sits on top of the communication data within an organization and analyzes and structures communication information for individuals. This allows you to share this information selectively with your co-workers and others in your network. We specialize in mining hidden value in an organization's network. For example, if you want to contact Uber, Affinity makes it easy to pinpoint which person in your organization has the best connection to someone at Uber who can set up an introductory meeting. These things are a great help.

Affinity is a relationship intelligence platform, and there are three main factors our customers love about us and that makes us successful. First, we are the most automated relationship management system on the market. This means we save our business customers and their teams enormous amounts of time when they're trying to manage a pipeline of some sort. Gone are the days of manual data entry. We can allow our customers to focus on doing their actual job. Second, we help clients mine their network to discover hidden opportunities within it that they didn't even know were there. This allows them to leverage their real-time relationship graph to achieve a successful business outcome. Third, we help customers prevent dropping the ball on important relationships by highlighting data-points, such as missed emails from important prospects, communications going cold, and the like.

We currently have six hundred global companies using our product. Many of our clients are financial services firms and twenty-three percent of VC firms in the U.S. are our customers.

What kind of information does Affinity need? Do you also analyze phone calls?

Yes. If you use our app when conducting a phone call, we will analyze the call and it will be added to the system records. We are currently working on providing transcription services as well.

In order for our product to work efficiently, users need to give us permission to access their e-mail and calendar data. Once we have access to the data, customers can communicate using Affinity.

Getting access to this kind of data seems like a lot to ask of a company. How do you ensure security and privacy?

You're right, it is a lot to ask. When we first started the company, no one would give us access to the data we needed. We worked hard to ensure we had the right security and privacy protocols in place. It took us over a year to get to a place where we were truly trusted by our clients. We are one of the first companies in our area to be General Data Protection Regulation (GDPR) compliant.

Data security is crucial both to us and to our customers. We have compiled an extensive list of measures we have taken, and continue to take, to ensure data security. This list is accessible to the public via our website. It consists of a ten-page list of the numerous precautions we're taking. This includes everything from encrypting and anonymizing developer databases to having internal controls over who can see what information.

Now we serve some of the largest institutional banks, work with FCC regulated customers, and serve VCs in the U.S., the UK, Germany, and France. It's taken us a while, but it's a great feeling to look back on how it all began and see how far we've come.

How do data privacy regulations affect your business?

We deal with sensitive communications data that, in many ways, forms the intellectual property of our customers. I think it's great that regulations like GDPR exist to protect consumer interests. The whole world is moving towards a model similar to the one that the EU adopted. As a vendor, you must put in a lot more work to stay compliant with the different regulations. We think this is time well spent, as it helps protect our customers from any privacy breaches or violations.

How did you develop your product and customer relationships?

It took us a while to figure out what kinds of products people were willing to buy. You can easily develop a product that works spectacularly for three or four customers, but not for a prospective new customer. That is when you realize that tweaking a few parameters can adapt your product so that it satisfies more and more customers.

Another thing that's important is to get feedback early and often. This helps you see if your product is something that would be desired by customers, and if not, how it could be altered so that it does. We initially went out and showed it to fifty potential customers and got their feedback. This helped in the next series of designs we made.

What is the future of CRM?

Great question! We're living in an amazing time. Data processing and Natural Language Processing efforts are at their peak. I believe we're just scratching the surface on how the CRM space will evolve. There are several key areas I think will be impacted.

First, there will be a drastic reduction in data entry from teams. This includes everything from automatically logging calls, creating contacts and notes from call transcriptions, and status updates on deals. Considering all the activity that the reps are doing now when interacting with a CRM platform, I don't imagine they will be doing much of it at all.

Second, CRMs will help employees prioritize their deals. It is easy for reps to get overwhelmed when deciding which deal they should be focusing on. With the amount of information available today, CRMs should be able to go from being systems of record to actual prescriptive platforms where they help the sales rep throughout their days, reminding them which deals to reach out to and where there might be a potential for improvement. Last, CRMs should make it easier to get new accounts. There is still much to be done by most, if not all, CRM companies, but the CRM will be a game-changer in the long-term.

How are you ensuring your company is prepared for the future?

Before e-mails became a reality, we were using many different methods of communication. Based on some of our internal research, approximately ninety percent of our clients communicate via email and calendar. There is always a possibility that in the future there will be a new disruptive communication platform and e-mail will become insufficient. Already there are a lot of new forms of communication popping up like Slack, but they are mostly internal, which is not our focus. As a company, we are focused on communication that occurs between employees and other third parties outside of their organization. We believe that in that domain e-mails will remain dominant. However, if that changes, we will adapt our product and make the necessary changes in order to evolve and grow.

Imagine a world where you can tangibly use your network to help get your job done on a daily basis. Thinking about that world keeps me excited every day and that's why we're building Affinity.

Mega Growth, Mega Markets

Interview 4

Disruption in e-Mobility

Vish Palekar

President and CEO of Mahindra GenZe

Written by Siegfried Balleis, Joerg Robert, Christian Grenz and Michael Fischer

"Freedom and convenience brought us an exponential growth of cars on the street. To solve congestion and parking hassles, cities need to re-imagine their mobility paradigm from cars-oriented to people-focused."

— Vish Palekar

Dr. Vish Palekar is a seasoned executive, an entrepreneur, and a strategist with a career spanning over twenty-six years. Vish has held leadership positions in companies like Cummins, GE, Mahindra and Mahindra, and Bloom Energy. He is passionate about electric mobility, clean energy, and automation. Vish is one of the pioneers in 'New-Mobility' and a strong proponent of democratizing electric mobility. He has championed connected electric two-wheeler mobility, particularly with an emphasis on e-bikes and electric mopeds as a method of personal transportation for short distances. He believes that electrified, shared, and connected multi-modality will become the future of transportation, as people seek flexible clean options, particularly in urban areas.

California is at the forefront of driving regulations and customer behavior aimed toward a zero-carbon future. In addition, as the fifth largest economy in the world, California has its share of challenges, including traffic congestion. In this chapter, Vish Palekar provides his thoughts on the global and local trends of shared and electric mobility. Vish discusses the disruptive forces facing the mobility ecosystem and the various approaches available to alleviate the challenges through multi-modal shared and electric transportation alternatives.

What is the new-mobility paradigm?

As part of the industrial revolution, we created this incredible form of mobility called the automobile, along with an unparalleled network of roads and highways. To a great extent, we are victims of our own success. Given the freedom and convenience they offered, cars became the predominant mode of transportation in most western countries. Therefore, we continued to design most of our cities around the automobile. The result of this exponential growth led to increased traffic and parking hassles around urban centers like San Francisco, often with cars holding one driver and three empty seats. As one billboard put it "You're not stuck in traffic, you are the traffic".

The solution to this surge in the number of vehicles lies in reframing the problem. Most people, particularly millennials, are simply interested in moving from point A to point B, and fifty percent of trips in San Francisco and most urban centers around the world are less than five miles long. In addition, the environmental damage brought about by climate change would suggest that all vehicular trips be efficient and with the fewest emissions possible. To address these needs and the corresponding challenges, cities like San Francisco have re-imagined a mobility paradigm that focuses on people, not on cars. They have created a conducive environment and policy aimed at facilitating shared and electric multi-modality, both for two-wheelers and for cars. This has alleviated some of the traffic challenges. Several "smart" cities in the U.S. and Europe have also adopted a similar approach rather than a solely car-oriented solution that focuses on adding more lanes to keep the cars moving. This change in problem definition has changed the issue at its core, enabling novel and disruptive solutions for traffic and environmental challenges.

Besides the change in the core purpose of transportation to move people, I believe technological innovation will play a crucial role over the next decade, thanks to advances in Internet of Things (IoT), embedded controls and AI amongst others. These disruptions are captured in the acronym CASE (Connected mobility, Autonomous transportation, Shared services, and Electrified). The advances in these technologies are likely to be the main driving forces in the personal transportation industry, and the influence they have is dependent on the specific type of transportation mode in question. Based on one analysis, each automotive company today may have to spend close to fifty billion dollars over the next decade in order to be competitive in all these disruptive changes. The scope of these advances and the uncertain outcome and effect on consumer/driver behavior presents significant challenges to many of the key players in the industry.

Why is Silicon Valley the perfect incubator for the new mobility?

I have lived in many parts of the world, but to me, Silicon Valley is one of the most exciting incubators of innovation and scale because of the ecosystem that has been developed. In most parts of the world, people focus on the business plan, but Silicon Valley focuses first on the business model. Focusing on the business model involves an understanding of customers, monetizability, operations, and economies of scale. The nature of startups and venture capital is such as many innovations will fail, but in Silicon Valley, this failure is celebrated and learned from. One of the outcomes of this mobility is what is referred to as the "unbundling of transportation". Many smaller form factors are being electrified before converting to an autonomous capability while the reverse is likely true for larger trucks and vehicles driven over longer distances. This business model innovation is a Silicon Valley creation and serves as an incubator for global ideation. The other differentiator is speed of execution. Silicon Valley drives product-market fit and iterative business model thinking faster than anywhere else making it the perfect incubator for the world.

Where is connected mobility going in the next five to ten years?

The key is IoT, in other words, machine-to-machine communication. Everything's going to communicate with everything else. The key advances include improvements, not just in the hardware, but also in the software. In addition, companies are wrestling over how to design an ecosystem of connected elements that delivers beneficial and monetizable information to customers. Connectivity is likely to be pervasive; cars are becoming connected to our phones not just for infotainment but an all-encompassing experience including unique location-based services, smarter diagnostic and maintenance, and reduced insurance costs. A vehicle to everything (V-to-X) architecture is driving connectivity to external elements such as streetlights, traffic signals, and other cars enabling safer and automated driving features, GPS and map-based driving optimization, and on-road services. This connectivity is also opening a path to personalized playlists and other services and products that can enhance our way of life.

An important element in the design is consideration for processing a significant amount of data. These considerations include edge and cloud-based architectures to reduce latency and power needs, faster processing speed, and complex AI based computations. 5G is going to be a key enabler. On the software side, there is a critical need to identify and separate safety-critical software from non-critical software. While non-critical software applications may not be incredibly robust, safety-critical software must work without compromise and be secure from hacking. OEMs are designing these features in all their new vehicles to enable a connected mobility ecosystem and deliver vastly improved services and safety transforming our driving experience.

What are the challenges of connected mobility?

Some of the challenges include uniform connectivity protocols, safety, security, and data privacy that IoT is going through a lot of innovation itself; data from each connected application is growing exponentially and the processing information is required to be sent faster and cheaper. The advent of 5G is going to be a key enabler for these applications. The potential for hackers to access the network and disrupt the vehicle or services, steal personal information and impede the safety of the driver or the vehicle, is one of the key challenges of a connected ecosystem.

What are your views on third-party smart car software developers vs. in-house smart car software development?

A lot of different technologies go into engineering and manufacturing these vehicles. The biggest concern is who controls the car platform. Do the car makers allow third-party platform providers like Apple or Google to control the experience with the likes of CarPlay or Android Auto respectively, or do they try to develop the software themselves? If the carmakers decide to develop the platform, they must recruit, train, and develop the resources themselves. Traditionally, most manufacturers did not have the type of engineers required for such complex tasks and tech architectures in-house. These activities were often the core competence of third-party providers such as Silicon Valley tech companies.

However, given the long-term strategic importance of this platform, OEMs have rapidly built teams to define the secure platform and the interfaces themselves aligned to their brand and customer propositions. In some cases, these third-party providers have been used by OEMs but invariably this has tended to not be a long-term strategy and resulted in a pivot to OEMs controlling their own platforms.

Another reason for this dynamic is that the software platform must provide a differentiated utility. Lots of people can create software that adds layers to a car that can handle asset management, has a user interface, and can stream music. The challenge arises when companies try to use this technology to make the car more reliable and easier to service. These utilities need the platform to access the critical components of the car and this can only be achieved and enabled safely by the OEM over a long period of time. Hence although third parties have an important role in driving the technologies, most OEMs tend to control the platforms through in-house development and teams.

What does Silicon Valley offer to the car manufacturers?

While the software building process and resources are being figured out by car manufacturers, they might rely on external third-party suppliers. These companies are often in Silicon Valley or also referred to these days as "Software Valley", considering how much the area's focus has shifted from hardware to software. When it comes to cars, as mentioned earlier, there's virtually no room for error in the software, making this a difficult development.

What other aspects are important to smart cars?

Safety, security, and convenience are critical factors in design and implementation. The availability of Bluetooth connectivity and IoT provides a broader spectrum of utility, not only for the driver but for the passengers as well. Along these lines, Apple recently announced a TV platform which will be accessible to both driver and passengers.

Another area of improvement is automation, which is helping improve safety measures in vehicles. In some cases, the vehicle can adjust its course if it recognizes the danger of an accident ahead. All these advancements not only help customers feel safer but lower the cost of their insurance as well. The availability of sensors with higher accuracy and fidelity that offer constant 360-degree awareness will keep improving the levels of automation. For example, using AI in the next generation of software, cars may soon be able to recognize traffic lights that are currently out of commission and adapt to that situation.

Where does the future lie for micro-mobility in providing the last-mile solution?

In addition to independent providers, every car company is getting into micro-mobility and trying to figure out what is an optimal short distance or the last-mile solution. There are several new form factors that are playing a role in this complementary modality for personal and shared use. These predominantly include the use of electric bikes, kick-scooters, mopeds, or rickshaws. Almost half the trips in most urban centers are less than five miles and these micro-mobility form factors play an important role in these short-distance trips. In addition, the ability to run shared services with these two- or three-wheelers is more cost-effective and hence growing around the world. Another important use case for micro-mobility is likely to be the delivery space. In the U.S., we call this the gig economy. Increasingly people want their food, beer, or groceries on-demand. These services can be effectively delivered over the normally short distances using these vehicles. Given the improvement in safety, utility, and cost-effectiveness of this clean form of mobility, it is likely going to be a growing trend in most urban cities around the world.

What are your thoughts about the electrification of vehicles?

I do not think there is any doubt that electrification will be the driver of the future. I think it is a question of how quickly this will happen and at what cost. As the cost of batteries decreases, things will move rapidly in that direction.

Inherently, the efficiency of electrical motors is greater than the efficiency of any other type of engine. The question is how to get to the same scale and cost-effectiveness as that of the combustion engine. The combustion engine became the predominant driver of our vehicles over the years and the ability to reproduce it cost-effectively helped drive its scale. As the number of electric vehicles grows, the same will undoubtedly happen to the motor and other components of the electric vehicle helping it replace its polluting internal combustion engine.

Electric motors have a better feel, and almost everyone that has driven an electric car loves it. It is faster, more powerful, has fewer moving parts, and has lower service needs.

Tesla has been an early innovator and helped accelerate the proliferation of electric vehicles. In addition, several companies, including BMW, Volkswagen, and Mercedes amongst others, are beginning to introduce similar new cars and driving consumer interest.

Another driver of electrification is the availability and access of charging including fast charging. This includes home and workplace charging as well as charging at shopping malls and highways similar to the network of gas stations that are pervasive all around the world. Governments and private enterprises are finding ways to grow the availability of these chargers and making them accessible for consumers at home to remove any friction from the purchase of electric vehicles.

What is the primary reason for the proliferation of electric mobility? How long will it take to roll out electric vehicles on a large scale?

We are doing this, obviously, to reduce harmful emissions and our dependence on fossil fuels. We're just starting and have just reached the two percent market share level. Everybody is starting to predict that we will rapidly go electric within the next five to ten years. This will accelerate in the U.S., where there are over seventeen million cars sold every year, and within the next three to five years every company will offer a variety of electric vehicle models to replace the internal combustion engine.

What are the market driver of electric mobility?

There are three: government policies, availability of chargers, and battery costs. Governments all over the world are working toward adopting electric vehicles through investing in the development of EVs, offering tax benefits to incentivize electric vehicles, and deploying regulations in order to slowly phase out fuel-based vehicles. The deployment and availability of chargers at home, workplace, shopping areas, and on highways is also being accelerated and helping drive the acceptance of electric vehicles. Simultaneously, batteries have played a major part in the roll-out of electric vehicles. Costs for lithium-ion (Li-ion) have decreased by seventy percent in the last seven years and is projected to decline even more over the next few years. The decline in costs for batteries allows manufacturers to produce more EVs at reasonable prices. The positive impact of progress made in all these three drivers is rapidly lifting the acceptance and adoption of electric mobility.

How available are the resources needed to build batteries?

Battery storage is a critical resource for the growth and scalability of electric vehicles. One of the preferred types is the Lithium-ion battery. These batteries come in various form factors but are predominantly in the form of cylindrical, pouch, or prismatic cells. They also include various chemistries that serve to maximize the energy and/or the power efficiency on a per liter and/or per weight basis depending on the design of the vehicle. A critical element of these batteries is a small amount of cobalt which is a necessary ingredient that allows for better energy efficiency. Many experts believe that the fuel of the future will be cobalt. It is quite scarce, and about eighty percent of the world's cobalt is controlled by China. Its availability or other replacements that are both cost-effective and energy-efficient will likely be the drivers for the batteries of the future.

What will the differentiating factors be between the trends of the future?

Great question! I think this will be dependent on how all the earlier-mentioned factors will come together. On one level, the question will be how to connect these vehicles. Who is going to be in control? The other factor is the question of perceived value and speed of disruption. If cars become autonomous, vehicles will become commodities, and ownership models will likely become less attractive. Perhaps new business models such as fleets and sharing will become pervasive.

As a general trend, people want the ability to move hassle-free from point A to point B. Vehicle ownership is no longer the favored option, and people are much more willing to use shared services.

This leads us into shared mobility. This is a fast-growing area of interest, especially in the U. S. The two industry leaders, Uber and Lyft, both of which started their businesses only a few years ago, have grown rapidly. An interesting niche segment of this market are the micro-mobility solutions, particularly electric bikes and kick scooters.

Why is carsharing, carpooling, and micro-mobility gaining momentum so rapidly? It's because people want options; they want multi-modality; they enjoy flexibility and freedom. Another influencing factor is the cost of ownership. This cost is increasing, especially in urban areas, thereby creating many opportunities for ride-sharing services, connectivity, and electrification.

What will derive the growth and development of charging infrastructure?

It's important to understand the three different levels of charging. Level 1 charger is generally installed at home and derives its power from the standard household outlet. You use a cord that plugs into your standard three-prong outlet and it takes approximately eight to twelve hours to fully charge the vehicle. Level 2 is mostly seen in public parking areas, residential and commercial settings and are often small fixed-in-place charging stations. It takes approximately four to six hours to charge. Level 1 and Level 2 are AC chargers, compatible with all-electric vehicles and use the vehicle control system to regulate the charge. Level 3 AC or DC chargers are greater than 22 KV and can provide an eighty percent charge in about thirty to forty-five minutes. These are found only in public or commercial settings and often drive the charging rate based on the vehicle design. As a general rule, the number of charging stations needs to grow so that we can have enough chargers available every two miles just like the gas station infrastructure of today.

The providers of charging services need to be paid adequately for the availability and operation of this critical driver for EV growth. Different business models are driving the deployment and adoption of charging stations. These include government funding or subsidy, traditional retail pricing for charging, or nontraditional models such as monetization of branding and Wi-fi services. OEMs are also getting involved in charging as an enabler and generating additional value for their customers driving incremental vehicle sales and service revenue.

Do you think Tesla played a role in jump-starting the EV industry?

Silicon Valley in general and Tesla in particular are laser-focused on making cost-effective electric vehicles. Tesla has been so instrumental in making this happen that we should be celebrating what they have done. The battery cost is getting down to below a hundred dollars per kilowatt hour primarily driven by Tesla and some battery suppliers. Looked at from an innovation standpoint, Tesla has been able to innovate and scale up innovation. Strategy and execution are critical in driving such large-scale innovation and Tesla's pioneering role in jump-starting the EV industry is indisputable.

How do you visualize the future for traditional automobile manufacturers?

Traditional auto manufacturers are resourcing and adding the capability for all of the CASE disruptions being faced. Tesla has led the innovation in the U.S. and the traditional OEMs have tried to play catch up, losing the early share in U.S. geographies such as California. Similarly, the German car manufacturers who have been amongst the best in the world for over thirty years are banding together to accelerate their progress. I am energized by their efforts here in the U.S. and globally. When you combine good engineering with a recognition of business models and innovation models, you are bound to come out a winner. Traditional car manufactures must embrace change and focus on their core business while at the same time build the capacity for new form factors and vehicles.

How do you foresee the future of hydrogen propulsion? Will it take over EVs?

Hydrogen propulsion and fuel cells continue to be promising technologies for the future but face infrastructure headwinds for deployment in mobility. Hence, they are not commercial, except in niche markets, where the infrastructure can be made available. In the short term, this is unlikely to replace the EV momentum, as battery prices are dropping below a hundred dollars per kWh, and the scalability of the EV solution is easier than any other renewable propulsion technology. However, hydrogen could find its way as an immediate solution for heavy-duty applications given its ability to be stored and the need for longer ranges while driving.

Is the car going to be our smartphone of the future?

The mobile phone must be integrated into the car experience. People have gotten used to living with their phones, and most consumers do not want two devices. Our research shows that people prefer to have just one device to aid in running their lives for them whether in the car or outside.

The car has to work seamlessly with the smartphone. At a minimum, this includes the infotainment experience, connectivity, and voice-activated commands that are likely to converge between the vehicle and the smartphone. Vehicle identification and adjustment of controls will mimic the changes that are happening in a smart home and will give the user a personalized and seamless experience.

Do you see a possibility for today's car industry to become the extended workbench of the software industry now dominated by Alphabet, Amazon, IBM, and Microsoft?

Just as it happens with any tectonic shift, established incumbent companies often have a hard time innovating. The present market leaders have expectations to meet with their present products and business models and customers to satisfy. They must show strong financials to keep both shareholders and stakeholders happy. A fifty-billion-dollar investment over a decade is a hard pill to swallow, and it is even harder to convey the reasons behind it in a satisfying manner to stakeholders interested in short term financial results. Therefore, innovation usually occurs externally. We will see new companies enter the market. The incumbents will try to form joint ventures to minimize their investments or begin to look to startups for solutions. They will need others to make the first moves and take the initial risks because for them the focus is likely to be near-term revenue targets and profit margins.

Most executives in this field are in their late forties or early fifties. They have spent decades in an industry that emphasized the production of efficient cars with combustion engines. For these leaders, it will be very difficult to adjust to the new trends and to gradually change their mindset.

The car industry must redefine itself and must do it quickly. In this process, it needs to define its core competencies and have a strategic point of view for the future. While there are significant moats built by the OEMs, with such rapid technology disruption, competition is emerging from other unconventional companies such as Alphabet, Amazon, IBM, Microsoft, and Apple as they try to capture and control the software and data platform working with the OEMs.

What impact does this have on the labor market and on the social environment?

The emergence of connected, autonomous, and electric technology has led to fundamental shifts in the supply chain, manufacturing, and the service competencies needed in this new digital era. Designing and manufacturing electric vehicles will require a completely different skillset in the labor force from those of their combustion counterparts. The use of shared and autonomous vehicles can cause displacement of the driver pool that is available today. One can obviously retrain people to a certain extent, but these changes have the potential for creating more serious social issues. What will happen to the millions of people around the world who now derive their daily income from transporting other people? These are serious challenges. The changes in management, including retraining to adapt to the new digital environment, are critical issues for both governments and communities.

How can we avoid the social disruption that appears unavoidable due to this digital revolution?

The disruption of mobility through CASE will have a significant social impact on people around the world. This is likely due to large shifts in modes of drivability through autonomous vehicles, reduced number through sharing of vehicles and dedicated fleets and different manufacturing skills needs from factory transition to electric and connected vehicles. Governments will have a major role in addressing the impact of this social change by designing educational campaigns and retraining programs for students and employees who will likely face a displacement or loss of their jobs because of digitalization. In a perfect world, we would all individually recognize that big changes are on the horizon and begin retraining ourselves, but this will likely not happen and will need some proactive help from governments and corporates.

I am worried about developing countries with large underserved populations like India or Brazil, with its vast pool of people who perform the less-appreciated and lower-paid work. They will be radically affected by the coming digital era. In the U.S. that workforce represents maybe a couple of million people per year, whereas in India it is fifty to one hundred million workers every year. Unfortunately, there are no easy answers. Change is the only thing that's unavoidable in this world and we must learn how to adjust to these changes in a socially beneficial manner.

This is a complex issue that has a large geopolitical impact, which requires policy implications for most countries. Retraining programs are part of the solution and clean energy itself be a job-creator. These issues need to be fully addressed and expanded upon. Manufacturing of sustainable products has a multiplier effect and governments are likely to focus heavily on creating manufacturing jobs locally, resulting in changes around the concept of globalization. Localized job creation in emerging low-paying economies will become an important factor. Countries must also build a larger service economy and harness the innovation and skills of its people with new products and services to offset the pressure from the manufacturing economy.

What is the future for other areas of transportation, such as ships and airplanes?

The transition of different forms of mobility to cleaner fuels or electric mobility will depend on several factors: the size of the motive power and the constraints around it, such as the cost of batteries, packaging constraints, and range and safety considerations. In addition, external factors such as charging ecosystems, maintenance, and service considerations will influence the rate of change. It is likely that smaller vehicles, like two- or three-wheelers, will transition faster than four-wheelers. Following four-wheelers will be the larger vehicles such as heavy-duty trucks and buses including fleets. Vessels and airplanes that are likely to be in use for long periods of time may be the slowest to change to all-electric but are already transitioning to hybrid configurations.

Why does California set such ambitious goals toward renewable energy while the rest of the world lags behind?

The 2045 goal is ambitious and difficult in many ways, but California has huge advantages. For one thing, it's the fifth largest economy in the world and presents both a marketplace and a supportive policy environment. This allows OEMs to manufacture electric cars, electric buses, and electric trucks for the large California market. In addition, the energy sector is being redefined, led by California entrepreneurs in the clean-tech sectors. California has set ambitious goals for both 2030 and 2040. It is leading the push toward a zero-carbon future. To achieve its goals, California has led in the creation of an innovative business environment, with incentives such as carpool facilities for electric/hybrid vehicles, tax incentives, and cap-and-trade incentives. It has also reduced the subsidies for fossil fuels and advocated strongly for a coalition of like-minded economies and countries. Many countries have acknowledged this and are now beginning to follow California's lead and roadmap towards a zero-carbon future.

Creating a Sustainable World through Innovation

Danny Kennedy

Sungevity Co-Founder and Former Greenpeace Activist

Written by Christoph Heynen, Fabian Sperling and Michael Fischer

"Activists and entrepreneurs are not as different as you may think."

— Danny Kennedy

Danny Kennedy is the managing director of the California Clean Energy Fund (CalCEF), one of the well-known funds focused on clean energy. He is also the CEO of New Energy Nexus, a network of incubators, accelerators, and funds around the world, concentrating on clean energy start-ups. Danny co-founded Sungevity, a global leader in the residential solar industry, and is the author of "Rooftop Revolution", a best-seller in the field of photovoltaics. As a serial entrepreneur, Danny is highly regarded within the Silicon Valley community and all around the globe. He is a pioneer of the cleantech industry and is creating a better, and more sustainable future by combining his entrepreneurial spirit with past experiences as a Greenpeace activist. Danny holds a Bachelor of Science in Human Geography from Macquarie University, Sydney, Australia. Feel encouraged to follow Danny Kennedy on Twitter – @dannyksfun.

D anny tells us how he, an Australian Greenpeace activist, became a venture capitalist, why hydrogen cars don't stand a chance against vehicles with batteries and why reaching the 100% energy self-sufficiency target in California is a worthwhile nut to crack. He also addresses key technologies for energy generation and storage, such as solar PV, organic hydrogen storage, and li-ion batteries. He explains the vision behind CalCEF and CalSeed and analyzes the relationship between the consumption of oil and war in the Middle East.

How does California stand up in terms of clean energy?

California is the fifth largest economy in the world, right after Germany. Based on GDP we´re bigger than Great Britain, France, and Russia. California has set itself ambitious goals: We have passed a law last year, stating our electricity consumption must rely entirely on zero-emission energy sources for our electricity by the year 2045. To keep up with this ambitious plan we must be thirty-three percent renewable by the end of the next year. We reached thirty-two percent over the past year, so we are on target. The new governor has continued his predecessor`s legacy and passed an executive order, forcing companies to be carbon-neutral by 2045. We are on a very aggressive ramp to find, fund, and foster companies that can contribute to the vision of renewable energy, electric vehicles, platforms, ports, trains, planes, and carbon-neutral agriculture. California has a tremendous agricultural presence. People don't realize we are the breadbasket of America.

What is the "California Clean Energy Fund"?

The "California Clean Energy Fund" (CalCEF) deals with the early-stage companies showing significant growth potential. We provide support to great entrepreneurs, like Marcus Lehmann, the co-founder and CEO of CalWave Power Technologies – a company involved in harnessing the power of ocean waves to produce electricity and freshwater – and help them succeed in any way possible. Our focus is to build an ecosystem with incubators and accelerators, to get entrepreneurs whatever they need to increase their chances of success. CalCEF is intertwined with the Californian Government, as they provide the funds that we invest. Currently, we run a program called CalCharge with the National Labs, the Stanford linear accelerator (SLAC), Lawrence Berkeley, and Lawrence Livermore to advance energy storage in the state. We also run a testbed initiative with the

University of California, to assist start-ups moving through the "valley of death", around verification and measurements of their prototypes. Earlier, we helped start the Cyclotron Road, a fellowship program that supports leading entrepreneurial scientists from around the world. We've invested in forty-six companies over the last eighteen months.

What is the "California Sustainable Energy Entrepreneur Development" Initiative?

The "California Sustainable Energy Entrepreneur Development" (CalSeed) initiative was funded by the California Energy Commission, as an early-stage grant funding program that aims to accelerate California's clean energy goals. CalSeed is a grant program because we didn't want to complicate things with equity. We are basically the state's private sector related R&D commercialization arm. Earlier we used to fund through venture capital funds and deal with warrants or have non-diluted stakes that were converted into equity, but it was too complicated. We wanted to access a larger pool of companies. That's why we decided to run it as a grant program. We provide grants up to six hundred thousand dollars each in the areas of smart energy, software for grid management, appliances for energy-efficient buildings, and storage. We've spent approximately five million dollars a year in start-ups to do that sort of work. There are some occasions where through New Energy Nexus we do an equity play. For example, in Indonesia, we created a fund for start-up businesses, mainly because there is no one else providing that service. We had four million dollars from a philanthropist to start a fund there and attempt to turn it into a twenty-million-dollar fund. In a matter of a few months we turned it into a one hundred-million-dollar fund, it is quite a big deal in the clean energy space. In India, we funded a three-million-dollar facility for micro-grids. There is a lot of potential for solar innovation in India because there's a lot of sun and rooftops, but they lack the funding. Finance companies couldn't get a grip on the off takers, they required other funds to come in first so they could evaluate companies. We came in with three million dollars with net zero percent interest rate to prove out the market. We do a lot of financial innovation to try to help companies progress.

How do you ensure that the grant money is used wisely?

In the beginning we managed this program in a more academic environment, but we have strayed away from that. We run the start-ups through accelerators, like the Cleantech Open, and they don't receive all the money upfront, it's milestone-based payments. We try to keep them lean and keen, not just give them a runway and say, "go have your experiments and see you in two years." We make them work for the money. California has become excellent at incubation and acceleration, mostly to feed the venture capital, but we've also adapted to helping start-ups show results quicker.

What is California's clean energy bill and what are its policy implications?

California's clean energy bill mandates that one hundred percent of retail electricity be procured from renewable sources by 2045. The bill is very fascinating in its ability to put companies on the spot. Fossil fuel companies can say it's impossible and the government responds with "it has to be done, otherwise you're in violation of the law". As a responsible law-abiding corporation, they have to comply with the one hundred percent clean energy law. Unfortunately, with the current technology and available solutions, it is not possible to achieve these goals. Even the California Energy Commission agrees that, today we have the know-how to reach eighty percent of the clean energy goal, ninety percent is a stretch, and one hundred percent is impossible. We need new technologies and novel solutions.

Policy implications are huge. The local counties have already initiated projects to meet the objectives. Alameda County, with a population of 1.6 million residents, introduced a program, called consumer choice aggregator (CCA), that demonopolized the energy industry. Under the program, PG&E will be replaced by one hundred percent clean and locally produced energy by 2030. Likewise, Los Angeles approved a 1.3 gigawatt grid scale clean energy storage project after Aliso Canyon gas leak, where 10,000 people got sick, in what is known as the largest hydrocarbon gas release in American history; much larger than the Deepwater Horizon leak or the Exxon Valdez leak.

California also wants all cars and trucks to go electric by 2035. It all started with Tesla being the disruptive force, but other car companies are fast adapting. Tesla today is the biggest employer of manufacturing workers in the state of California, thirty-five thousand people, and the biggest manufacturer of batteries in America. Volkswagen, the biggest car manufacturer in the world, adopted Tesla's CEO's, Elon Musk's, rhetoric, committing to an all-electric fleet by 2026. Germany is being forced away from diesel because of Tesla.

Clean energy is desirable not just from the perspective of cost savings but also from the perspective of community health, pollution, and climate change. However, to make it a reliable and consistent resource, we need to take a closer look at the long-term seasonal storage technologies. We are experimenting with alternate chemistries such as the lithium-sulfur and Metal-air batteries. These batteries are relatively large, with a small number of cycles, and you can charge and discharge them for weeks and months at a time providing great economic utility. Even software companies are involved in creating better solutions for demand management.

Keep in mind, the whole reason for the energy transition is to get ahead of the climate curve. If we wait another five to ten years to make choices, we´re dead, literally our children are going to be in trouble because we are having debates. At the turn of the century, there was a legitimate conversation. Is it going to be carbon capture? Is going to be nuclear? Is it going to be wind or solar? Is it going to be wet renewables? Is it going to be something else? Some have negative learning curves, and they become more expensive the more you do them e.g. Nuclear, while others have positive learning curves, they become ridiculously cheap, the more you do them. I think we need to stick with those and deploy those methods at scale and get them out there as fast as we can, so our children have a shot.

How does hydrogen, as a source of zero-emission, fit into the picture?

As far as cars are concerned, the market has already spoken. There are 700 hydrogen cars on the road versus 700,000 electric vehicles just in California. Toyota and other companies that pushed for hydrogen are now going the EV route because of consumer preferences. Yet, I think hydrogen will find some applications in aviation, shipping, and a few other industries. Electric cars do not play a major role in displacing barrels of oil from the global economy. We also need to change buses, planes, and trains. I think we'll use hydrogen to do that because, there's a natural, wonderful thing called electrolysis. We need to do more of it, but I don't think automobiles will be a use case. There have been major advancements in the storage and transportation of hydrogen in so-called liquid organic hydrogen carriers and their dispensing at the regular gas stations for use in hydrogen cars. As an investor, however, I immediately see the red flags. I don't believe in refitting the fueling station infrastructure with another liquid fuel. Also, as I've previously mentioned, the individual vehicle market has already picked electric over hydrogen.

With batteries, are we switching one limited resource with another: fossil fuel to lithium?

Fossil fuel and lithium are both rare, limited, and finite but you can recycle lithium. Once you burn fossil fuels, it's in the atmosphere, gone forever. Lithium can be recycled over and over again. California has large reserves of lithium. Below the Salton Sea, which is near the Mexican border, there's an enormous aquifer with an abundance of lithium. We haven't tapped that for industrial purposes yet, but lithium is the linchpin technology for energy transition.

How competitive is renewable energy to conventional energy generation?

Over the past twenty years, the main enabler of the solar and wind industry's growth was government tax credits. The government allowed tax write-offs on investments made in the designated renewable energy products. They even allowed these tax credits to be transferable, thus creating a large financial market for trading tax credits. Tax credit for wind and industrial tax credit for solar have totaled tens of billions of dollars by now. They will eventually go away and these industries will have to compete without them, moving forward.

Solar and wind have become increasingly cheaper than the newer versions of carbon-based energies. We produce electricity in Iowa at 1.3 cents a kilowatt hour. No coal plant can compete with that. This led to more money being invested in wind and solar projects versus oil, coal, and gas projects, since 2012. In the last two years, 16 gigawatts of coal plants have been shut down because economically they can't compete with wind.

Do you see a connection between conventional energy and wars?

If the Middle East were producing broccoli, I doubt we would have much of a history of intervening there. In 2011, General Wesley Clark, commander of NATO, wrote a forward for my new book: "We in America have spent our blood and treasure for one hundred years, along with the lives of our young men, to protect the supply lines of these inefficient machines." In 2019, the budget for military expenses was seven hundred billion dollars, that's two billion dollars a day! Think of what we could do with that budget; address healthcare, the inequity, homelessness, clean energy, all that could be paid for in an instant.

What will it take to limit the impact of climate change? Do you see any progression being made towards this?

You can debate the numbers, but to get European, American, Asian, and African economies clean, we're going to have to spend approximately a trillion dollars a year for the next twenty-five to thirty years. The non-profit organization Ceres initiated the "Clean-Trillion-Campaign" to bring together investors, businesses, and policymakers to mobilize a trillion dollar a year investment in clean energy. A trillion dollars of value creation annually is equivalent to a thousand one billion-dollar annual business. Only one of the start-ups I've been involved with over my career has done one billion dollars a year. Ninety percent of companies that start with a good idea do not profit at all. With everything we do, with all the incubation, training, support, and money for start-ups, we probably double or at best triple the rate of survival. They go from ten percent survival rate to thirty percent survival rate. This is a numbers game; we need more companies trying new ideas in clean mobility and electricity businesses.

Can you give us examples of disruptive technologies that will shape the future of the world?

It is a period of disruption. I think the electric scooters made by GenZe are as disruptive as solar and wind were to electricity over the last decades. Right now, the Chinese are building a freeway from Beijing to the site of the 2020-21 Winter Olympics, which is going to be a solar highway and the pavement will produce power. There are five companies bidding for 20-kilometer segments of the 100-kilometer stretch. The German company that's bidding for 20 kilometers, is doing induction. As you drive over it, it powers the buses. It is not the end of the pursuit, but it is going to be with economies of scale. I think electricity costs will be nullified. It will become a public resource. Just like Wi-Fi which used to be expensive and only available to a few. Now it's on the street for free. Electricity will be like that within a couple of decades because of its aggressive learning curve.

Could you share your experience transitioning from being a Greenpeace activist to an entrepreneur?

When I decided to make this shift in the early 2000s, I was living in San Francisco. We ran a campaign to receive one hundred million dollars of bonds issued by the City of San Francisco for solar and wind on Hetch Hetchy, which is a reservoir. The hundred-million-dollar bond was a citizen referendum in the 2000 election for the city of San Francisco. We, Greenpeace, organized to put out the vote for this. We got seventy-three percent of the community to vote for these bonds. I've been involved in politics since the early 80s and I had never seen anything receive seventy-three percent of the vote. I realized solar is like catnip. It makes people excited and want to do it. After that I was all about it, and I'm still obsessed with solar companies.

Greenpeace was one avenue where we used capitalistic market tools to change society. As an activist, I used to run the Australian offices where we launched ships to the Southern Ocean to get in front of harpoons. Over the span of thirty years the opinion on killing whales went from "this is just what we do" to "it being a bad and a wasteful idea". Watching whales from ships was far better. This shift was thanks to a business argument made by the International Whale and Dolphin Watching Association. Many fishing companies headquartered in Boston, Sydney, Cape Town, and Santiago now use their boats to take people on whale watching tours.

Another time I used market strategies to help people was when I used to run forest campaigns in the Solomon Islands. I chopped down a tree, turned it into ten thousand chopsticks, and sold them for more than the island could get for its entire forest. Business strategies work, so I made the change from an activist to an entrepreneur. I still think of myself as an activist, the tools have changed, the game is still the same. I'm simply utilizing companies as campaigns.

If you had the chance to invest a billion dollars, which sector would you invest in?

I would invest in bus fleet charging stations. In the US, current tax reforms will unleash an abundance of cheap capital for so-called opportunity zones, such as low-income tracts. The city of Oakland currently has thirty of them. Bus depots generally tend to be in poorer neighborhoods making them ideal locations for setting up the EV charging infrastructure while having a positive impact on the environment and the community.

I would also invest in recycling batteries for EVs. There aren't a whole lot of VC's willing to sustain the costs. Now the Indian and Chinese governments are doing this at scale. The company NIO sold eleven thousand vehicles last year to the Chinese middle class. They are amazing. The entire battery stack is hot swappable. You drive into a station, a robot comes in, takes the batteries out, puts in another one and off you go – less than three minutes! Full diagnostics on the batteries. You know what we do in America with EV packs when they don't work? We ship them to Oklahoma, and we try to recycle the metals. We don't reuse the batteries, there's not a second life strategy. It is obviously an enormous emerging market and space if you assume twenty to sixty percent of vehicles are going to transition to electric in the next decade.

Mega Growth, Mega Markets
Interview 6

Revolutionizing Ocean Wave Energy

Marcus Lehmann

CalWave Founder and Passionate Surfer

Written by Michael Fischer

"American innovation and German diligence could take us to whole new heights"

— Marcus Lehmann

Marcus Lehmann is the co-founder and CEO of CalWave Power Technologies, a Berkeley-based startup and one of the leaders in Wave Energy. CalWave was founded in 2014 and is based on a "wave carpet" concept developed at the University of California at Berkeley. The idea behind it is that the up-and-down motion of the waves can drive a piston pump attached to an "absorber carpet". CalWave's technology was further refined when they entered the Department of Energy's Wave Energy Prize, a competition to help refine wave energy and gain efficiency. CalWave captured one of the top prizes.

I n this interview, Marcus tells us about his transition from Germany to Silicon Valley. We wanted to know from him what made him take the risk of a hardware start-up in "Silicon" Valley. Why would wave form of power generation make the breakthrough and how can San Francisco become a model city for wave energy. He gave us his views on the path towards commercialization, and the untapped potential of America's oceans. We talked with him about the vision behind CalWave and the challenges one has to face when developing cutting-edge technology. The U.S. has yet to see a fully commercial wave energy facility, so there's a lot of room for growth.

Please tell us about yourself.

I graduated from Technical University, Munich in 2013 with a 2019 and I've spent several years in California, working as a research assistant at the University of California and the Lawrence Berkeley National Laboratory. I founded the CalWave company in 2014. I have German engineering skills combined with California's entrepreneurial spirit.

From your experience, do you believe the U.S. mindset is different from that of Germany?

Yes, I believe there are differences. The German approach is very systematic and analytical. The U.S., especially California, has more of a trial-and-error-approach. At least this has been the tendency in the past, though we can now witness Germany's awakening to the large impact that creativity has on success. Combining both attitudes, American innovation and German diligence could take us to whole new heights.

Can you tell us a little bit about wave energy and what sparked your interest it?

The industry of wave power is still new compared to the wind power plants developed a decade ago. Many different technologies have been tried and developed for harnessing the power of wind. The three-blade upwind design emerged and became standard, then was equipped with pitch and yaw control to be effectively shut down. Wind power started to write its success story amongst renewable energy sources. For wave power, such generally accepted technology has not yet been standardized. Due to the lack of dominant and feasible designs for wave converters, the Department of Energy (DoE) established the Wave Energy Prize. This was the first time a standardized set of performance metrics was analyzed by a third party. Over ninety-two technologies joined the competition nation-wide and we were among them, representing the University of California at Berkeley. The DoE selected the inventions based on general life cycle analysis and practical implications. They tested the best twenty entrants in a 1:50 scale model in a water tank. According to the tank testing, simulation data, and financial feasibility studies, the judges announced the nine finalists and proceeded to test them on a 1:20 scale model. In 2016 we were awarded the prize, due to exceeding the target threshold of 2, with a result of 3.6. We showed a potential path towards utility-scale of wave converters. Right now, we're working on the first open-ocean demonstration.

How can the use of wave energy help a city like San Francisco?

To fulfill all the electricity needs of San Francisco, we need around 1.3 gigawatts (GW) installed capacity. There's not a lot of space for wind and solar power since San Francisco is facing the ocean.

If we look at the geographic location of the city we can see that San Francisco is one of the best locations for wave energy. Wave energy also has the advantage of being thirty to sixty times more power-dense than wind power, so less land is required. Swell doesn't depend on whether it's day or night, which makes wave energy a highly predictable resource. We know up to two weeks in advance how the resource will look. Wind and solar, on the other hand, can change within seconds. This presents huge challenges for these utilities.

Let's imagine we place one of our units in Ocean Beach in San Francisco. One unit could produce enough power for one hundred and eighty homes and could save us a thousand barrels of oil per year. To cover the entire electricity needs of San Francisco we would need to cover around twenty to thirty miles of California's coastline.

What is CalWave's vision and what are your goals?

Our vision is to provide twenty to thirty percent of the global electricity demand by using wave power. Europe and the U.S. have great locations for this source of renewable energy. Our main goal is to solve the growing utility-scale storage issues we are facing with current renewables alone. Wind turbines can only produce energy if there's a breeze and photovoltaic (PV) solar modules can only produce energy during the daytime.

Where do you think California is heading in terms of renewable energy?

California's administration anticipates one hundred percent renewable energy by 2045. We have no suitable long-term storage level to supply this demand without facing power blackouts. With wave energy, however, we have a tool to solve short-term storage as well as utility-scale storage. Fluctuating solar and wind power requires a lot of energy storage, and lithium-ion batteries seem like the obvious choice, but they are far too expensive, not to mention their limited production capacity and material supply. A two-and-a-half trillion dollar investment on batteries would be needed for California alone.

The National Renewable Energy Laboratory projected that California would get from forty to fifty percent overall renewable energy sourcing. That solar energy would take approximately 10 GW of storage. I acknowledge that the prices for storage are coming down and production capability is being developed, but I did a back-of-the-envelope calculation and the results are not good. A great example would be that for an electric vehicle (EV) battery-focused factory to build 10 GW of storage, it would take 1,700 years of production capacity. Batteries are fine for the EV market, but for utility-scale power, we need a lot more zeros. The only path to one hundred percent renewables is through diversification of our generation portfolio and that's why we founded CalWave.

What kind of technologies are used for wave energy?

The development of wave power generation systems is more complex than other forms of renewables. You can't just build them and test them in your backyard to find out if they work, as one could do with wind turbines or solar panels in the early days. It takes a much more rigorous and systematic approach to solve this problem in the field. Offshore operations are more expensive and require better planning. From a purely architectural perspective, we can cluster all wave converter technologies into two categories, surface devices, and bottom devices. Surface devices are floating on the surface and moored to the ocean floor, while bottom devices are directly mounted to the seabed. Both technologies have their drawbacks. Bottom-fixed is not an option for California, for environmental reasons as well as limited site availability. Surface devices have no means to be shut down effectively in storms, which leads to overdesign of structural components and mooring systems.

We carefully studied the history of the wind industry and the first developers of the wind turbine as we know it today. The moment wind became industrially viable and scalable was when pitch control was introduced. Pitch control is the technology used to operate and control the angle of the blades in a wind turbine to adjust for wind changes. From that point on, we were able to shut down wind turbines remotely without needing anyone to be on-site.

Wave power must meet the same criteria as a wind turbine in terms of high performance and remote shutdown. Our patented solution operates while submerged, allowing it to survive stormy seas while causing no visual pollution or posing any collision danger. We are installing our systems further offshore, where the waves are longer and hold more energy. Concepts closer to the coastline look simpler at first, but the waves already have double the energy just off the coast. The water is deep further out; therefore, offshore power plants need a special anchoring system to keep the technology floating underwater. This makes it possible to withstand heavy storms such as from the pitch and yaw regulation of a wind turbine. The energy density of wave power goes down exponentially with the water column. This means that with a slight change in water depth we can decrease the loads exponentially, giving us control over the excitation load. In times when we want to produce, we have it in the highest energy-dense region. During storms, we can shut it down.

Furthermore, we see that wind and solar are both subject to hurricanes. Our fully submersible wave converters allow us to survive hurricanes, unlike the solar farms that are often blown away. Thus, another market for the wave converter is created, that of disaster relief, as resilient backup will be needed

Can you briefly explain how your wave converters work?

The tidal energy resource is not as highly distributed as wave energy, which is available everywhere in the U.S. and on the western EU coasts. When we first investigated wave power, we were looking at the coastline from a bird's-eye-view. Within muddy coastal sections, the waves broke earlier, and they wouldn't travel close to the beach as the other waves did in areas with a less muddy seabed. Waves have more energy out at sea. The closer they get to the shore, the more energy they lose. While the waves travel over the mud, they load force onto the seabed. In other words, they make the mud vibrate. Simultaneously, the waves lose energy. It's similar to a shock absorber. Our conclusion was that we should use that same principle to generate power.

How are wave converters connected to the main grid?

Right now, California gets a lot of solar energy from Arizona, and I recently attended a seminar on the Natural Resources Defense Council (NRDC) on this topic. They're working on a further grid extension so that our utilities can increase. In the future, the grid could get so big that we could even handle Canadian pump storage. I don't think that's going to happen, considering the economic and political perspectives. It's always beneficial to operate on a decentralized or state level. The utility-scale storage options in California are limited. Instead of investing in new storage, it would be far more beneficial to count on direct power supply.

Are there any restrictions on placing the wave converters?

There's an economic restriction; we need a water depth of at least fifty meters. This is necessary to securely shelter the converter. When the water depth is less than half of the wavelength the waves start to interact with the seabed. This means that some of the energy is lost.

In the case of offshore wind farms, we would just go to where they're currently located and use the infrastructure those windfarms have built or are floating on. If we start a wave converter from scratch, let's say on small islands, we can be much closer to the shore. We pick our sweet spot as close as where the shoreline drops to sixty meters. In California, the sea depth drops quickly so we don't have to be that far out.

Are there any benefits to partnering with others working with renewable energy?

We are seeing the benefit of co-locating with wind farms. Two-thirds of the cost of a wind farm is for everything but the wind turbine itself. This includes the entire cabling, permitting, electrical infrastructure, and grid connection. Using both technologies at the same location would not increase this fixed cost, but it could double the amount of power generated.

Stanford University did a study regarding the combined output profile of wind and wave which shows capacity factors could go up by eighty percent. Partnering with leading offshore wind developers who are currently looking for innovations in that field would be the smartest way to deploy our systems at scale.

Considering that your plants will be submerged in seawater, what expenses, in terms of maintenance, do you expect to accumulate as compared to your initial investment?

In a co-located plant with offshore wind, we can work together and split the costs. We have plenty of tools available. We can run open-source, multi-parameter optimization on clusters and we can conduct multi-computational fluid dynamics (CFD) studies on High Performance Computing (HPCs). These were not accessible a few years ago. With the costs of Internet of Things (IoT) going down, predictive maintenance, remote maintenance, and robotic maintenance will be efficient and cost-effective. A partner firm in tidal energy works on a self-propelled tidal turbine which can self-install, reducing the labor costs of installation and maintenance. Offshore gets expensive when you have human intervention. When we're finally on the farm level, we can adopt robotic technology that allows us to keep the operating expenditures (OPEX) lower by combining OPEX costs with wind turbine operators.

Who are your target customers?

To be competitive with solar and wind we must find a systematic path toward higher production volumes. We must target markets where we can provide additional value, such as islands or Navy bases with high electricity prices as well as remote power. We're also in touch with St. Croix in the U.S. Virgin Islands, which has high electricity prices. Currently, power purchase agreements (PPA) on islands for solar plus storage cost twenty to sixty cents. This will be achievable with our first products. We are in touch with Gump Station, a UC Berkeley research center in French Polynesia. Once we do our first pilot test in 2021, we could replicate these units.

What will be the main market that you address?

We must find a way to have larger production volumes so that we can have a significant impact on greenhouse gas emissions. The most powerful locations are here on the West Coast, followed by Chile, the European Union, Australia, and New Zealand. Island nations are predestined for wave energy as they represent eleven percent of the global population and they run mostly on diesel fuel, which unfortunately produces the same amount of emissions as coal does. Even if all the industrialized nations found a way to get weaned off coal, that eleven percent would continue running fossil fuels and have high electricity costs. On smaller islands, wave converters would add enormous benefits to the baseload. We did an analysis for Sri Lanka, which has a grid capacity of about six GW. They are already forced to curtail significant portions of their solar at twenty percent. So the path toward one hundred percent micro-grids is a very challenging one, with just one generation resource.

Can you tell us about CalWave's recent achievements and what do you envision for the future?

In 2019, CalWave received two additional multi-million dollar awards by DOE to build a commercial scale drive train in parallel to our open water demo and to design the next generation of our submerged pressure differential WEC and investments from High Tide Foundation and others. In 2020, CalWave's "xNode" was awarded the Grand Prize of the discovery stage of the Ocean Observing Prize to enable the "Ocean Internet of Things" and successfully deployed the anchors for the open ocean pilot at Scripps, San Diego.

We're on schedule to commission our open-ocean pilot in California in early 2021, and planning to offer xNode devices to our first customers for Autonomous Underwater Vehicles (AUV) recharging and other entirely novel ocean science missions. CalWave's solution and IP represents the next generation of transformational ocean energy technologies needed to finally unlock the vast carbon-free energy resources that exist in our oceans all around the world.

In your opinion, how far advanced is the project?

In 2012, we built our first prototype, together with fellow students, with only what we could find in the laboratory. Since then, the project has developed significantly. In terms of NASA's 9-level technology and readiness level system, we are now between levels 4 and 5. This means we are already testing prototypes and carrying out the first scaling experiments.

We are currently funded by the U.S. Department of Energy, with a 48-month contract. We are therefore planning up to and including the year 2020 and are expecting that we will need another year to extensively test the technology. Theoretically, we could go into serial production in 2021.

Why do you believe wave power will play an important role in the energy mix?

We need to diversify our energy production. Here in California, we not only have in abundance the resources of solar, wind, and wave but geothermal and biogas as well. I believe that the future will include a mix of all forms of renewables. I think energy production should take on the same attitude that you find with good farming. A farmer knows that monoculture never really contributes to building sustainable soil quality. In California, wave power could become its third-largest renewable resource, but it's still completely untapped. The resource is sixty times denser than wind and solar. It has no daily variability and it runs 24/7. There is some variation over the year, but we have no real daily variations. It never drops below forty percent capacity, and that's exactly the baseload power we need to achieve a higher percentage of renewables. It's extremely predictable, which is attractive to the utility companies, and it's close to where we need the power. In California, most of the population lives near the coastline. In the U.S. overall, sixty percent of the population lives within six miles of the sea. From a world perspective, three-quarters of the mega-cities are close to a shoreline. Eighty percent of the population lives in direct proximity to it.

From an entrepreneurial standpoint, what are the most important lessons you have learned?

Silicon Valley is built on digital startups and there are some examples where the hardware area has been successful. There was the Clean Tech Bubble prior to the 2008 downturn when a lot of VCs invested in clean tech. Many of them had been previously successful in IT, and they thought they could do the same with hardware. That's just not the case. If hardware fails, you can't just run an update and fix it; you have to change your entire production line. Those involved with the Wave Energy Prize learned from these hurried approaches and developed a program where scaling is done much more gradually and systematically. Collaboration is essential in order for us to grow, so we're working with most of the national labs and industrial experts in our field.

Tell us what motivates you the most.

In one of his TED talks, Al Gore stated that the World Economic Forum considers that climate change presents the greatest danger to the global economy. Gore concluded that humanity is facing a severe moral challenge and that every community needs to act rapidly to address this challenge. Our wave converters offer a much higher benefit than just producing electricity for cities. The future for sustainable energy in cities lies in the utilization of all available local resources. To address the huge challenge presented by climate change, we must set a moral example. San Francisco is a thriving coastal city that has a chance to become the global exemplar of what a fully sustainable city of the 21st century can and should be.

Part IV

Success Stories

Napa Valley – The Silicon Valley of Wine

Tom Davies

President of V. Sattui Winery

Written by Tobias Salbaum

"The Napa Valley experience goes far beyond wine – it is the experience of the arts, good food and the beauty of nature. All these things combined make up the Napa brand."

— Tom Davies

Tom is the President of V. Sattui Winery. He was among the first five employees hired at the winery and his great business sense and thirst for knowledge lead him to the very top. Tom graduated from Chico State University in 1979 with a degree in business management.

V. Sattui, a pioneer winery in Napa Valley, exemplifies resilience and excellence, catering to over three hundred and fifty thousand annual visitors, nearly two hundred thousand mailing list customers and over forty thousand active wine club members. Their extensive wine offerings feature sixty different types of wine, resulting in over sixty-five thousand cases produced annually. But their success cannot be credited solely to their quality of wine. As soon as you enter the winery grounds you experience an extraordinarily welcoming environment. Not only are you provided with world-class wines, but you discover an on-site marketplace, featuring over two hundred cheeses, house-made charcuterie, and extensive gift shop and accessories. V. Sattui's aim is to provide their guests with an unforgettable experience.

The goal of this interview was to discover what made the Napa Valley the "Silicon Valley of Wine". Over a glass of Pinot Noir, we discussed with Tom the key enablers of his success as well as the history of V. Sattui. We spent time with Tom at his stunning winery and took in the elements that make Napa Valley one of the world's great wine regions. We learned the importance of product development, differentiation, and the benefits of offering complementary products. He discussed the history behind their unique products, such as their one-of-a-kind Madeira and Angelica, a brandy-infused wine. We talked about the challenges this dynamic and complicated industry faces: long product development cycles, the increasing cost of land, infrastructure, and how Tom continues to create blue ocean wine in a red ocean competitive space.

How did you start your journey at the V. Sattui winery?

I had recently graduated from college and was home for a visit when my older brother asked me if I had any plans for my future. Looking back at my college experiences at Chico State, I realized I had always been passionate about wine and thought it was a good match with my business degree. I sent resumes and cover letters to all the sixty wineries that existed at the time in California. Only three replied. Two wineries responded with generic rejection letters. The third one was from Dario Sattui.

My interview took place over a game of ping-pong. I lost the game but landed the job. . I was hired on as a wine salesperson, head corker and part-time cellar worker, with a starting salary of five dollars per hour. Though the pay was laughable, Dario's enthusiasm, vision for the winery's future and sharp mind attracted me to the job. That night I went back to my tent with a bottle of Amador Zin, a wedge of Pepper Brie, and a loaf of bread. I remember sitting there thinking, "Well, this is pretty cool!" I landed a job at a winery in Napa Valley with the opportunity to learn the wine business from the bottom up!

What makes Napa special? Could you compare and contrast it with other wine regions?

There are many amazing factors that make Napa special. We are able to produce more varieties at a much higher level here in Napa Valley as compared to other parts of the world.

It has a lot to do with California sunshine. The proximity to San Francisco Bay moderates the temperature during the summer, so we end up having cool nights and warm days. We have many different microclimates within the Napa Valley, over a hundred different soil types, and we rarely have rain during the growing season. It is unusual to have an off-vintage year because the weather is so cooperative. The great years of Bordeaux happen only when they have Napa-like weather. This is why vintages are so important in other parts of the world, as Mother Nature often doesn't always cooperate.

There are many great wine growing regions in the world. What's unique about a wine is that it is from a certain place. The wine should reflect wherever it was grown and produced. That's what it's all about.

How do you see other wine eco-systems evolving globally?

As we get smarter about making great wines, we can identify the reasons of their success. Once we find other areas with similar soils and climates, there's no reason why we can't make great wines of the same kind at those new locations.

Some of these wines, especially the international varieties like Cabernet, are becoming hard to identify to an origin. There is a signature to a Napa Cab, but other areas have figured out the way we make it, so you sometimes lose that sense of origin. Napa is a very special place to grow wine, but climate change, economic forces and unneeded and hurtful regulations can jeopardize our future.

This is scary for those of us who have paid a premium to be part of the great Napa Valley. It is expensive to make wine in Napa, as land prices are approaching a million dollars an acre and cost of production is much higher than other growing regions in California that also make great wines. That is why we put a lot of effort into making the best wines possible and work hard to market the Napa brand.

How does entrepreneurship manifest itself in the Napa Valley?

We had pioneers who took a risk and brought wine here when it wasn't all that popular in the U.S. They built a great brand, emphasizing excellent quality and everything that went along with it.

Unfortunately, Dario's story and those of other pioneers is almost impossible to repeat, due to the skyrocketing cost of the land. The cost of entry into the wine industry in the traditional sense, where you both grow the grapes and make the wine, is over. It is just too expensive to undertake.

We still have so many interesting people choosing to come to the Napa Valley to grow grapes and make wine. It takes a special kind of person to give up the success they achieved in other walks of life and take the investment risk of coming to the Napa Valley and work hard to potentially make little or no money.

To start here today, you must think outside the box, and many people are still willing to do that. They are starting to outsource their grape growing. Why can't you have a winery in Alameda? Why can't you have an urban winery? You can make wine anywhere. You may even argue that making wine in the Bay Area may have some advantages; having manufacturing and bottling in proximity to transportation hubs may be the wave of the future. We have this beautiful valley and yet our highways are filled with industrial-related traffic on two-lane country roads. The valley should be about growing grapes and having a world-class destination for visitors to learn about and enjoy our wines.

How has Silicon Valley affected Napa Valley?

It has had a tremendous effect. You are collecting successful people from all walks of life into one place. Wherever they came from, whether they were manufacturers, doctors, academics or bankers, they were all very good at their jobs. They took a chance on coming here and risking the wealth they had amassed. If you look at these highly motivated people who are willing to assume risk, you find that they are very interesting people, and interesting people usually bring culture along with them; not just the wine culture, but music, art and food. If you love wine that often means you travel the world whenever you can. It is a combination of people with a real thirst for enjoyment and knowledge, a thirst far beyond wine.

These fine people who come here each bring something very special to the area. For instance, Chuck McMinn has a winery called Vineyard 29. He owned Covad, a company specializing in DSL in Silicon Valley. He has been instrumental in creating a bike path that winds all the way through Napa Valley. We have twelve miles finished and the next twelve are ready to go. It is costing a million dollars a mile to build, but it'll be worth every penny. Chuck McMinn is a perfect example of a guy who came here and made it his mission to bring something special to Napa Valley. In his case, it is by vigorously championing this superb bike path.

This mentality grants us the gift of having all these bright, community-minded and forward-thinking people in our area. They have set up strict zoning laws to keep the developers out which will hopefully prevent what has sadly happened in Santa Clara. That area was once the agricultural breadbasket of northern California. Try to find a plum, cherry or apricot orchard there today. All gone! Farsighted zoning laws are the contribution that has most helped Napa Valley become what it is today.

How do you go about selecting a particular varietal and or wine to produce?

One part of being successful in business is innovation. Unfortunately, we often get too caught up in the day-to-day happenings of our businesses, like keeping up with orders and overseeing employees or checking in with our salespeople. A lot of time is spent away from the craft. I am trying to take some of the time I now have to ponder what actions will help our business five to seven years from now.

The easiest way to explain the process would be through an example. We have a new Russian River Pinot Noir called Collina d'Oro. We love Pinot Noirs from the Russian River. They have a particular soil, a rich gold soil that helps produce high quality Pinot Noir. Once we decided that this was the direction we wanted to head, we found a real estate agent. We also hired a viticulturist to identify microclimates well-suited to Pinot Noir. We came across a place near the town of Forestville, a little fifteen-acre parcel that had been an old Gravenstein apple orchard. We identified it as a great location, and began doing some soil and water tests to determine whether it fit our needs. Once we found that it did, we purchased the property. Fast forward to today: we just released the first vintage last year. From start to finish it was a ten-year project. The time from when you first identify a wine to produce to having a bottle of that wine in your hand represents a tremendous commitment of time and equity.

We just planted some Chenin Blanc and some Albariño. Chenin Blanc was one of the more popular varieties in the Napa Valley 50+ years ago; I doubt if there are more than 20 acres left today in the valley. Chenin Blanc produces a deliciously crisp white wine with notes of mineral, straw and stone fruits. There are a few producers out here now who are starting to make it. We are taking the chance that something like this wine might make a comeback. We like the variety; it is great food wine and has the ability to age to many years.

We also have our marketing and our management teams involved in these decisions. You bring marketing in to get a perspective on our customer requirements, to forecast potential demand and to identify trends. We need to identify the products that are selling for us, and those that are not. Riesling represented 25% of our sales many years ago. It is an amazing grape; some argue that it may be the greatest grape in the world. It produces wine that lasts forever. This kind of grape can be made in different forms. Put simply, it is a dynamic and versatile grape. Despite that, the Riesling market has completely fallen off the face of the earth and I am not sure why. It can be made into a very crisp, very dry wine or one that is sweet and fruity. All we know is that that the variety does not sell as well as it did before. A lot of it is due to current trends. Who knows; it might come back. We see this cyclical trend over time. I found a wine in our cellar recently that we made 14 years ago. I named it Concinnare. Its name originates from the Latin word for harmonious. We blended Chardonnay, Semillon and Sauvignon Blanc together. It was an interesting blend, but it didn't sell and we never made it again. I believe the wine would have been more popular today; A lot of it comes down to timing.

Can you shed some light on how the wildly successful wines Madeira and Angelica were born?

Madeira is one of our most unusual products and it is certainly unique within the industry. It was one of the first wines Vittorio made in his winery in San Francisco. He marked the beginning of Madeira when he started making wine in the late 1800s or early 1900s. That winery was closed during prohibition. The new Madeira was born out of Dario's fascination with his grandfather's wine. When the old building in San Francisco was shut down, it was taken over by some of Dario's relatives. As a young man, he would visit these relatives and he discovered that there were still some barrels of the old Madeira left in the cellar. When he restarted the winery in Napa Valley, he was able to obtain these barrels. The question remained: How to create a new product from only two barrels. He was lucky to find that Martini Winery had some old Sherry. This was not identical to the Madeira, but it was compatible. They were willing to sell Dario some of the then 30-year-old sherry dessert wines. He added some of this 100-year-old Madeira to each of the individual barrels. That's how the full process of Solera started. The best way to explain the Solera process is by thinking of a big stack of barrels. The very bottom level of them contains the very oldest ones. You take a few gallons from the bottom levels and then top it off with syphoning from the barrels above it. By doing it like that, you never fully extinguish the oldest wines. You develop this mother, and you keep adding younger wines to it. Eventually, these younger wines begin to take up the flavor of the older ones. What has started off as a couple of barrels has now grown into close to four thousand barrels. Every year we produce new wine that we add to the solera. Some of these will not see the bottle for another 30 years. This process represents a tremendous investment, and no one in their right mind would start it now.

The idea of producing Angelica, a brandy-infused wine, came from a friend. His family has been making cognac for four generations. He decided to come to Napa Valley in the early '80s and we became friends while he was helping us with some work. He tried to sell his small-brand cognac during tastings at wine and liquor stores, but he was going up against noted brands like Hennessey, so no one was really interested. He shared a wine called Pineau des Charentes with us. It is a specialty product that you only find in Cognac. As the story goes, there was a barrel of juice left to be fermented in the wine cellar. Somehow a cellar worker accidently put some cognac in it. He was embarrassed about the accident, so he hid the barrel away. Five years later, they discovered the barrel and soon realized that it had transformed into an amazing product. He shared it with us and I thought it was delicious and that it would sell well in California, so I asked him to help us with the project. We started using Muscat grapes and juice, but the question remained as to where to come up with brandy. We ourselves were not a brandy producer.

There used to be a brandy producer here in the Napa Valley called RMS. Remy Martin decided to make cognac in the Napa Valley back in the '80s and they had some beautiful copper stills in their winery in the Carneros region. It is rumored that it was so good that the quality was surpassing what was being made in France. We don't exactly know why, but they shut the place down and destroyed the copper stills. They were left with thousands of gallons of this amazing brandy. We jumped on it. We introduced this brandy to the juice and aged the wine for 7 years in French oak. If you simply mix them without aging, you get two separate tastes, one of juice and the other of brandy. Once they age, the alcohol and the juice become wedded as one.

From an entrepreneurship and business point of view what unique strategies have you employed to grow both your profit and revenue and to distinguish yourself from others?

As an entrepreneur, I find that the ability to control costs is extremely important. I believe everyone gets too caught up in how to increase sales. While it is certainly important to grow, cost control is just as important. Would you rather increase your sales by a dollar or would you rather decrease your cost by a dollar? When you decrease cost you get the whole dollar, but at best you only get fifty percent of the dollar that comes from increasing revenues.

We realized early on that if you use distribution channels to market your product it eats up a large percentage of your profits. To counter this, many wineries either increase the consumer price of their product or upgrade their facility so they can utilize economies of scale to make money. None of those options aligned with our vision of an affordable, warm and welcoming experience, so we decided to go another route and began selling directly to the customer. Surprisingly, it worked and this remains our signature distribution method to this day.

Over time, we added in two more sources of revenue. We became one of the first wineries in the nation to start a wine club. Members of a wine club would receive benefits such as access to private tasting rooms as well as receiving one or two bottles a month. This allowed us to sell to customers over state lines without the use of distributors. Despite our success, it was troublesome launching the wine clubs. Each state is like a different country with different laws and regulations.

The other method we added to our business model was selling wine futures. This method worked on two levels. First, it allowed us to have a better idea of the projected sales of certain batches. Second, it provided a memorable experience for the customer. Once the customer bought a wine future, they had the chance to taste it from the barrel at different stages of the process. Now the customer can witness the evolution of the product; how it moves from grape juice to authentic V. Sattui wine.

We buckled down on social media and were one of the first wineries in Northern California to hire a social media marketing manager. Personally, I am not a big social media person but I am smart enough to recognize how important it is.

Tell us about Vertical Integration.

Another vastly important element of maintaining profit margins is lowering production cost. In agriculture and in the wine industry, vertical integration (owning parts of your supply chain), is a key element of cost effectiveness. We have invested a lot of capital into buying farmland in the Napa region. This allows us to insource seventy percent of the grapes we need. To put it into perspective, we can grow high quality Cabernet for around $3,000 a ton. Outsourcing the same product costs an average of $9,000 a ton, with some highly-prized vineyards demanding over $25,000 a ton. That is an enormous difference and it's why most wineries try to spread themselves along the supply chain as much as possible. Unfortunately, this is becoming more difficult in today's environment. Back in the day, you could buy farmland for around forty thousand dollars an acre but now, due to the increased interest in the Napa Valley lifestyle, the most coveted land sells closer to one million dollars an acre or more.

Have you thought about ways to minimize traffic in Napa Valley and still give wineries the economies of scale to manage costs?

I have been working with a few farsighted vintners on this issue. The selling and marketing of wines belongs in proximity to where the grapes are grown, but it doesn't make sense to have large-scale production in these rural areas. Large corporate wineries are filling our highways with trucks and trailers and commuting production workers. Most winery workers live in the city of Napa, or in Sonoma or Solano counties, so it would make sense to make wine in an industrial area, closer to where people live. Our current congestion may be the demise of Napa Valley; our little two-lane roads are getting jammed up.

It is important to consider alternative forms of transportation in order to ease the traffic. The wine train is a great idea for alleviating the number of cars on the roads, but we should focus on consolidating large-scale production in South County and keep the upper Napa Valley for the beautiful experience it provides.

Moving production to the southern portion of the valley is ideal, especially for wineries that distribute their products from American Canyon, which is most of the major wineries. It makes no sense to make the wine up north and then transport it south. Making the wine near distribution centers would ease traffic, reduce costs, and is better for the environment. You can make great wine just about anywhere if you find similar soil conditions and similar climate conditions. Even though the Napa Valley may have a great reputation for

Cabernet, that doesn't mean it's the only place you can grow high quality Cabernet. In fact, I recently tasted a great Cabernet from Solano County.

One obstacle we must take into consideration when looking into moving our operation is the cost of land. How can you make a profit when you pay a million dollars an acre? We continue to push our local government officials to make changes to a few of the outdated regulations in order to ease the burden on us. For example, we have a 120-acre ranch in Carneros and we want to plant another twenty-five acres onto it. We wouldn't be cutting any trees because they were all burned down in the wildfires; it's all rolling hills now. We're going to spend approximately half a million dollars in due diligence, with biological reports and erosion control plans. The process is already into its third year. How could any new winery afford the time and capital needed to do this? The only reason we find it acceptable is because we didn't have to pay an exorbitant price for the property.

New wine product development is naturally a very long-term investment. What are the key lessons you have learned in this area?

Our production and business grew concurrently with the number of people coming through our door. One of the mistakes some businesses make is that when they see the level of their business, they forecast it and ramp up the production based on that. If that is the case, if anything changes you're saddled with excess inventory. We were always a little behind demand in the sense that we often sell out of products, but we never made more than what we were selling. I think it is important, especially in the early years, to balance your inventories. In the wine business, forecasting accurately is especially difficult because you are making decisions today for products that will probably not hit the shelves until seven years from now. We recently had meetings regarding planting new varieties, focusing on what millennials are going to be drinking. Is the focus going to be on Albariño, or is it going to be something else? Maybe a new blend that no one's ever made? We're trying to make these decisions despite knowing we are not going to have results for seven years.

How do you go about building a good wine team in terms of labor issues?

Napa Valley is an expensive place to live, but still we have managed to build a great world-class team and run a successful business with over two hundred thirty employees. One of our main concerns is to pay people well and to treat our employees beyond expectations. That is very important.

As is always the case, labor is a big issue, but not so much on the technical side. If we were to go out and look for people who can run our vineyards, run our production, make the wine, and provide technical help, well that is a little easier to come by. For the pool of people interested in working in those technical positions, even coming in from outside the industry, Napa is an attractive location. We do have challenges filling the jobs where the pay may not be high enough to live in this expensive region.

How do you cater to a wide range of customer base from millennials to the boomers?

The question is, how do you cater to both groups? How do you appeal to the younger millennials and give them the experience and the authenticity they are looking for? It is difficult, because aside from age, we also have many different ethnicities visiting the winery and people who are new to wine. We take into consideration the fact that older people may want a more sophisticated enclosed environment, whereas the younger generation prefers being among people in an open environment. It is challenging, but it gets down to great customer service and treating everyone well. Welcoming everyone is a very valuable key to how I run this company. We have always been that way.

We are fortunate to have younger people visiting V. Sattui. I worry about other wineries not understanding this dynamic, especially the wineries that have focused on the one-to-two hundred dollars per bottle price range. How does that relate to the younger generations? Of course, that can be a profitable model, but the boomers are getting older. I am now serving our third generation of customers. We have always had the ability to cater to the old and young. Maybe it is because of our scenic picnic grounds or the feeling of openness, the sense that we are a winery for everyone.

Are there any valuable lessons you learned over the years that are helping you during the current COVID-19 storm?

As in any business, success is greatly dependent upon your ability to change. If you don't change, you're out of business. A perfect example was the 2008 recession. Before the recession, our main method of marketing was email advertising, as approximately half of our sales are off-site. We sell a lot of wine directly to consumers which they can have shipped to them. Up until 2007-2008, sales were on fire. We would send out an email and receive hundreds of orders in a single day. This number of direct sales was huge for a winery of our size. Then the recession hit and there were hardly any orders coming in at all. We started wondering what we should do now. People were coming for tours and tasting, but all the offsite sales across the country pretty much stopped cold.

Right before the recession we hosted a fundraiser for Rudy Giuliani, and I had purchased cigars from his favorite cigar shop on Columbus Circle in New York City. A month or two later, the crash happened, and I received a call from the cigar store asking if I wanted to buy any cigars. That's when the light bulb went off. Maybe we could phone our customers? Normally, I wouldn't have thought it could work. Generally speaking, if anyone calls me at home or at work trying to sell me something, I hang up. What made the light bulb go off was that this guy was calling to sell me something I truly like; that was the difference. Today, twenty-seven percent of our sales are generated by phoning our customers. We continue to send out emails and use social media, but the fact that we could reach out by phone to our customers maybe two or three times a year added great value to us and built excellent relationships with the customers.

We have a group of ten people who call our customers from a little farmhouse. The relationships they have built over the phone is probably greater than some of the relationships we have here on site. People from Florida or Texas only get out here maybe once every year or two, so this way we can maintain contact with them and build on our relationship, generating continuing sales. Our ability to change during the 2008 recession allowed us to pull through it. We must be willing to step outside our comfort zones and try new ideas if we want to overcome obstacles and continue to grow.

With the current situation of the COVID-19 lockdown on our hands, our online and phone presence has never been more important. Our customers love it. We tell them we're just checking in to see how they're doing, and they seem really happy to hear from us. Our customers want to keep in touch with us. With the new technologies available, keeping IN touch with our customers has never been easier. We have really been doubling down on our social media presence. We have a couple of videos already, and we plan to have a Zoom conference with our customer base next week. We are doing cooking demonstrations this weekend, and I have done a couple of quick videos for our Facebook page. A lot of the wineries are now doing virtual tastings, which seems to be getting the buzz right now. I want to try different things, as I find some of them kind of boring with two people just sitting around talking about the wine for forty-five minutes. The key is to figure out how to make virtual shows more exciting and more interactive. Eventually some of these virtual tastings may take off and that might be another way that people can connect with our product without having to come to the winery. Even though nothing is ever going to replace the in-person experience, there are a lot of new and interesting approaches available for us to try.

You have learned a lot about the wine business over the years and have achieved great success. How do you share this knowledge with your surrounding community?

For the last fifteen years, we have adopted our local middle school and every year we have brought in the eighth-grade class for the entire day to show them the wine business. During these events we discuss the importance of agriculture, show them how wine is made, how grapes are grown, and throw in a little bit of the science behind selling.

We also work with the Napa Valley grape growers on a program called Fields of Dreams. The program assists young people who have graduated from high school or are in their first year of junior college and participate in an externship at the winery for a month.

We became involved with NEXT (Napa Educator Externship), which is a joint venture with Napa Learns, Napa County Board of Education and Workforce Alliance of the North Bay. During these three-day-long externships, we give teachers the opportunity to shadow professionals in the industry. They shadow people at wineries, restaurants, and hotels to learn the requirements of the job positions and the requirements needed to prepare their students. We are dedicated to this program as it is our way of giving back to the community and keeping the local spirit alive.

At V. Sattui we have created a curriculum containing several elements: agriculture and the wine industry in our community, understanding the Napa visitor experience, communications and marketing for direct-to-customer business, grape growing and winemaking, and the economics of growing grapes and making wine. We have been trying to cultivate industry education and understanding locally, as I believe it's important for people in the community to understand how precious and important agriculture is to our community. Our goal is to instill a sense of pride in the valley.

Your advice to entrepreneurs pursuing a career in the Napa Valley?

Let me just say that finding myself here in Napa Valley and working in marketing and sales has continued to be a wonderful experience. For me, it's what it's all about and it's extremely satisfying. While I would never minimize the importance of making wine, I find that for me, it's a greater challenge to properly position it and market wine. Thirty or forty years ago, there were hundreds of distributors and brokers in the wine business. Now there are two of them who control nearly 50% of distribution. If you are a new winery trying to get a start and find your way, you must learn that a large broker won't be jumping at the chance to represent your small new brand. It's so important that you learn how to sell direct and not be afraid to try a number of different sales avenues until you discover what methods work best for you. This has been our model from the start and we've done tremendously well with it. It is up to you as a fledgling winery to create your own path and never be afraid to try out new ideas. Be bold and you can succeed. You may take a few tumbles along the way but get up and keep trying and you will find your own way to success.

Your final thoughts on Napa?

At the end of the day, the success of the Napa Valley as a world-class destination is directly tied to our world class wines. But we also have done many things to retain and protect the specialness of the Napa Valley well into the future. Much of this has to do with the fact that over 50 years ago, we protected the land against development. With the AG preserve, we have protected thousands of acres from commercial or residential development. We will never have any more homes on the valley floor, and very few more up in the hills. We have protected the beauty. As an industry, we long ago understood that the Napa Valley experience goes far beyond wine. It is the experience of the arts, great food and the beauty of nature. All these things combined make up the Napa brand. It is truly a very special place and we are very fortunate to be a part of it.

From Teaching to Entrepreneurship

Sukhi Singh

Founder of Sukhi's

Written by Amaranta Quintero and Ákos Balász

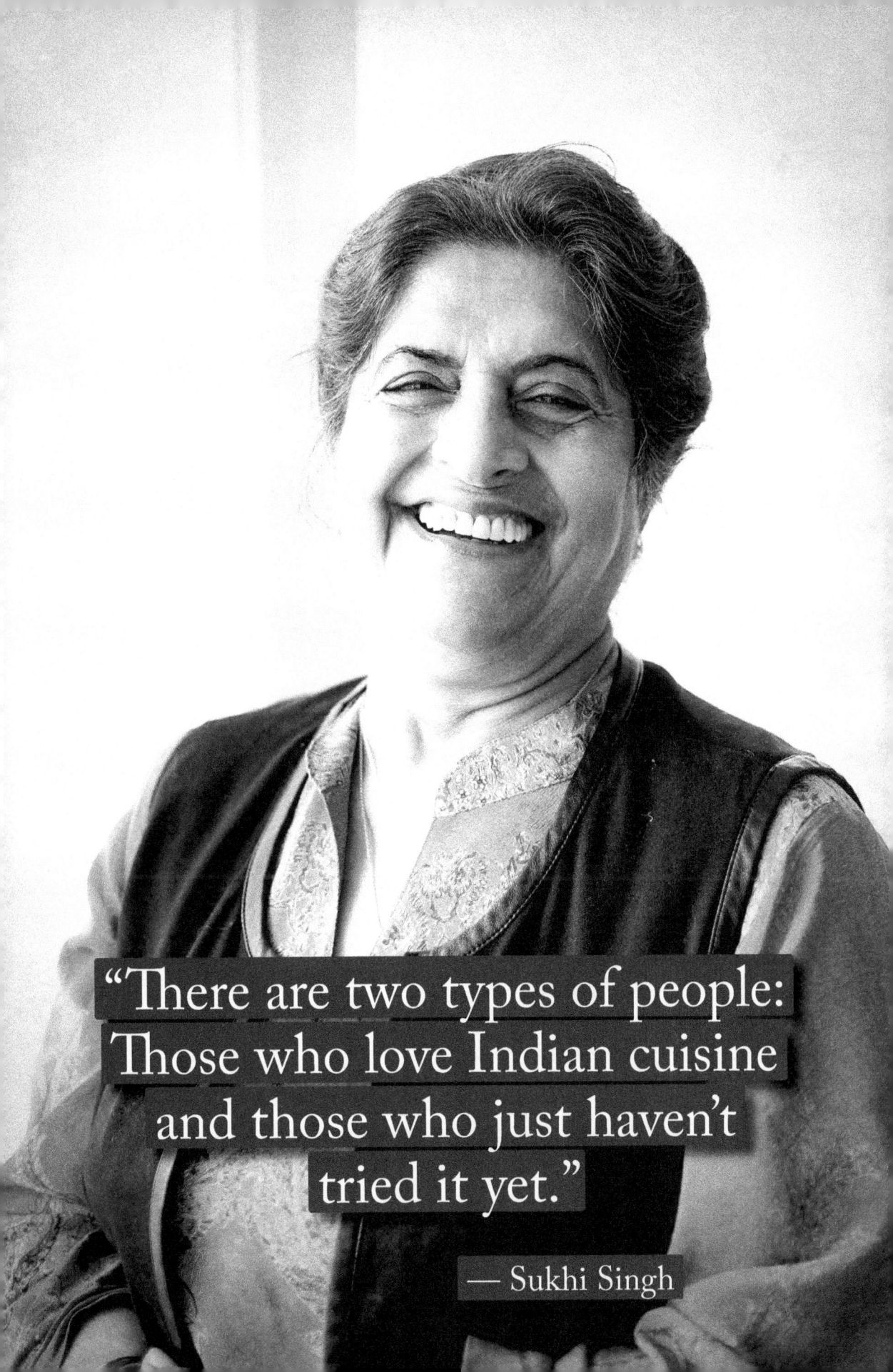

"There are two types of people: Those who love Indian cuisine and those who just haven't tried it yet."

— Sukhi Singh

Sukhi Singh is the founder of Sukhi's, an authentic Indian cuisine purveyor headquartered in Silicon Valley. Sukhi's began with her vision of providing the younger generation with an easy way to put on the table tasty, authentic, and natural Indian food. From that original vision, the company has grown beyond all expectations. Sukhi's five different product lines are distributed to over 4,000 stores nationwide, including large stores like Safeway, Costco, Whole Foods, and Meijer. They distribute over 14 million samples annually.

In this chapter, Mrs. Singh relates her journey from the ground to the top of the food industry. She provides her unique perspective on what it means to be an entrepreneur in the food technology industry and what's needed to succeed in Silicon Valley. Though she joined the entrepreneurial arena later in her life, her resilience and determination have gained her great respect within the business community. As someone who left her home country of India behind to pursue an entrepreneurial journey in the U.S., she shares her unique and valuable insights.

She explains what has kept the fire burning in her heart, a fire that allowed her to grow her passion for authentic Indian food into a multimillion-dollar brand. Through this interview, we get a rare insight into her journey. She touches on such topics as which marketing channels to choose, what guerilla marketing tools to deploy, and how she, as a David competed with the Goliaths. Sukhi provides her unique perspective on what it means to be an entrepreneur in the food technology industry and what is needed to succeed in Silicon Valley.

How did your journey into the food industry begin?

My husband was in the Indian Air Force and we were posted in London. He would pine for Indian food and as much as I enjoyed cooking, I didn't enjoy spending hours in the kitchen every night. As a result, I would prepare sauces, in advance, and keep them in the fridge to use over the next few days. This allowed me to keep up with my busy schedule and yet, quickly cook and place our dinner on the table every night.

After spending some time in London, we moved to the United States and bought a deli in Oakland, California. We ran the deli for two years and during that time, I began selling my sauces at nearby markets. My goal was to alleviate the fear of Indian cooking, where one might have read in cookbooks that fourteen ingredients are needed to make an Indian dish. I made the sauces, each with their separate packaging of spice mix, making it easy for anyone to create a delicious and authentic Indian meal. This is how my journey started and the products began to take shape.

How did you acquire your first customer?

My sister had a party at work, and she asked me if I could prepare food for the occasion. Little did I know that the husband of one of her co-workers was the manager of the Berkeley Bowl, which, at the time, was one of the most prestigious ethnic food stores in the Bay Area. He loved my food so much that he asked my sister to convince me to sell my products at his stores. At the time I didn't realize how big of a breakthrough it was. The fact that my product was selling out, week after week, without any marketing, proved that I was doing something right. I had a feeling that I needed to work hard on this to make it succeed. I negotiated with my husband about investing two years of my life into it, and if it didn't work, I'd quit. He wasn't a big fan of the idea due to financial insecurity, but over the years he has learned to trust my instincts.

What were some of the challenges you encountered and how did you deal with them?

Over the years, I have learned not to take no for an answer. People will tell you that you can't do it, but if you feel it in your heart that your dream is worthwhile, you should go for it. You will find a way to make it work. A perfect example of this was our first challenge, which was to find a kitchen to make the sauces. I had reached such a volume that I could no longer make sauces at home and we didn't have enough income to rent a commercial space. Most people would have given up, but I told myself that there has to be another way. I was talking to an Indian restaurant owner when she mentioned that her restaurant was open six days a week and she wasn't using her kitchen on the seventh day. There was my solution! I convinced her to rent me her kitchen for that one day a week. It was a win-win situation. I would go there, early in the morning, and work hard all day to make my sauces, which we would sell during the rest of the week. We would make about 200 cases during that one day and spend the rest of the week selling the products.

Another lesson that I want to share: As an entrepreneur, you must find the "hole" in the market and fill it. I was truly fortunate that during the time we had the deli I was able to realize that people loved to eat Indian food, but nobody likes spending the time involved in making it. This was the "hole", or market, that my sauces filled. With my products, you only had to combine the vegetables or meats with my sauce, cook it for ten minutes, and you had delicious authentic Indian curry.

The dot com boom made the timing just right for us. Emerging companies in the area, like Microsoft, attracted talent from India. These newcomers missed the taste of home-cooked Indian food, and the chefs working in the campus cafeterias were not familiar with Indian cuisine. This gave entrepreneurs like me a whole new area to cater to. The dots connected.

Was it difficult to obtain funding for a business in the food industry?

Learning from our deli experience, I decided we would be self-funded, no matter how much it slowed our growth. At the time, we didn't have any money to invest and we weren't established enough to attract investors. We sold the product during the weekends and used the money to buy supplies for the next batch, during the week. After the initial success, I decided to apply for a bank loan. I met with the president of the Bank of California, not realizing how unprepared I was; I didn't even have a business plan. After the meeting, I asked my brother-in-law to help me come up with one which took us about a month to put together. My loan was approved for thirty thousand dollars and I used the money to register for a food show in San Francisco. It was fifteen thousand dollars to buy the supplies, three thousand for the flyers, and five hundred for photography. After looking over the costs and attending the show I realized I was competing against the industry giants and if I went head-on, I didn't stand a chance. It was a great learning experience which made me switch my strategy from going after large stores to selling through local channels first.

What made you decide to get involved in farmer's markets?

We needed to pay rent, utilities, and bills for our offices and to do that we needed cash-flow. I heard about the farmer's markets in our area and decided to explore them. My initial concern was who was going to buy Indian food at seven o'clock in the morning? After some research, I found a farmer's market that operated during the afternoon. I paid four hundred dollars for registration and set up the shop there. On the first day, I made three hundred seventy-five dollars and realized that I had found my cash cow. There was no looking back.

How did you build relationships with markets and grocery stores?

The opportunity presented itself during a Christmas party I was catering for. Within a short time, the food had disappeared and a gentleman came up to me, praising my food and asking if I had considered marketing my product. He coincidentally happened to be the sales manager at Morehouse Mustards and we exchanged contact information.

He told me that there was a Safeway store on Marina Boulevard in San Francisco that approved their own purchasing for the store. He suggested I use them to get my foot in the door with Safeway. I approached them, got accepted, and their customers loved my products. That year I branched out to thirty Safeway stores because of the connection I had made at the Christmas party.

What persuaded you to venture into refrigerated and frozen foods?

My epiphany occurred while I was conducting a demo at a Whole Foods store. A woman told me that she loved our product and we got into a conversation. I asked her how often she uses our product and she told me about once a month. That's when I realized she was only going to buy one bottle for three months. I checked to see what else was in her basket and saw four frozen meals. I thought to myself: "She'll be back next weekend to buy more frozen meals. This is an opportunity I need to explore!"

As I mentioned earlier, you must find the "hole in the market", create a product to fill it, and build your business plan around that.

At the beginning I was determined to only use dry ingredients to avoid refrigeration. This allowed me to ship it myself and make larger profits for cash-flow. This was crucial because the moment you involve a distributor you say goodbye to at least thirty percent of your profits.

How did you form partnerships with larger stores?

Once we started growing and we were financially strong, I decided it was time to move into larger stores. I was calling stores every week and marketing my product. The culture and willingness of people in the Bay Area to innovate was, and still is, key. People here are not afraid to try out unknown brands; they have a large appetite for risk. Mainstream

California stores were enthusiastic about my product. The goal for my first year was to get into one hundred stores in the Bay Area and I got into one hundred and ten.

How did you scale from a family business to a national operation, with customers like Costco and Whole Foods?

In 2000 a Costco broker approached us at the farmers' market and asked us if we were interested in selling samosas and naan at Costco. At this point, we had just started stepping into refrigerated products and we put together a three-portion meal for Costco. Luckily, there wasn't a lot of competition at that time and the product was very successful which led to strong growth. Since then, Costco has been a wonderful partner to work with.

We had a similar introduction to Whole Foods. They approached us at the farmers' market. Initially, we sold at their hot bars, which offered an array of warmed up-food for shoppers to choose from. These foods are something people can pick up on their way home from work that's ready to put on the plate and serve. We built solid relationships on the unbranded prepared foods side and then leveraged our success into the branded areas of frozen and refrigerated foods. Today you will find a strong Sukhi's presence across the store.

What obstacles did you face when working with small and large retailers?

Both types of retailers are important and come with their own challenges and rewards. Smaller retailers give you a chance of building a strong relationship, great placement, and feedback from retailers and consumers. You can work with them to test new marketing programs and new products based on your needs. You have more influence over the retail conditions like pricing, placement, promotion. Overall, there is more flexibility albeit low volume.

Larger retailers offer you a lot more distribution points so that you can reach more consumers, but they have a rigid program around retail conditions. If you already don't have a solid program to show movement through sampling, promotions, etc. you can get discontinued despite heavy investment to get on the shelf in the first place. You should have solid proof points on the opportunity with your products before investing in placement with a large retailer.

A great approach would be to test your product and programs in smaller retailers before moving to larger retailers. Both are important in your eco-system.

What are some key partnerships that enabled you to grow and scale.

In the life of every new business there comes a point where you can no longer run your business alone. You must be able to realize when that point comes, and you must identify what your role is and hire talent for the roles you can't do yourself. We have been able to build a great executive team at Sukhi's that started with my children but then expanded quickly. Each team member added a new skill set that allowed us to grow and scale.

Our customer relationships have also been very beneficial in our growth. By partnering with our customers, instead of just selling them products, we were able to gain insights into what consumers were looking for much faster than we would've been able to notice ourselves.

How do you keep innovating?

We keep evolving to meet the market's changing situations to promote our company mission and products.

I first started with dry products to reduce the amount of time and money it took to prepare authentic Indian cuisine. Once the dry products became popular and consumers continued to express their love of our products, we knew we needed to move into refrigerated products. This tapped into a larger market which brought new challenges, such as figuring out how to produce and distribute refrigerated products. As we continue to learn the requirements of producing and distributing frozen authentic Indian cuisine, we are diversifying by adding new dishes and recipes to our product lines. This path is more in line with our vision of offering our customers an easy way of providing delicious authentic Indian food with natural ingredients.

If you had to describe your journey in terms of stages, how would that look?

It has been a marathon. We have thirty-years of hard work behind us with no outside funding. It began in the 1980s when we bought the deli. That decade's theme was ideation, and we spent it learning the basic lessons of starting a business and taking the first steps. The 1990s were really about establishing a solid base, a platform on which to build our business. We learned how to sell our products, we rented our first kitchen, and we set up the manufacturing processes. Beginning in 2000, it became about building the company to obtain larger-scale clients. We gained Costco as a customer. Our main focus became optimizing our distribution channels and figuring out what worked and what didn't. From 2010 onwards, it became about scale and growth. At this point, we experienced a massive growth on the solid foundations we had built. Everyone has a different approach to attaining success, and this was ours.

What was the "secret sauce" that went into your success?

Hard work. That is really how success in business happens. The majority of our customers came to us through execution at the ground level. It wasn't me sitting in an office making "strategic decisions". I built this business from the ground up by sheer unadulterated execution. We were always looking ahead and we were enjoying every second of it. I found something I love to do and it's apparently something I'm both good at and able to make money from. Since Indian food was not a mainstream cuisine here at that point in time, it was really a blue ocean product with little or no competition. My advice to aspiring entrepreneurs is to find that hole in the market. You need to discover a need not being filled by the competition and work to fill it. Finding that blue ocean, that wide-open sea, is the key to success.

How has the coronavirus affected your business and how are you navigating through the storm?

From a business view, the focus right now is to just sail through the turbulence. Food is an essential business and we have been lucky from that standpoint. While some parts of our business are doing well, others like our Foodservice channel our down.

It will be very interesting to see how everyone recovers from this. Even when things start to get back to normal, the question will remain: can we keep things financially viable? How do we stay profitable while enforcing the new health protocols? Turbulence like this also presents unbelievable opportunities. For example, this is a great time to look into potential mergers and acquisitions and to look for companies that are in need of financial stability and might align with your strategy. We must continually reinvent ourselves. We must look for new products, new partnerships, and new channels to utilize what we have already built.

What do you see next for you?

I have reached the point where I am starting to take a step back from day-to-day operations. Now I mainly focus on coming up with new products and recipes. I am transitioning the company to the next generation, allowing new family members to engage and reinvent while supporting their growth through mentoring. It's a great next step and I am excited about it!

Navigating through Pandemic Times – The Pinterest Story

Jeremy King

Head of Engineering at Pinterest

Written by Ákos Balász, Nitin Aggarwal and Michael Fischer

"We are living in a time of uncertainty. There are companies that are growing 20%-50%-100%, while at the same time other businesses are failing."

— Jeremy King

Jeremy King is the senior vice president and head of engineering at Pinterest. Over the years he has held several leadership positions in some of the world's greatest organizations. As the chief technology officer at Walmart, Jeremy led the digital transformation of the company. Prior to that, Jeremy was an executive vice president of technology at LiveOps and vice president of engineering and software development at eBay. Jeremy holds a bachelor's degree in information technology from San José State University.

I n this chapter, Jeremy explains how this unsettling and highly volatile phase in history is a great opportunity for people with fire in their hearts and an appetite for innovation. Jeremy advises on skills that will be in demand, companies that will flourish, mentorship, and how to differentiate between those which will rise higher and those that will sink.

Jeremy shares the seven secrets to create a successful corporate startup, with over 200 students from the San José State University, the Friedrich-Alexander University Erlangen-Nürnberg (FAU), and the Lal Bahadur Shastri Institute of Management. These principles, developed by Jeremy over decades of experience, helped him start the digital revolution at Walmart. We conducted this interview in April 2020, at the peak of panic and hysteria caused by the first COVID-19 lockdown in the US.

My Journey

I grew up in North Carolina, but I spent most of my life here in Silicon Valley. We moved here when I was quite young. My dad worked for IBM and my mom was an artist. I consider myself lucky that I was present during the time that the internet was evolving. At the time, I worked for a company called SynOptics communications, probably the only competition to Cisco at the time. At SynOptics, I discovered the World Wide Web and notionally got my MBA experience largely because I worked on the company wide SAP project for two years. It really helped me understand the inner workings of the business, not only from the system's standpoint, but finance – and how it becomes integrated with sales – manufacturing and planning. At the same time, I also met my long-term mentor, Maynard Webb, who was the CIO at that time. He and I remain friends to this day. I stayed with the company for a long time, maybe a little bit too long. Perhaps I should have jumped out a year or two earlier, while the internet was still booming.

For my next experience, I signed on as the first engineer and the fifth employee of a company called Petopia, an E-commerce, infrastructure, and internet company. In 1999-2000, we built the first version of Petopia from scratch with just a few engineers. We raised $126 million dollars, filed to go public, and instead went bankrupt. This was another MBA type of experience where you go through the entire process of taking a company public but end up having a fire and asset sale! We sold all our assets to Petco and I stayed on to transition the website.

Luckily, Maynard joined eBay and invited me over, which was a great experience for me. At the time, eBay was the number one website for E-commerce in the world, and Amazon was still going through its growing pains. You could argue that from a business model perspective, we (eBay) failed, but this was where I really learned how to scale. As head of the architecture team, I was managing about 3,000 people in the organization. We acquired and integrated a huge number of companies with eBay systems. These included PayPal, Skype, and a dozen smaller companies as well.

After seven years, my mentor, Maynard, and I left to go to another startup called LiveOps. I was really enamored with crowdsourcing. Everybody knows what it is now when talking about the gig economy, but back in those days, nobody had heard of it. I thought we were at the beginning of a really big trend, but it turned out we were too early. The trend is still risky for investors and they are still arguing about whether people in the gig economy should be classified as employees or contractors. LiveOps was an enterprise software company, so not only did I get to learn a little bit about enterprise software but also about how to keep systems up at five nines (that is, functional 99.999% of the time) and how to construct systems of that type of scale. We never actually reached five nines, but we got four and a half nines several times. Five nines is an incredibly hard thing to achieve at that scale.

Then I got this crazy call from Walmart. Fortune one! The biggest company in the world! I told the recruiter that if I got to talk with the CEO, I would take the interview because at that time nobody knew what was going on with Walmart. Walmart E-commerce didn't really exist then; they had ignored it for ten years. I luckily got in there and was able to create Walmart Labs. I spent the next eight years rebuilding Walmart's internet presence. I told myself that I'd be there for six months or five years depending on the level of commitment, but I stayed there for nearly eight years..

Since leaving Walmart, I have been at Pinterest. At Pinterest, our mission is to bring everyone the inspiration to create a life that they love. Now, more than ever, people are using it to get inspired every day. When people want to get off social media and figure out what they really want to do with their life, they go to Pinterest. We are big; we passed up Twitter and Snap this past year in the number of active users. More than 50% of our users are outside the U.S. and over 80% are on mobile. Our site is huge, with 240 billion pins, 5 billion boards, and 400+ million active monthly users. We just launched a couple of things that help make shopping easier. Personally, I use Pinterest almost every day. I do a lot of home automation work and I am building a wine cellar. We also want to make sure that people can use our site for a lot more things than just home renovation projects. We have recently launched the Today Tab and it's filled with categories like creating a great home office, working from home, learning yoga, and many more. A lot of people are new to those things and they're using Pinterest as their inspiration. We are a pretty well-known brand, standing at number 3, according to the 2018 Prophet Brand Relevance Index.

I recently penned down my thoughts about the things that I learned, about being at a start-up, then at the largest company in the world, and now being at Pinterest, again as a start-up. This chapter will be about lessons for CTOs on how to create a technology startup within your company, even if you are not a technology company.

The New Normal (or the Abnormal): In the context of COVID-19

We are living in a time of uncertainty. When you look at the charts, there is huge volatility across the board. You just have to look at the stock market to gauge how volatile it is. There are companies that are growing 20%-50%-100% while at the same time other businesses are failing. Amazon Web Services (AWS) and Microsoft Azure are having a hard time keeping up with the data center space. We live in an extremely abnormal time, and from an IT perspective, we would prefer to make things boring and have a lot more predictability. But right now, that is not happening with a lot of activity going on. You are seeing winners and losers across the board. Overall retail sales have dropped almost 9%, the biggest drop since the government started keeping track in 1992. But there are winners also. Health and personal care stores, groceries, and general merchandise stores fared well, growing sales by 4.3% and 6.4%. There are other categories that are seeing a huge drop. Clothing sales and home furniture are dropping massively across the board. When you look at companies like Uber, Lyft, or GM, you see that they are experiencing an incredible shrinking of the gig economy companies. Uber's global gross bookings are down 80% from a year ago. Lyft saw similar trends, with their business down 75% from last year's level. It is amazing how fast these companies are having to adjust, and you see Uber and Lyft changing their strategy to home deliveries instead of ride-sharing. When you read the news, the question is how long Uber, Lyft, and Airbnb can even survive in an environment like this. So they have to adjust dramatically and people working in these companies are moving frantically to transform their businesses. It took a pandemic, but Netflix has generated profit for the first time. They managed to increase their viewership and decided to stopped their own TV services and as a result, they are not spending as much money. But the question remains, will this help them survive long-term?

Pandemic's Impact on IT Budget: Students close to graduating may be getting nervous about the current environment. However, the tech job market is impacted by the IT budget and when you look at IT and engineering, in particular, a small majority of companies are saying they are not impacted, or they are actually increasing their budget. Thirty percent of the companies, including Pinterest and Google, are saying their impact on budget will be short-lived. Short-lived means they have slowed hiring, being more deliberate about the headcount of those they are bringing on. Companies are really investing in technologies that help people with an elastic workforce, a new term introduced to support work-from-home (WFH) needs, cloud migration, and digitally optimized workforce. While technology investment at many companies is increasing in IT and engineering, companies have slowed spending in other areas, like sales or marketing, because sales activity is very unpredictable right now. I don't see investments in the technology space really slowing down or slowdown, if any, will be relatively short-lived. The decreases, of course, are showing up in areas like travel, airlines, Uber, and Lyft. However, I think they will come back relatively quickly. In summary, the short-term priority for companies is to support WFH and create an elastic workforce. The mid-term priorities are migration to cloud, project slowdown, and digital optimization.

We did a survey and one of the questions we asked was "Are we able to support you when you are working from home?" Most people inside the company are feeling supported. However, the number one problem people are having is when they have small children. Two working parents and two small children can spell disaster. You have to invest in childcare, entertainment for your children, all the while having to juggle with work, reduced hours, or sabbatical in order to get through these difficult times.

How do we get out of this?

Ron sugar is a very well-known board member. Comparing the present moment to other turbulent periods in history, Sugar said, "I see the coronavirus unfolding as a three-act drama":

1. Triage: Every company is in triage right now. The primary focus throughout this should be on ensuring the health of employees and garnering as much liquidity as possible.

2. A period of transition: Transition will probably be on an 18-month cycle. The focus will be on how to get the workforce back safely, given the increased likelihood

of regulatory and plaintiff litigation. Of course, there are many companies that are unstable right now and there might be an increased number of acquisitions and mergers. We need to worry about prowling activists taking advantage of this kind of situation.

3. The new abnormal: When you look through history, every catastrophe was followed by a very long period of technological and social innovation. While it might be a little bit disconcerting right now, opportunities for engineering folks around the world to innovate out of this will be extremely high.

Seven Tips on How to Create a Corporate Startup

This section is inspired by the Wall Street Journal's story, "We Need to be a Technology Company: Wells Fargo Struggles with Aging Systems" and my work at Walmart.

Walmart is not a technology company; it is a retailer, but we also needed it to be a technology company. When I was there, the goal was to build a start-up technology company inside the world's largest company. In the end, every company is going to be a technology company. For those in IT, there are lots of opportunities across the board.

Tip # 1: The Environment

At Walmart, when I looked at the environment, even the basic capabilities of building a tech team weren't in place. Engineers were largely separated into different buildings and not engaged in the day-to-day business workings. They did not have the latest software; they had legacy laptops and computer systems. We never really had the capabilities that we all expect today, like Google Suite, Slack, or Zoom. All these things have to be built into the base before you can even start building an engineering post. Environment also includes feedback. The peer-to-peer environment has made the corporate world a lot more open to making sure that we are giving feedback regularly. Most corporations are on an annual cycle and that will need to change very dramatically.

Tip # 2: Culture

Once the environment is in place, you must start building the culture. Engineers don't want to work on a year-long or two-year-long product anymore. They really want to do integration and product management as well as move rapidly with iteration. We make sure we are using the right tools and sites, like GitHub, which are important in facilitating inner-sourcing. Another important aspect of a successful culture is encouraging a sense of collaboration. When I first started at Walmart, the culture was very territorial. If an engineer had gone through another engineer's code, found a mistake, and fixed it, the other engineer would often be unappreciative. This is not the type of culture that can foster innovation, so I had to change that mindset. At Pinterest, this aura of collaboration was already present. The employees at Pinterest are open to accepting help and advice. This culture of collaboration is something that you want to establish as early as possible in your company.

Tip # 3: Data Democracy

Access to data is really the key to it all. Too many companies do not have modern tooling and they don't train people to understand where the data is when they take them on board. At Pinterest, it is very common for someone to ask a question during a meeting. Right then, someone will flip open a laptop, run a query, and provide an answer immediately. Sixty-three percent of Pinterest employees, including HR, sales teams, and business ops, have access to our big data system and have run a query within the last sixty days. Therefore, it is important to have the data in the system available to anyone who needs it. I have always told people that they should learn SQL and Excel, even if you are in a business discipline because this access to data is extremely important, no matter what department you are in, be it HR, finance, or sales. Another essential element is openness. Many companies have not really done the work necessary to make the data available to their employee base. Oftentimes the data is hidden behind some rationale like: "This data is secured; you don't need to have access to it". There are a lot of well-known techniques for securing data in such a way that it remains safe for your company and yet allows employee access to it.

Tip # 4: Experimentation

Experimentation is about instrumenting your platform so that you can run a lot of A-B type tests. Companies like Airbnb and Booking.com are famous for this. Pinterest has a wonderful experimentation platform. I built this into the Walmart platform, and in retrospect, I have to admit it was extremely hard to do. At Walmart, we finally reached a point where we were able to run about 100 tests a month, while at Pinterest we are running 200-300 tests at a time. Building an experimentation engine is very important. It has to do with the instrumentation of your codebase from the very beginning and with how to segment users. If you want a good book on experimentation, read Experimentation Works, by Stefan H. Thomke.

Tip # 5: Risks

Your ability to take risks is dependent on the management structure of your business. It involves how you set up your corporate structure. The building blocks for taking risks are the things that I have already talked about: environment, culture, data, and experimentation, but it is also about how you set your organization up so that you have a small number of people in charge of decision-making. The number of people that you have in a meeting or in a situation requiring decision-making is inversely proportional to risk. If you only have two people who need to make a decision, it's easy to take a risk; but if you have 10 people involved, it's hard. Walmart did a number of things, not only building Walmart labs but also buying and integrating companies like Jet.com and Flipkart into the innovation engine. We also had an innovation team that focused on things that were more than three years out from the current platform, which we called Store #8. You should be looking for those inside your company or in future companies. Companies typically have research areas that continue to anticipate things that are more than three-plus years out. It's around a three-year cycle that you have to rebuild this innovation.

DRI is Apple's famous term that stands for Directly Responsible Individual. RACI (Responsible, Accountable, Consulted, Informed) is another well-known model for making decisions. It doesn't really matter which platform you use, but you should be setting these things up so that it is absolutely clear within a company who can actually make these decisions. That's the key part of the whole thing.

Tip # 6: Transparency

This is one of my favorites. When I was at Walmart, though I had ten thousand people working for me, in less than 30 seconds I could find out what any engineer in my company was working on. An employee would know a week before what she would be working on a week later. It was because we put instrumentation in. It was very important for me to understand where all the money was being spent before I would ask for another dollar from the organization. We had to set up teams properly, make sure we were budgeting, and integrating this in prioritization. Without this information, it is hard to prioritize and get a satisfactory outcome. At Pinterest, we have built our own tools internally, using a Google sheet. However, with now over 1,000 people, we are about to blow up Google Sheets and are considering new tools. We are looking at Jira and a number of other solutions.

Tip # 7: Hygiene

When I first joined Pinterest, we were talking about technical debt. Technical debt is essentially legacy platforms or systems that are no longer owned by an engineer, or things that are outdated and out of compliance. I was coming from Walmart, a 50-year-old company that was still running things on HP-UX, AIX, and main frames.

Then I came to Pinterest, which was 100% on AWS and in the cloud. But there still is tech debt inside of Pinterest. Part of the reason that tech debt happens is that you take your eye off the ball and you don't focus on hygiene. Twenty percent time is a well-known idea that comes from Google. Any engineer can take 20% of their time to innovate. My 20% time is hygiene time. If you are not spending at least 20% of your time ensuring that your environment is stable, current, secure, and performing properly, a year from now you will end up in a very bad place where you have to hugely invest in hygiene. The other thing I also tell CTOs is that you really have to reward and celebrate this work. Everybody loves things like shipping a new product to customers or some update to a data platform. With this type of work, the CTO should be the person who rewards and celebrates this kind of work so that it continues to occur.

Following are the responses from the Q & A session following the presentation.

How to get management to address tech debt? Especially in non-tech companies?

Non-technical companies have a hard time addressing technical debt. At Walmart, they were "milking the assets" that they had bought, in some cases, over ten years earlier. The best way to approach this is with data. From a hardware perspective, you can show that the total cost of ownership of a piece of hardware actually goes up after year three because you are consuming more power and more coolant than if you bought a new piece of hardware. On the software side, I usually bring it back to transparency where you are classifying the work that you are doing either as project work or "keep the lights on" work. Then you can show month by month, quarter by quarter, how much you are investing on what. Obviously, people want to invest more on the innovation side and less on the "keep the lights on" side. In our case, we were able to justify taking a pause, even on new application development for a month or a quarter, in order to get the technical debt down so the environment would improve. It is a challenge but it's a situation where you have to keep referring to the data.

How did you find your mentor? How do I find one?

My mentor, Maynard, and I are still pretty good friends. I figured out later, when I became a senior executive, that my mentees are the ones who can tell me what is going on in the company. As you grow up in the management chain, you lose touch with the day-to-day happenings like what teams are effective, what people think of management, and what people think of the hiring and the on-boarding process. I found that my relationship with my mentor stemmed from him relying on me. Even though he was the CIO and I was a hard worker and a project manager, he would come to me and ask me about a particular team and my thoughts about a particular problem. I was very open and honest with him, but never in a mean way. I wasn't pointing fingers or trying to get people fired; I just openly shared my views and pointed out issues I had encountered. I realized that I was naïve about what he was asking me. Oftentimes, he already knew the answer and I was just reinforcing it. I would not advise walking up to a leader in your company and saying, "Hey, will you be my mentor?". I would try to understand what their problems are and be a good source of information for them. And then you will find that a mentorship relationship will typically find its way into your dealings with each other. I don't think that Maynard and I ever formally made a mentor/mentee relationship. Currently, I have about six mentees in my company and we are a little bit more formal. There are six others that I grab lunch with from time to time, just to get their opinions on what is going on. In essence, know what you are doing, have an opinion, and don't complain about your boss.

What's the difference between somebody getting to your level and somebody just experiencing an average career? What does one do to better ensure success?

Part of the reason I was successful is because I became an "expert"; in my case, an expert in web platforms. At the time it was pretty low-tech stuff. I was doing Netscape Navigator and PERL, setting up our internet, and getting our internet environment stable. But in the process, I became the company's expert on the web. The people that I value and the people that I think accelerate through the company quickly are the ones who become experts in the XYZ system, a technology stack or an expert in an important part of the business. The folks that I see that are "doomed to be a senior manager/director for the rest of their lives" are people who jump into management too early. Very few people are the best leaders in the world and can lead any team of any size, even if they don't have the expertise. If you do a few years and then jump into management, my guess is that you will be a senior manager or a director for the rest of your life. Oftentimes you won't get to VP or executive level. I would encourage many of you to stay off the management track as long as possible. You can always learn later. Most people who have been individual contributors for a very long time also get great experience in understanding the differences between a good and a bad manager. So, technically, you are getting management experience and you can hold off for a very long time. You can always take on leadership roles later in your career.

What are your thoughts on outsourcing? Given the current environment, will more jobs be outsourced?

When I came into Walmart, I found a company that effectively outsourced nearly everything. Frankly, it was a disaster. I was able to change that perception. I would say: "You cannot outsource innovation". What I meant by that was you have to understand what's core to the business you need to insource and what is not core to the business you can outsource effectively. What I found on the Pinterest side was the exact opposite. One hundred percent of our team was made up of employees. It might have not seemed like it, but there were a lot of tasks that are not a priority for the company. Once you put something on maintenance mode, it becomes a pretty tedious job for an employee. These are just "keep the lights on" projects, and these are the things that you should outsource. Setting up operations with less than 30 percent outsourcing is a pretty good target to aim for as a company.

At Walmart in particular, we originally had the CTO and the CIO, the internal tools of the company, and the public facing tools of the company in the same organization. We built our own payroll system. You could argue that's absurd but at the time, there was nobody in the world who could handle a million paychecks a week, so we kind of had to build it. But that's not a core part of Walmart's business, why did we build our own payroll system and why did we continue to maintain it years later, as these you can technically outsource? However, if you are working for a company like ADP, or one of these payroll companies, this will be a core part of their business that is going to be insourced. So, it really depends on your perspective as to what's insourced and what is outsourced. It really is a question of perspective.

How do you know when it is time to leave a company?

If you look at my bio page, you'll see that I stay with companies for a long time. But generally speaking, I would suggest you not even start looking elsewhere until you have been with a company for three years. We used to say at eBay that if we got three years out of somebody, we should consider ourselves lucky. But today that's just absurd. Many of your peers who have graduated have gone out and started bouncing around between companies. I had someone come up to me and say that they have been with their company for two years. They like their job and the work that they do, but they want to diversify the companies that they work for. I view someone who bounces from job to job every two years as undesirable. I see them as a person I don't want to hire. Even after two years, you are just getting started. Frankly, you cannot really grow in your career until you get a good firm handle on how the whole company works, how the system works, and how you can become a good leader. Don't even think about leaving until you're at least three years in. The only exception to that is if you have a terrible manager or leader. If that situation lasts longer than 6 months, maybe you should simply exit. But just to be clear, most of the time when there is a leadership problem or a management problem within the company, the company is very well aware of it, and they're working on how they can affect a clean exit. If you jump after just a month or so, I would say you are making a mistake because the company is probably already working on it. I believe one of the reasons I reached the executive level is that I was willing to stay at companies longer than most.

Given the COVID-19 situation, what does the future hold for individuals looking for a career in IT?

I believe that the need for both engineers and IT professionals across the board will continue to remain very strong. The demand might come from different types of companies. A lot of people earlier on were joining the Airbnb and Ubers of the world, but now they might be joining bigger companies that have more cash on hand and are more stable. Many companies are scrambling to build out remote work capabilities. For those in the networking field, I would invest in understanding tooling and how it works. The sales cycle for tech products has shortened quite a bit because people don't want to spend a lot of time making decisions on things like a new VPN solution or what they will use for video conferencing. They go in, do an evaluation for a week or two, and then they write a purchase order. So you are actually seeing an acceleration of things like security software environments. We had to upgrade our VPN, hardware and everything, and we did it in two weeks. I do think there will be lots of places where there will be work available. I think over the next few months businesses will evaluate where they are, how much cash they are burning and how many customers they are keeping. In six months, it will shape up, but I remain optimistic about the IT sector.

When The Going Gets Tough

Vikram Takru

Co-founder & CEO of KloudGin

Written by Stefan Blos

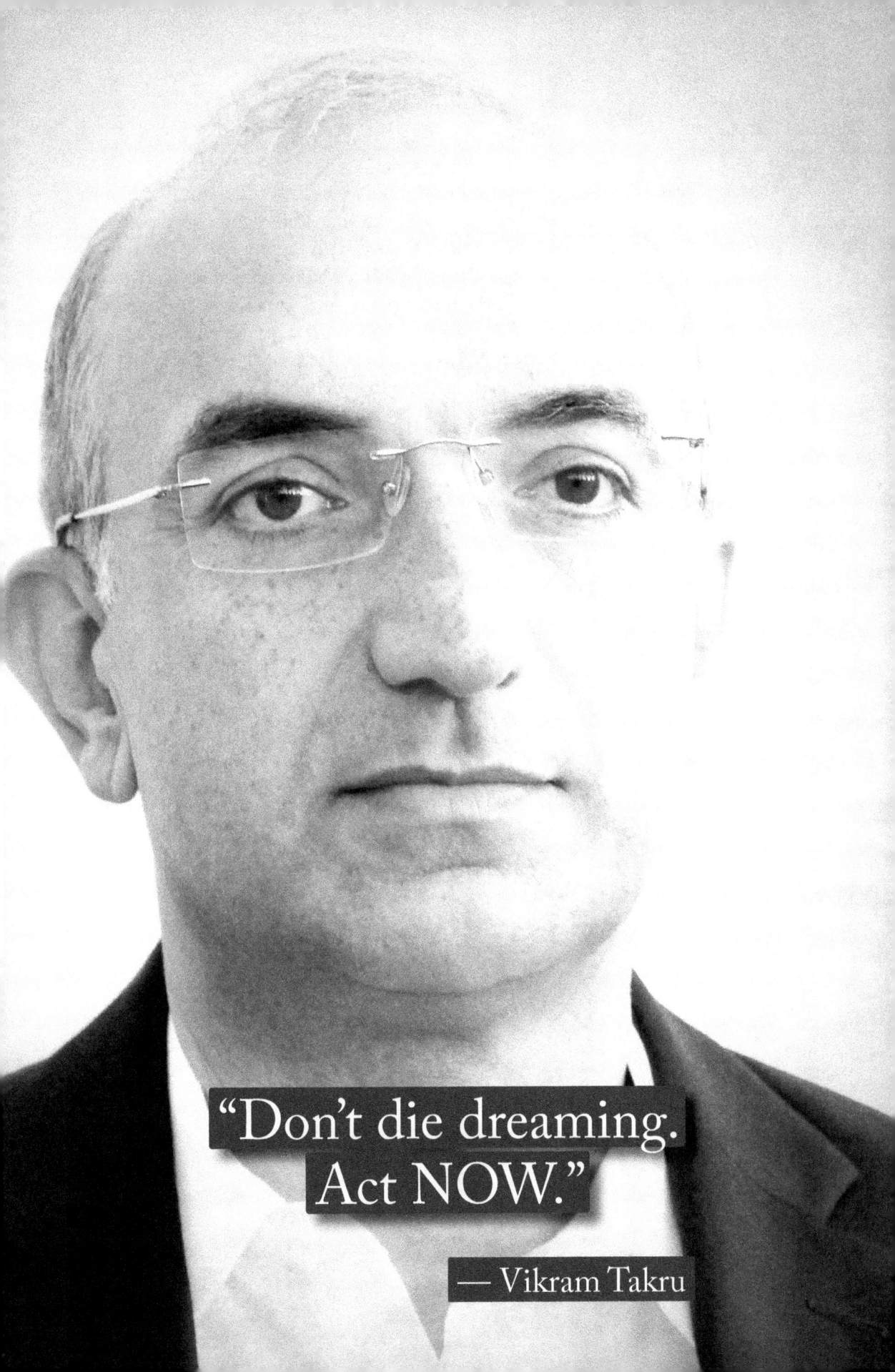

"Don't die dreaming.
Act NOW."

— Vikram Takru

Vikram Takru is a passionate entrepreneur and an industry thought leader with over twenty-seven years of Enterprise software experience and two successful exits. His latest venture, KloudGin, was founded with the mission of reinventing the customer experience and increasing operational efficiency by leveraging areas such as Big Data, Mobility, Machine Learning, Artificial Intelligence, Internet of Things, and the Cloud for large enterprises and SMB customers. The goal is to enable mobile workflows that apply to the unique needs of the industry and still remain simple and pleasant to use by non-tech-savvy users.

In this interview, Vikram talks about reinventing the customer experience and increasing operational efficiency by leveraging such areas as big data, mobility, machine learning, AI, IoT, and the cloud for large enterprises and SMB customers. Furthermore, he gives insight into his entrepreneurial journey that he faced during the downturn. He shares the obstacles and challenges he encountered and how he overcame them. He then shares the importance of channel partnerships for customer acquisition and business growth.

Can you tell us about your background? When did you know you wanted to do a startup?

I moved to the United States in 1991 and joined Oracle in 1996 where I later became the senior director of research and development (R&D). I was in charge of the department, building enterprise software, and by the time I left, twelve years later, earlier I was also a part of the IT Solutions consulting services department. Like many others, my focus was on becoming financially stable. I didn't care where I worked or what I worked on. Until my late thirties, I was building software day in and day out. I found myself putting very little thought into my work and was simply executing what was asked of me.

Then one day everything changed. I had an epiphany and realized that I did not want to wake up as a sixty-year-old man looking back on my life and regretting never having started my own business. Though I had no particular idea in my mind for my first start-up, I took a leap of faith. I like to call it the "escape velocity" because it was something that had been continuously building up until it finally propelled me to take the extreme step of starting my own company. It wasn't about money, although that was obviously an aspect to consider.

Can you take us through the process of founding your first company?

I had already been planning to leave Oracle and start my own company for some time. When leaving a company, it is important not to burn any bridges on your way out. It's just good business hygiene.

I left Oracle in late 2007, right before the 2008 recession hit. The recession not only affected people but even large companies were badly shaken by it. It affected the entire world. Suddenly the money just dried up. Consumers were too afraid to spend, and employees were being laid off in masses. Venture Capitalists were going out of business and no one knew where the recession was headed. I pondered about what I should do. I had two choices at the time; I could go to Oracle and ask for my job back or I could keep pushing forward. Considering that Oracle was laying off people as well, I basically had no choice but to keep pushing forward. Humans survive. When we are challenged, our basic instincts take over and we realize that we are capable of doing things that we never thought were possible.

The challenge that I had ahead of me was figuring out how to fund a start-up with no money, no market, and no customers. After observing the market, I realized that analytical information was a market that VCs were heavily funding. This type of information reports the health of a company, employee productivity, and what businesses are doing well. My partner and I decided to start a consulting firm collecting data on different companies and people. This seemed like the best route to go considering our main focus was making enough money to put food on the table. If we had started a company that produced a tangible product, we would not have been able to properly fund it and risked failing financially even before getting off the ground.

We wanted to assemble systems and deliver them in the best possible way. We were able to use some aspects of the recession to our advantage. The shattered economy reduced people's trust in established consulting firms, such as Deloitte and Accenture. Board members began to feel that these established firms weren't capable of effectively getting the job done, which gave us the opportunity to step forward and prove ourselves. In a normal situation, very few young and unproven companies would have been given high volume projects, but we were determined to approach them with a fresh outlook and an open mind.

How did you decide what kind of business you wanted to be in? Was it difficult?

We faced many ups and downs, but we learned one important lesson: focus on the "what". This is the hardest part. What are you going to build? What services can you provide? In everything we do as a company, we must know and fully understand the "what." The "how" is easy, because there are many tools and technologies available to help you deliver your products and services.

We knew that we had strength in Business Intelligence (BI) and analytics, so those became our primary focus. These tools helped us gather data, organize, analyze, and gain useful insights from multiple sources. Consumers were interested in this because they wanted us to give them the best practice needed to solve their problems. Since we were already familiar with the Oracle toolset, we decided that this would be our method.

What other challenges did you face after figuring out the "what"?

Getting your foot in the door and making money was one of the most challenging aspects. Why should somebody trust you? Why would they buy your product? This is especially true in the entrepreneurial world. Free is not an option; I don't believe in free. The other party must see the value of what you have to offer.

The question for me, as an R&D guy, was how to find customers. When we realized we didn't have the money to hire salespeople to build up our brand, we understood the power and value of network channels. We used Oracle BI software to narrow our focus in conducting analytical information services. This made Oracle one of our channels. We followed the Oracle sales team and helped their customers set up the Oracle systems, and provide them consulting services. Building accelerators added value to the sales process and helped us sell globally to large clients. One of our biggest customers at the time was General Electric. We started in their oil and gas division and eventually moved on to their aircraft and appliance divisions.

It's difficult getting your foot in the door but once people know what you can bring to the table, it opens up new channels. We focused on providing flawless customer service while at the same time trying not to make huge mistakes along the way.

When you enter a new market as a new player how do you convince customers that you can provide better solutions than those of established competitors?

Our strategy was to look for the companies that were losing deals because we figured that they'd be desperate to try a new player in the game. The goal was to have them try our product, love it, and tell others about how it helped them meet their quote and sell more. This provides marketing via word of mouth. Once you have six established clients, your network will have grown tremendously, since those six clients can convince many more potential clients to look into your company and give you a chance.

You scaled your first company to five hundred employees. How hard was it to keep a constant flow of projects in order to be able to afford their payrolls?

This was very difficult. Many of the people on our team had left large companies to work for us and they trusted us to put food on the table for their families. Every leader needs to take this trust very seriously. The strategy was not to be too reliant on large projects but to diversify our portfolio into different sectors and types of customers.

How do you build a great team? What characteristics are you looking for in employees?

Hire for attitude, not for skills. I hired some extremely talented and smart people, with high IQs, and I hired a lot of my friends. When I put some of them in a collaborative environment they didn't work well together. This is the time when you must make quick, sometimes difficult, decisions regarding hiring and firing. I had to fire some of my good friends, but thankfully, they still remain my friends. They knew, at the time, that I couldn't risk the future of my company, since it wasn't only about me but about all the employees, partners, and customers as well. You need to view yourself as a trainer and a mentor, realizing that if people are not working out the way you had hoped, then you have to let them go. Someone can sound great during an interview but may not meet your standards during the job. This is where the filtering aspect from your channels is extremely important. It's hard to find and hire talented people, especially here in Silicon Valley, and your trusted network is an invaluable resource.

The ability to adapt is also crucial. Considering that in a start-up things can change very rapidly. There will be chaos and there will be problems and you need people who can thrive in this environment. There are people who joined from VP roles at Oracle and Salesforce because they didn't want to wear the same hat day-in and day-out. They wanted a chance to play lots of different roles. Those are the people you need to find.

What happens when a mistake is made? How do you get past it?

Companies make mistakes all the time and sometimes they can be fatal. Most of those mistakes happen because someone ignored the red flags and didn't want to make the necessary corrections. Accepting that a mistake was made is one of the first steps in learning. After that comes brainstorming, seeking answers regarding how that problem might be resolved or could have been avoided in the first place. For example, when we first branched out into Delaware, we had mistakenly disbursed the wrong amount of stock to our employees. Unfortunately, this problem cost us around two hundred thousand dollars to fix. It was a tough hit to take, but of course, it was a necessary one in order to do right by our employees and the government.

How did the process of selling your first startup go?

I don't think anyone should build a company intending to eventually sell it. You'll be distracted and constantly looking for more investors or exits in your company. Focus on building the company, your employees, partners, and customers. Most of all, focus on building trust.

We were never planning to sell our business, nor was there any reason for us to sell. We were growing at a phenomenal rate and we were generating cash. We had just released our second product, which was going well, and then Oracle approached us. They realized that, after buying Oracle products, their customers were still coming to us, wanting us to provide them with the solutions they sought. The timing was perfect. We realized Oracle was the only one who could potentially buy us, mainly because we had made the mistake of building our entire operation on the Oracle stack and we relied heavily on them. That's when we decided to take the money and run toward investing in the next chapter of our lives.

What do you consider a successful exit?

A successful exit means different things to different people. There are multiple facets to it. First, you need to get enough money out of the sale to ensure that you and your family are adequately taken care of. Second, you need to make sure that all your employees are also taken care of. They offered their work, their knowledge, their time, and their expertise to give you the help you needed. Finally, you must be comfortable with the fact that you are not the one responsible anymore. You sold the company and by doing so you lost control over it. Someone else is now playing your game, and whatever happens next is not your problem.

How did you come up with the idea for your second company?

We were proud to have survived the 2008 recession and money started flowing from the first start-up in 2009. We decided to go back to the business we were previously in. We talked to a lot of customers and paid attention to their needs. This led us to build a pre-packaged analytical product called "Asset, Planning & Manufacturing analytics". It was able to analyze failure frequencies, mean time to repair, overall equipment effectiveness, and other related metrics. It also conducted financial analytics and provided a surface where all Key-Performance-Indicators (KPIs), and other finance and procurement-related information, were made available. We focused on the core business functions such as discrete manufacturing, process manufacturing, high-tech manufacturing, planning, and asset analytics. All of these were very closely tied to Oracle products. This meant that in order to use their tools we had to sell our product alongside theirs. This meant that we not only had to sell the products wherever Oracle went but that they also dictated pricing terms. Since we had just started building, we had no other option.

Another thing we took into consideration was the iPhone and the potential changes it was bringing about. We knew that when a mobile platform was released everyone in the world was going to change the way they viewed content. We decided to stop working on products that were tied to Oracle and build something completely different, and that idea became more and more clear. We built a product team and created a separate product company that created an array of products around these ideas. We started with building a ground-up cloud-first and mobile-first platform built for non-tech savvy field workers, as we saw all enterprise platforms were too complex and did not focus on 400m+ field workers who do complex mission-critical work.

Besides having a channel with Oracle, who else have you built network channels with?

I constantly try to find channels for complimentary products, such as KloudGin, which is completely in the cloud. Our entire code revolves around service contracts, field service and asset management, supply chain management, and similar areas.

We knew that Sage Intacct was a big financial accounting firm and that they were experiencing problems, one of the main ones being that they were competing against the Acumatica from Microsoft and other companies like SAP. Sage Intacct only utilized their accounting software, so competing against the big players all over the world was proving to be a struggle. We partnered with them and it was a win-win situation. They had the incentive and the success in closing deals on their own; they just needed our help providing the extra services that customers wanted. This was a great opportunity as there was mutual interest in growing and maintaining a network channel.

Did you ever consider going back to the corporate world?

There were moments when I thought: "Why am I doing this to myself?", especially with the financial crises going on. What kept me going was the escape velocity I had built up over the years. If I ever do have to go back to a larger corporation I would be very valuable to them because I have learned so much during my time as an entrepreneur.

There are many people who talk about building a start-up, but only a small percentage actually follows through with it. The ones who do go for it have their minds already wired toward doing that, so for them going back is not an option. It's a different world, one with its own set of problems and challenges.

You have acquired an array of skills and knowledge from your first two startups. Do you think you have perfected the method of founding a new company?

Every time you start a new company you think you have it all figured out. You do not! You are starting from ground zero every time you build a new start-up. One advantage you do have is that you will be more mature and will have gained additional skills and knowledge from your previous experiences.

It will be important to learn about new markets and establish new network channels. We weren't happy with having Oracle as our sole channel, so now we have dozens of channels. We have made new connections with our launches in Australia, South Africa, and the U.K. Oracle is still buying from us, but we are replacing them and their products with our own. Companies with big dimensions will always have problems that can be solved by smaller, nimbler competitors. That is what we have figured out and that's what we're counting on.

Trust is another key factor in building a start-up. If you create value, you will earn trust. This also proves true when it comes to your employees. You need to build a team of individuals who have varying strengths and skills. You may have friends, a co-founder, and so on, but the human dynamics in the start-up world are very complex. It's extremely important to know that the people you're bringing on board will work well with each other. Drive and mutual trust will lead to a successful company.

You recently started a third startup. Can you tell us a bit more about that?

For the third startup, we're building an enterprise SaaS (System-as-a-Service) space. It is aimed at providing a whole cloud platform for business processes around assets, customers, crews, and subcontractors. It builds an array of applications ranging from Field Service and Asset Management that allows it to compete with IBM, Oracle, and Salesforce.

We recently took our first round. While it was not a seed round, it was still a series A. We haven't announced it yet, but our VCs asked us when we were planning to do so, as well as asking us for a forecast. This is a typical thing for companies to do after raising money for a business. I told them that I didn't have a date and that we would wait until we felt the time was right.

We already have top multinational customers buying from us. I look at the amount of money coming in and that determines how many people we can hire every year. That's how we scale and, while it might be somewhat unorthodox, this is our method and we found the right partners who agree with us. This partnership allowed us to raise money when we didn't need it because we were profitable from day one. This is something that is really unheard of in the SaaS space, but we made it happen. We wanted to make sure we could grow comfortably while being profitable.

You said you found the right partners to work with. How did you decide who to accept investments from?

There are two kinds of VCs. In one group there are investment bankers who sit on the money they get from somewhere else. The other kind is those who have been founders or technology business leaders themselves. They have walked in our shoes, worked on their own companies, and know the dynamics of building a company. They are valuable to have as part of the start-up journey and they mostly risk their own money. They know what it means to invest ten million dollars in a company and the problems that will arise from scaling up. These are the kinds of investors I'm looking for and who I believe are the most helpful in building a company.

What are some typical questions you get from investors?

I can't say much about this topic because we didn't get a lot of questions from our investors. Their main concern was whether we would sell the company for two hundred million dollars instead of the four billion dollars they were hoping for. If the investors are savvy and experienced, they will know that there will, inevitably, be a lot of ups and downs. What you end up with will be different from what you had on Day One. When you tell an investor you know exactly where your journey is going, you are lying to them. All we could really tell them was that we were still at an early stage and we already have dozens of customers. Giving them some totally glowing outlook and prediction would be lying.

What would you recommend to young people who have just started their careers about how to approach entrepreneurship?

This will have a profound impact on your family. When I wanted to leave Oracle, I had a meeting with my wife and my daughter, and I told them that I wanted to take two years for myself to build a start-up. I explained to them that this meant I would not be as available to them, but I would be doing something I really wanted to do and that it would benefit our family in the long run.

If you ask my wife today, she will tell you, "Why the heck did I say yes? I had no idea what that really meant!" There were times when I would walk into the room and they would say something to me, but leaving the room I had no idea what they had said because I was completely zoned out. Once you start building you will need to focus all your efforts on leading your company to success, and that is what I was doing.

It is very easy to build a start-up when you're young because you don't have a lot of dependents. If you fail you can go back to your parents' home and continue on with your life. But at the same time, you have not experienced how the world operates and haven't seen the big picture, the long view yet. Don't try to build a start-up alone; you need a co-founder. Building a start-up is a very lonely process and when you have problems to figure out, you will want to have someone to help you who's equally invested. That person should be the complete opposite of you. One person might be all about sales and marketing while the other one is focused on operations and financing. Even when you have others working with the start-up, it's important for you to know every piece and process that exists in your company.

You have to be open-minded and constantly learning new skills outside of your comfort zone. I'm an R&D guy and didn't know anything about sales and marketing when I built my first start-up, so I had to learn. Although it was hard at the time, it is necessary if you want to expand your business, and it was also an invaluable experience in my life.

I know that there is no one answer to how you approach entrepreneurship but do remember that balance is extremely important. This is what I tell my daughter: If you are young and have thought of creating a start-up, you should begin your career with a small company. By that, I mean a really small one. You will get the training you need to build a successful start-up, and after three or four years you will have acquired the tools necessary to be able to start your own company. That is what is most valuable about this plan. It's working for me and it can work for you.

Entrepreneurial Excellence in Germany

Bernhard Beck

Founder of BELECTRIC

Written by Ákos Balász, Nitin Agarwal and Michael Fischer

"Even if your plan seems a bit crazy at first, you can make it happen, providing if it's physically possible and you work hard enough."

— Bernhard Beck

Bernhard Beck is a pioneer in the solar industry. In 2002, Bernhard and his colleagues started installing large scale PV module arrays, with new thin-film technology and created a whole new industry now known as utility scale solar power plants. His vision of large-scale photovoltaic (PV) power plants advanced solar technology from the most expensive energy source to a price point competitive with fossil power generation. He is the founder of Beck Energy, which later grew into BELECTRIC company group, the world´s largest solar EPC company in 2010 and 2011. Nearly 2 gigawatts of solar power have been installed worldwide, reducing over one million tons of CO_2 annually. Over the last two decades, Bernhard has developed over a hundred patents for applications in the energy business, now being used by international companies on a daily basis.

I n this interview, Bernhard explains how he, though only a college student at the time, convinced established scientists and the German government to support his new systems design approach, guiding the industry to higher efficiency and lower cost solar electricity. He describes what it takes to succeed as an entrepreneur, to create a new industry and how to build a team able to tackle the coming challenges. Bernhard, through hoch.rein Group and BOB-Holding, has been investing in new cutting-edge technologies such as electrohydraulic fragmentation and organic PV, which have the potential for establishing new industries. We asked him about these startups and what it would take to create a Silicon Valley-like environment in Germany.

What influenced you to become involved in the technology field and to pursue it as a career?

I come from a family of farmers. Today, farming is heavily dependent on technologies like modern tractors, GPS systems, autonomous vehicles, and many other emerging technologies. Growing up in this kind of an environment, and having a natural interest in science, I started working with analog machine-controlling circuits and electronics. Thereafter, I moved to software development and IT while gaining my German university entrance exam.

While I have never had much interest in school, I was always interested in technology. I was better at learning technology, hands-on, rather than from hearing a lecture at school. I started my studies at the Technische Universität Ilmenau – one of the best tech universities in Europe at the time. I studied media technology, which is a combination of electrical engineering, IT, and economics. During that time, I was reading a lot about renewable energy and was fascinated by the harvesting of energy from nature, just like farming,

What influenced you to focus your interest in technology to solar energy?

My very first contact with solar was in my sophomore year of high school when one of my teachers brought in a solar panel. By getting the chance to physically work on the solar panel I was able to grasp a basic understanding of it which then lead to a greater interest in solar technology and how emission-free clean energy works. So when I got to university,

I was already interested in renewables. I took an elective course with Dr. Bergman, who was running a small NGO promoting renewables in Thuringia. He showed us a small village with 1kW solar installations on every rooftop and we learned about his great vision for a 1MW solar power plant.

The following year, I looked into all kinds of renewable technologies such as wind, solar, biomass, and hydro. Comparing the complexity of each of these renewable sources, I came to the conclusion that solar energy would be the best answer to climate change if the cost of production could be lowered. At that time, the generation cost of solar energy was about 50 cents per kWh, which was extremely high, especially compared to nuclear energy or coal. This was the reason that solar represented just a fraction of a percent of the global energy industry. Nevertheless, it was a very simple technology to use. The sun hits the panel and you have an inverter that converts the DC power into grid-compliant AC power. You now have CO_2 emission-free energy. The next step was to bring the cost down and I challenged myself to find ways to do so. I was a student without any experience in building solar systems, but I was good at physics, so I started doing analysis and calculations.

Solar systems back then were extremely inefficient. The performance ratio – the actual energy output vs the theoretical output – at the time averaged 60-70%. That's low compared to today, where you see ratios easily over 80%. I started calling German weather authorities, asking them for high-resolution irradiation data to gain meteorological information. I started programming a physical performance calculation tool to find out how to improve the ratios. My calculations showed that with modifications of system design, adapting PV panels and inverters together correctly, combined with efficiency improvement of inverters, you could achieve more than 80% performance ratio. With the support of the German government, I decided to set up and run a large-scale demo to showcase the usability of my new concept. The government had created a program subsidizing pilot projects for demonstrating enhanced environmental technologies. I applied to the Federal Ministry for Environment, Nature Conservation, and Nuclear Safety, explaining my plan to increase the performance ratio to 80% and my interest in building a pilot project for Germany´s largest privately-owned solar power plant. Many people told me I was wasting my time, but fortunately, I was able to prove them wrong. I was probably the first person focusing on the PV system's efficiency from a holistic point of view, rather than looking at individual components of a solar plant. After I had explained myself, I received a confirmation letter from the Environment Ministry, the Minister of Environment himself confirming, that I would receive the requested subsidy, allowing us to build our very first high-efficiency demonstration system on my parents' farm.

Once I got the approval, I went to SMA Solar Technology, to convince them to get a new type of inverter that would match my design. I was there with a senior expert engineer who was responsible for inverter development, and I told him their current product specification didn't work efficiently with the latest PV panels and explained how inverters could be made more efficient. While we were in the midst of our conversation, Guenther Cramer, the co-founder of SMA, came by. He listened for a while and then asked just the right question: "Let's say in theory that we are able to build the inverters as you specified; what order volume are we talking about?" I told him we needed 37 inverters with 3kW AC power. Surprisingly, this order volume was already large enough to start a new product line at SMA, so we ended the negotiation process and got straight down to business.

The new addition of inverters was not the only thing that made this project stand out. We also programmed and implemented an online-access, real-time monitoring system for all inverters, with a webcam for checking weather conditions as well. This was likely the world's first online solar monitoring solution with seconds-based live data. We were able to stream all this data and footage, thanks to a direct satellite uplink, making us among the very few people in Europe with this capability.

Did you start BELECTRIC right after your pilot project's success?

Once the pilot was over; I went back to finish my studies at university. However, I was still approached by people because they were either interested in the technology or because they needed technical support. I had to balance between academia and work, making my day-to-day life very complex. That's when I met my business partner – Thomas Neußner. We identified the need for utility scale solar plants to enable low cost solar energy generation. This sounded absurd at the time, considering that the cost of solar power generation was 10 times more than both fossil and nuclear power. We discussed what it would take to make it happen. We figured it will take big ground-based solar power plants to achieve economies of scale, it should be energy-efficient and much simpler to build. We started from scratch. Our thought was to design the full system, using state-of-the-art technology to build it. We tried to answer the question of how to lower the cost. We identified that the key influencers were the raw materials incorporated in the system design as well as the efficiency of the full system. This pointed us toward thin-film technology with approximately 5% module efficiency. Even though the technology had much lower space efficiency than silicon wafer-based modules, it was offset by savings in expensive semiconductor raw materials. We decided to use cadmium-telluride as the energy converter in our solar modules.

After we had a detailed engineering plan for what to build, I told Thomas we should start a company together – a classic start-up. Understandably he was not a big fan of the idea, considering we were planning to disrupt a market that was controlled by big players like Shell, Siemens, RWE, and other large utilities. We were trying to sell a system that had never been built before now and we needed customers to finance this long-term without any proof of concept. Not very promising! When you have a new technology, it is difficult to find customers willing to pay for it on a very large scale. Thomas told me if I could find a customer, willing to take the risk related to a very first implementation of our new system, he'd agree to the start-up. At this point in his life, Thomas had sold his former business and owned a large stake in a utility company; he could have enjoyed a secure and comfortable, private life. For him, jointly developing a new energy technology with me was more of a hobby. He was pretty sure the startup would never happen. Within a few days, I had found a customer who was willing to bet his money that we could build the largest thin-film solar power plant in Europe. I worked hard on this, and as soon as I got the signature on the contract, I went to Thomas and told him that we could start Beck Energy tomorrow because now we had to deliver to our customer. He was a bit uneasy at first but was soon fully on board.

What challenges did you encounter in those early days?

The early days were a period of both opportunities and challenges, ups, and downs. The day we mounted our first solar panel, our supplier, Antec Solar, went bankrupt. Luckily, we had already received deliveries of solar panels for our first project and were able to keep our commitment to our customers. We did have intentions to subcontract the mounting steps but soon realized that no subcontractor could build what we had designed. This forced us to invent 3-D pile driving, now broadly used throughout the industry. We invented the wiring harness solution, tools to mount panels, and simple components like module clips. Many of today's standard products in the solar industry were developed in the early days of Beck Energy and many new technologies were introduced by us. Being the first customer of First Solar, we made it possible to establish thin film photovoltaic (PV) modules in the global energy sector and significantly lower the price of solar power generation.

We certainly never intended to be out in the field building these plants ourselves. We only wanted to design and sell them. Once we actually got down to construction I was on the phone for days, trying to find someone able to drive piles into the ground and fulfill our specific needs. We had already created and produced our steel works with circle-shaped holes, allowing no tolerance between parts and components, but with the intention to enable fast mounting. We were under the impression that it would be no problem to drive something into the ground with a couple of millimeters of tolerance. It turned out that the best offer I had at that time was a 15cm tolerance level.

The customer was getting nervous, seeing that even though the material was there, no assembly work had been done. We had to tell them that the machine needed to build this plant has not been invented yet. We were left with no other choice but to invent it ourselves and we didn't have much time. We spent many days and nights in a workshop, designing and welding a machine that could match the required tolerance level. We had no idea how the end-product would look; we just knew what our metrics were, and we created it based on those. That's how we ended up creating the first 3-D ramming machine, which worked very well and supported us in many follow-up projects.

The next challenge was constructing a much larger solar power plant in autumn with very bad weather conditions. We had to make measurements within a millimeter's accuracy, all the while standing with our feet sunk deep in mud. Back then, GPS had an accuracy of half a meter or so, best case 10cm. Not even close. At first, we just measured manually. We were only able to put down 5 piles a day, provided that we worked from six in the morning to ten at night. That was a perfect example of a difficult time when you have no option other than to just push on through, and we did just that. Finally, through a number of successes and occasional failures, we were eventually able to put down twenty piles a day. At that point, we embarked to construct our first 1 MW site and made this the future footprint for large scale solar power generation.

What prompted you to start a solar business?

The motivation came from seeing my parents work on the farm. Running a farm means that you are self-employed, but your profits are heavily dependent on weather conditions and your cost structure in technology. You can't have much profit if you just grow and sell crops. You must constantly innovate your procedures and technologies if you want to make profit. For example, my father was also providing services with special machines for forestry and winegrowers. I had modified some of these machines in my teenage years, trying to optimize functionality and provide a unique service to our customers. Growing up in this environment, I formed the mindset of: "If you aim for something and are willing to fight hard for it, there's a chance you will make it happen; but without a clear aim and focus you will eventually become lost." It's not much different than innovating renewable power generation.

Even if your plan seems a bit crazy at first, you can make it happen, provided it is physically possible and you work hard enough. I was always driven by the goals that I wanted to achieve; both in my personal and professional life. In business, you will encounter failures along the way, but at some point, you will achieve your goals. Just look at people like Elon Musk. He knows what he wants and he goes after it. This is the entrepreneurial spirit that makes the difference between success and failure. You have to have that fire burning inside you. I've always wanted to make a positive change in the world and looking back today, I am very proud that I've been a part of the global solar revolution, fighting against global warming for two decades now.

Of course, it is easier to take risks when you are younger and you don't have a family to take care of. I was running Beck Energy and attending university at the same time for more than a year. I reached a point where I had to decide to do either one thing or the other. Staying up with my courses was becoming more of a challenge because work was taking up too much of my time. And I could not focus on work properly because I wanted to study. I finally chose to drop out of university. Many entrepreneurs face the challenge of deciding to leave university and are successful without a professional qualification. Such a decision can only be made if both your heart and mind are calibrated toward an entrepreneurial instinct. Sometimes I wish I had graduated university, but today I am sure I made the right decision.

What was the biggest enabler of BELECTRIC and Beck Energy?

It's all about timing. Every technology, every idea has a timing element. Many people believe that creating a great product or innovation is the key, but in reality, you also have to time your innovation appropriately. If you innovate too late, you're out of the game. If you innovate too early you won't be able to move it into the market and your competition will have time to adapt. You need to have both the innovation and the patience.

Whether or not you have a great innovation doesn't matter as long as your timing is correct. Timing and customer access are what make or break businesses. When we started BELECTRIC it was the right time: we had the right innovation, a committed team, and the product that everyone wanted. We never raised money; our growth was purely organic; we did it ourselves; what we invested and what we earned was ours to keep.

One of the keys to success is building the right team. How did you build your team, and how did it influence your business model?

Thomas, my first business partner, was the first visitor I had when I was building the pilot project at my parents' farm. With his background in the utility business, we had a profound discussion about the energy sector and this eventually led us into a long-term partnership. Separately, Daniel Ziegler, a financial wizard with a tax advisory background, and Wolfgang Sarré started a solar company with a focus on financials. They noticed that people were investing in solar and it was producing significant cash-flow. When the cash-flow is larger than the depreciation, you have a profitable investment. For solar, two decades ago, this was a very new way of thinking. We teamed up and leveraged our strengths into a real business. When we started, we were not friends in the traditional sense, but we had absolute trust in each other as business partners and working as a team. Everyone brought a different perspective and a different way of looking at issues and challenges which was very important in order to succeed as a company. Our company culture was built throughout this culture of discussion.

One of the fascinating technologies you are currently working on is electro-hydraulic fragmentation. Impulstec as well MAB Recycling uses this tech to recycle electronics and Li-ion batteries. Could you tell us about this technology?

Our startup Impulstec, following a decade of research, developed and introduced the electrohydraulic fragmentation technology in the market which enables us to achieve almost complete battery recycling. With this technology we can efficiently harvest the active materials of the cell. We successfully tested it with one of the battery suppliers to recycle the production line waste. The end result of our recycling process was that we returned the waste right back into the production – reaching nearly a 95 percent round cycle. In my opinion, the key to low-cost battery recycling and great utilization of the harvested material is the ability to round cycle the active material of the cells. I am pleased to support the most advanced recycling technology, avoiding the use of acid and chemicals. We just use water and electricity. Our process is green and completely technology-based, sparking implementation interest in various industries around the world

During the years you invested in multiple technologies, what was the most interesting one?

BELECTRIC was known as the thin-film company. When we started I decided to use advanced thin-film technology to power our solar power plants. We wanted to make sure our solar power plants were net energy positive. Following this path of thin-film solar technologies, I was fascinated by organic photovoltaics – OPV – as it is plastic-based and it consumes far less energy to produce than any other power generating technology on earth.

In 2012, we managed to acquire a bankrupt solar energy company, Konarka Technologies. My partner, Thomas, noticed that their OPV technology was primarily developed in their German subsidiary in Nuremberg, Germany, which was near our headquarters. He called me and we made an extremely quick decision and ended up with a solar energy technology that was later awarded a Noble Prize.

One of the arguments against OPV is its lower efficiency. How do you counter this weakness?

I don't think the efficiency matters, nor is it necessarily a weakness. It can also be a strength to operate with low efficiency but with extreme low light capability. The OPV technology is simply misunderstood by most people. These OPV cells can produce some electricity even if you place them under a table inside a meeting room. They don't need to face the light source directly. Regardless of their location, if there is any illumination at all the electrons will begin moving. A silicon solar cell would never be able to provide electricity in an indoor environment, especially not beneath a table. It is not a question of peak efficiency, but more a question of enabling various new applications.

All our devices and products in daily use are more and more affected by Internet of Things (IoT) technologies. But IoT devices are limited in reality. Microchips are great and they are gradually expanding but their expansion is limited because of their need for an electrical power supply. The only reason that not every item has a microchip is because of their need for a power source. But let's look at it through the lens of this new OPV technology. Think of a glass of beer, for example. You place an OPV sticker on the bottom of the glass. You could also have a printed temperature sensor and a circuit microchip for wireless radio transmission on it. This would signal a bartender when your beer is getting warm. He would use this information to bring you a new cold beer, and you would gladly pay for it, simply because it tastes better cold. Doing this would result in a better customer experience and result in higher bar revenue. A simple thing like a sticker under a glass could turn the glass into an IoT device and would optimize the whole business of how your drinks are best served in a restaurant.

OPV isn't just a product. It is an enabler of new kinds of businesses. As this logic was pretty obvious, we called the company OPVious. There are hundreds of applications that are simply not possible without OPV and many more to be invented. Just a decade ago the lithium ion battery enabled the broad use of smartphones and gave us our first step toward mobile use of microchips, software, and communication. However, we lose this mobility daily because we need to charge the battery and head back to the charging cable. OPV technology will unlock the microchip to the free world – without cable or charging – and enable future technologies and business models.

Are there any breakthrough startups that you are currently working on?

Since the last decade, I have been working on a data and software-driven technology, called Gridbotics, which significantly increases the power line capacity of the grid. It is a very disruptive technology and the first real grid innovation since Nikola Tesla. With our technology, many more renewables and electric cars can connect to the same grid at the same time without limiting their power injection or demand. Simultaneously we are able to improve power quality and power line capacity. With this new technology, Gridbotics can drastically reduce the need for new power lines, thereby solving the global problem of grid integration in the energy transition.

The current smart grid technologies and solutions do not increase the grid capacity, but instead, they allow managing a capacity limited grid. Gridbotics taps into the physical network capacity and enables an improved interaction between supply and demand. We digitalize the grid edge to enable a new and better method of software-based grid management. Our developed advanced algorithms will make the difference in grid management of the future.

**You were one of the key people in making this wonderful event and collabora-
tion between SJSU and FAU happen. How did Silicon Valley influence you and
why are events like this important?**

When I was younger, my first trip outside of Europe was to Silicon Valley. I was absolutely fascinated by it, trying to absorb the culture and the technological environment as
much as I could. Coming from a conservative German environment, experiencing Silicon
Valley and seeing what is going on there, was definitely an eye-opener. This was one of the
best experiences that pushed me toward becoming an entrepreneur and I wanted to share
that experience with the students from FAU.

In Germany, you typically complete your formal education, start working for a large
company and end up toiling in an office every day Monday through Friday for the rest of
your life. That's a different model from the Valley's "fight-for-success model". This obviously aggressive way forward offers people a wider variety of opportunities. Anybody can
be successful if they don't stop after their first setback. I've had many failures throughout
my career. The question is whether you stand up again and you have more successes than
failures. That's what gets you to the positive side of life. Sometimes failures create an expensive learning curve, but any kind of failure offers some gain in knowledge. It helps you
become both agile and efficient by not wasting time with hesitation. This is what sharpens
your business acumen over time.

There are a lot of opportunities for business and technology start-ups in Germany,
but the mentality of most people is not the same as you find in Silicon Valley. I have
a lot of dear friends in the Valley, and I know it's not all riches and gold; it's a very tough
environment.

In the Valley, the way you deal with setbacks is different than in Germany. Here, we
tend to make fewer mistakes, but we end up moving deliberately carefully and end up
becoming slowly less creative and innovative. It's the mindset of Silicon Valley that drives
entrepreneurship and spurs people on to take more risks in order to achieve success. There's
no energy wasted on frustration when something doesn't turn out exactly as you expected.
Just because someone tells you it can't be done doesn't necessarily mean it's true.

Many entrepreneurs have managed to realize the impossible dream and a lot of them
are from Silicon Valley. We need to inspire young people to take on the challenge and
create better and more innovative technology. That's the epicenter of this, FAU-SJSU, program. We are trying to help these students overcome this sometimes overly careful, even

stodgy German mindset. This is what both FAU President Joachim Hornegger and I had in mind, and it became the central focus of this program. We are doing everything we can to make sure we get students over there to breathe Silicon Valley air, to trigger them to learn how best to gain further knowledge, and to mobilize them to achieve an exciting and successful entrepreneurship.

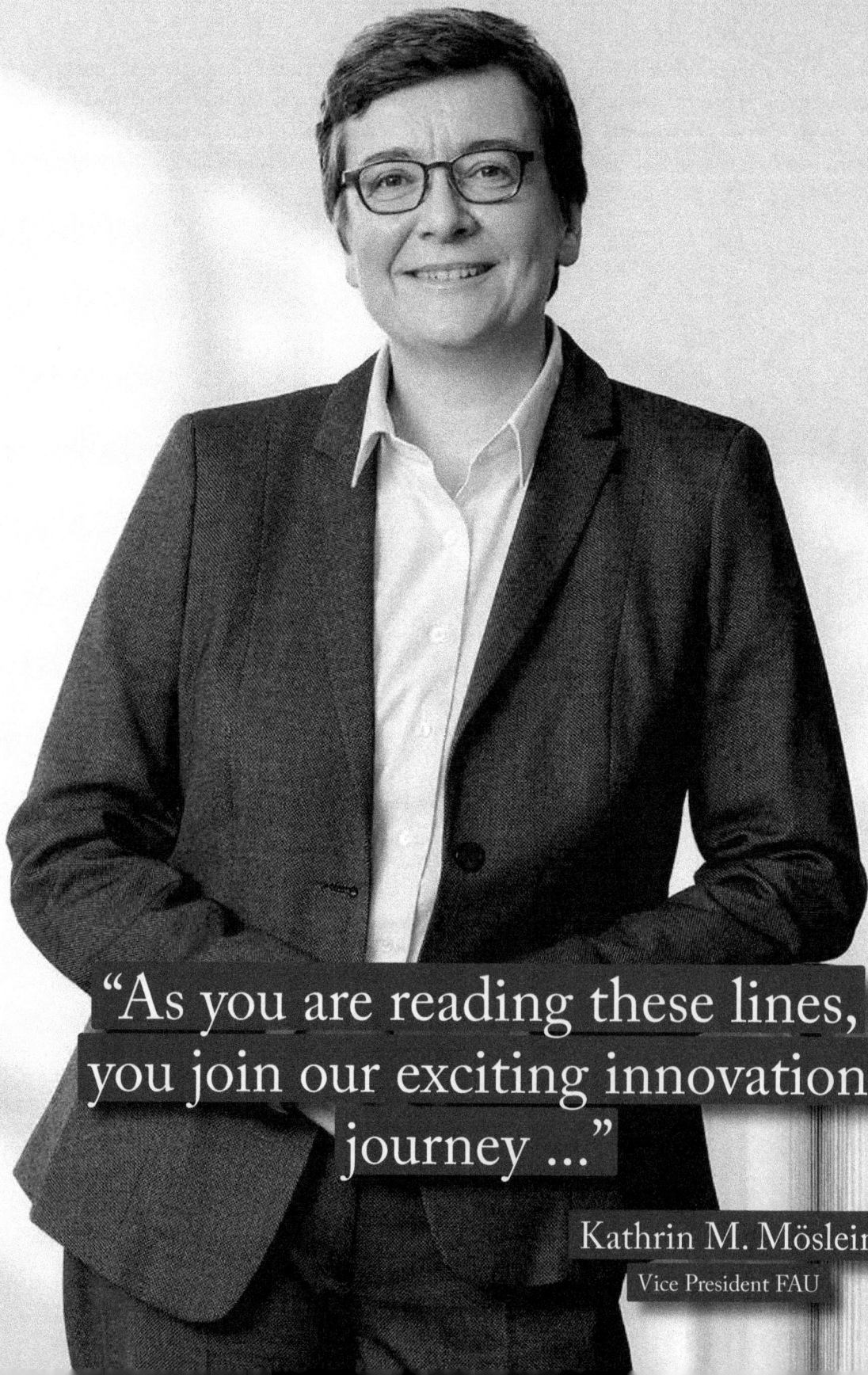

"As you are reading these lines, you join our exciting innovation journey ..."

Kathrin M. Möslein
Vice President FAU

Afterword

Kathrin M. Möslein
Vice President
Friedrich-Alexander University Erlangen-Nürnberg (FAU), Germany

As you are reading these lines, you join our exciting innovation journey: a journey that started when Joachim Hornegger, Dan Moshavi and Gurmeet Naroola met over a coffee in the Bay Area; a journey I decided to join when I discovered the smell of this coffee on twitter while sitting on my balcony in Nuremberg. I instantly knew I had jumped on the right innovation train, after I met Gurmeet on Skype for the first time: what an inspiration!

Even though we had never met before, we were quickly able to identify shared connections, friends, long-standing colleagues, and joint ideas. This next part of the story is where our FAU students got involved. We all know that ideas are nothing without implementation and, thus, we needed the best innovation talent we could find. Our FAU students enrolled in the idea translation class 'Innovation & Leadership' are simply the best when it comes to turning ideas into value. Fully inspired by our journey, a big cohort of enthusiastic Master students of different schools and disciplines from across our university accepted the challenge. FAU student, Markus Schober, with FAU and SJSU created an inspiring format for a broader collaboration between both institutions: the FAU Silicon Valley School. The first FAU Silicon Valley Spring and Fall Schools attracted participants from all parts of FAU. We had over 100 scholars, staff, students, and professionals from partner organizations apply for the first FAU Silicon Valley School. Unfortunately, we could only accept 30 of them, but we did make sure to find the most committed, curious, and open-minded applicants. Fast-forward to today, the FAU Silicon Valley School is a regular offering at our FAU Academy.

Our innovation journey was really able to pick up speed in the Spring of 2019, once Bavarian and Bay Area innovators met at SJSU for the first FAU Silicon Valley School. The mission was clear: hit the ground running, collaborate, innovate with a focus to co-create knowledge events, books, start-ups, and make "One and One equals Eleven". This was the springboard for our co-creation of innovation. This book is essentially an output of that. It is a tangible innovation in the form of a book. In fact, it is our very own 'facebook' – a 'boundary object' that opens up this newly created innovation network for you, the reader. The journey will continue as participants work on joint innovations, joint start-ups, etc. … the innovation train is gaining full speed.

Creating this book was a bigger task than many of us expected, but we were able to work around the obstacles by innovating and creating smart solutions. On the FAU side, Michael Fischer took the lead and was an unstoppable force in his commitment to make the dream come true. Thank you, Michi! Your energy and perseverance are simply impressive.

I can't help but smile when I see the product that came out of simply sharing ideas over a cup of coffee. So many innovators from our different ecosystems shared their knowledge, experience, expertise, connections, and drive – thank you all! Let's continue to bundle our unique strengths and live the FAU motto "Knowledge in Motion" to turn ideas into value and co-create true innovations.

Now, the time has come to invite you, the reader, to join our journey, to become a member of our innovation network and to share our belief that in innovation and co-creation "One and One equals Eleven".

Kathrin M. Möslein
Vice President
Friedrich-Alexander University Erlangen-Nürnberg (FAU), Germany

www.ingramcontent.com/pod-product-compliance
Lightning Source LLC
Chambersburg PA
CBHW051115200326
41518CB00016B/2513